YOUR INFANT WILL NEVER LOOK THE SAME TO YOU AGAIN...

After you learn THE SECRET LANGUAGE OF YOUR CHILD, you will be able to understand, appreciate and communicate with your child in amazing new ways. The language of pre-speech is a language of gesture, of posture, of expression...and by learning it you will be demonstrating to your child your willingness to enter, and participate in, a world of wonder previously closed to adults.

*   *   *

David Lewis, co-author with Dr. Robert Sharpe of several works of behavioral psychology including THE SUCCESS FACTOR, recorded more than eight miles of videotape in researching THE SECRET LANGUAGE OF YOUR CHILD.

**How Children Talk
Before they can Speak**

THE SECRET LANGUAGE OF YOUR CHILD

DISCARDED

DAVID LEWIS

BERKLEY BOOKS, NEW YORK

This Berkley book contains the complete
text of the original hardcover edition.
It has been completely reset in a type face
designed for easy reading, and was printed
from new film.

THE SECRET LANGUAGE OF
YOUR CHILD

A Berkley Book / published by arrangement with
St. Martin's Press

PRINTING HISTORY
St. Martin's edition published 1978
Berkley edition / June 1980

ISBN: 0-425-04547-1

A BERKLEY BOOK® TM 757,375
Berkley Books are published by Berkley Publishing Corporation,
200 Madison Avenue, New York, New York 10016.
PRINTED IN THE UNITED STATES OF AMERICA

Dedication

To my mother with much love and gratitude.

Contents

Contents

Acknowledgments

Many adults and hundreds of children have helped me, directly and indirectly, in the preparation of this book. Its real creators are the under-fives of Britain, America and Europe, whose body language I was able to record. To them, and especially to the numerous supervisors, helpers and teachers at the pre-school play groups, nursery schools and crèches, where I was able to film, my very grateful thanks.

I owe a particular debt of gratitude to my brother Richard and his wife Trisha, not only for producing three such charming research subjects as my nephews Sam and Kiran, and my niece Tamsin, but for allowing their home to be transformed into a cross between a laboratory and a television studio. Sincere thanks are also due to Jane Barlow and her baby daughter Josey whose progress from the first week of birth provided much useful material.

I would also like to thank Jane Booth-Clibborn, her helpers and the mothers of the play-group which allowed me such extensive filming facilities. I am also grateful to them for agreeing to the publication of still photographs taken from those recordings.

I would like to express my warmest thanks to Professor Hubert Montagner of the Laboratoire de Psychophysiologie at the Université de Franche-Comté, Besançon for allowing me access to his research material. His pioneer studies of non-verbal communication in the under-fives has transformed our knowledge of infant silent speech.

I am also delighted to record my thanks to Joyce Robertson, who with her husband James runs the Robertson Centre in London. Her helpful comments and permission to quote at length from her paper *Mothering As An Influence on Early Development* are greatly appreciated.

I am grateful to the CIBA Foundation for permission to use material presented to their 33 Symposium on Parent-Infant Interaction and published by Elsevier/Excerpta Medica/North Holland, Amsterdam. My special thanks to those quoted for allowing me to use their findings and comments: Dr A. Bentovim, Department of Psychological Medicine, The Hospital for Sick Children, London; Dr T. B. Brazelton, The Children's Hospital Medical Center, Boston; Dr J. H. Kennell, Case Western Reserve University, Cleveland, Ohio.

My thanks to Professor R. Birdwhistell of the Annenberg School of Communication, University of Pennsylvania, and his publishers for permission to quote from his book *Kinesics and Context: Essays on Body-Motion Communication* published by the University of Pennsylvania Press.

Also to Dr Jaroslav Koch and his publishers for permission to quote from his book *Total Baby Development*.

I should like to thank Wendy Gibbs and her family, and Mrs Martin and her family, for allowing me to use family photographs. All the other photographs are my own work. The line drawings were made by John Adams. Finally my thanks to Colin Sayers for his technical advice and assistance, and to Jane Massey for typing the manuscript.

THE SECRET LANGUAGE OF YOUR CHILD

1 How Children Talk—Without Saying A Word

Two small boys had been playing silently together in the park sandpit while their mothers chatted and watched them from a nearby bench. After some twenty minutes I overheard one woman remark to her friend: "What a shame Alan and John aren't able to talk yet. They would be having so much more fun."

Her companion nodded in agreement. Then she laughed: "Well, we can hardly expect a couple of two-year-olds to hold an animated conversation, can we?"

The answer to that question is an unqualified *yes*! That is exactly what one can expect to happen when the very young get together. In fact a lively conversation had been taking place between those small boys without either of the watchful mothers even noticing.

Surprising? Not really. You see, although Alan and John had been talking volubly to each other for most of the twenty minutes they were together, neither boy had spoken a word. Not that there was anything remarkable about either those two-year-olds or their fluent exchange. We now know enough about infant conversations to realize that while they may be tongue-tied where words are concerned they are by no means dumb. All infants will converse with one another given the opportunity.

Recent research in Europe and America has confirmed what sensitive parents may have suspected for years.

Long before children can speak they are able to talk to each other with ease by means of a silent and secret language.

I have called it a "secret" language because, although a few academics now know a little about it, most people have never heard of it. Even the parents of young children who are able to see its ABC used every day are usually unaware that such a method of communication and self-expression exists.

But if discovering the existence of the secret language comes as a surprise, learning about it can be an immensely rewarding experience. For once you understand how silent speech works, it becomes impossible to look at small children in quite the same way ever again. The previously familiar interactions of childhood, the games and quarrels, the tears and the tussles, suddenly acquire a whole new world of meaning. Acts of behaviour which might once have been dismissed as senseless and disorganised can be seen for what they are, highly organised acts of self-expression and communication between socially competent and sophisticated human animals. "I felt as if I had been blind for years and could suddenly see properly," commented the mother of a three-year-old girl after she had come to understand her daughter's silent speech.

The purpose of this book is to show everybody with an interest in the very young how they can learn to "see properly."

To explain how you can observe, understand and use one of the least known and most frequently misunderstood systems of communication on earth: The secret language of your child.

Soundless Words—Silent Sentences

Infant conversations are rather like the ideal Victorian child. They can be seen but not heard. The "words" which make up the language's considerable vocabulary are directed not at the ears but at the eyes. They are soundless signals created by means of a wide repertoire of body movements. When these signals are correctly formed into phrases and sentences, they have no need for accompanying speech to convey their meaning. Vivid dialogues can be constructed using only a smoothly flowing sequence of visual signals.

Small children speak volumes without a word passing their lips. But that does not mean the muscles of the mouth take no part in silent speech. On the contrary, while the small child, like the adult, talks using the whole body, all the facial muscles have an especially important role to play. Let us look at just a few of the many ways in which they, and the other muscle groups, can be used in silent speech.

The sides of the mouth can be turned up to produce a very wide variety of smiles. These can communicate emotions from extreme delight to anxious uncertainty, signals which may welcome or congratulate, thank or attempt to placate. The edges of the mouth can be turned down to show sadness, disappointment, disapproval and many other more negative feelings. The lips may be tightened to indicate anger, or drawn back from the teeth to intimidate. The mouth can be opened wide with the muscles kept taut in fatigue, or made wide but relaxed during uninhibited play. The forehead can be tensed in bewilderment or smoothed in bland disinterest. The eyebrows can be raised quickly and briefly as a greeting or lifted slowly and deliberately in elaborate astonishment. The eyes can gaze aggressively or flicker nervously. The whole head can be tilted to invite friendship or turned to reject an approach.

Moving down the body, raised arms may request an adult's help; clenched finger may signal fear, limp hands indicate fatigue, and rapidly moving arms show frustration, rage or joy. The trunk may be bent forward as a sign of domination or held straight during nervous hesitation. The posture may become as taut as a ramrod in the face of an attack or remain as relaxed as a tumbler's during mock tussles. These are just a few of the scores of body signals available to the infant who has learned how to use the secret language correctly.

As with words, their meanings can vary according to the emphasis placed on them and the sequences in which they are used. If body talk is to be effective, every movement must be properly performed and the whole message as carefully choreographed as a ballet. When this is done the signals provide a system of communication and self-expression which is as satisfactory and flexible as any spoken language.

It is true that toddlers cannot use these signals to discuss last night's television programmes, grumble over the weather, or gossip about a neighbour. But only an adult would regard such limitations as significant.

All the toddler's social needs can be met by using silent speech.

With it, the very young child is able to make new friends, organise games and win the co-operation of other toddlers when a team effort is needed. In the nursery it enables a pecking order to be established and maintained. The dominant child can exert leadership over the group and the anxious child can appease aggressors without a word being necessary. The signals warn other infants that a child is angry, or miserable, frustrated or fed-up. They can be used to show affection, repay a kindness, return an insult or protest at an injustice. The only time the language seems to fail is when the child uses it to talk to an adult. Then there is a good chance of a breakdown in communication and the child runs the risk of being either misunderstood or ignored completely.

For the strange thing about silent speech is that while its signals are usually crystal clear to other infants, they frequently make little or no impression on grown-ups. Adults often appear unable to get the message, however clearly an infant sends it out.

How Can We Be So Wrong!

If you have ever tried to argue about your bill with a French waiter, without being able to speak a word of French, you will begin to appreciate how an infant feels when his signals are met with indifference or incomprehension! Just as we tend to believe that all foreigners would be able to understand what we are saying if only they were a bit brighter or tried a little harder, so must the very young child conclude that adults are being either stupid or deliberately uncooperative.

The child sends out messages any two-year-old could understand without difficulty, but the grown-up either takes no notice or behaves in an entirely inappropriate way.

The infant signals: "I want to be friends . . . I would like to play a game . . . I am tired . . . I want to help you," and if there is any response at all it may well be a wrong one. The friendly child is irritably dismissed. The playful child is told not to be troublesome. The tired child may be urged to greater activity. The helpful child is scolded for being in the way! It does not always work out like this of course. But every time it does happen the confused infant must feel that the adult world is puzzling and unfair.

This is not the only way in which lack of knowledge of the infant's body signals can lead to trouble for the toddler. Grown-ups watching the very young at play may draw the wrong conclusions about what is going on, simply because they misinterpret what they do see. For example, I have watched friendly exchanges between admittedly boisterous infants and then heard other adults condemn them as aggressive. Equally, I have sometimes seen infants use blatantly threatening signals and then receive parental praise for being so affectionate. This did not happen because the adults present were unobservant or insensitive to the way the infants were behaving. On the contrary, most of them were both interested and involved. They had simply not learned enough about the signals of the secret language to place an accurate interpretation on what they saw.

The danger here is that an infant may be labelled as aggressive or anxious, friendly or unsociable, when quite the opposite is true. Such labels, however undeserved in the first place, tend to stick to children and affect the way adults respond to them. After a time it can happen that the children start to behave in the way which grown-ups seem to expect of them. Those considered to be aggressive really do develop into bullies, those regarded as fearful withdraw more and more from social interactions. One can only speculate on the number of older children and adolescents who are genuinely aggressive or isolated as a result of such inaccurate adult judgements during their infancy.

Another problem which can arise as a result of ignorance of the basic secret language signals is that an adult may send out messages to the young child without realising it. These inadvertent messages can have far more dire results than a verbal mistake between adults. For example, if you call a German a *schielendes unikum* under the incorrect impression that this is a compliment, the insulted person is likely to point out your error in a fairly forceful manner. You can then apologise for having called him a "cross-eyed twit" in the first place. But if a similar mistake occurs using body language, the small child will probably be quite unaware that you never intended to say what you did. If the message runs contrary to your mood at that time, it can cause confusion. If the inadvertent message is threatening or angry, it may produce misery. For example, a grown-up unintention-ally signals: "Let's play . . .". The delighted child responds by starting a game; but the adult, who is too busy or too tired to play, irritably rejects the approach. The child is naturally bewildered and upset by this refusal. The adult thinking that the infant is sulking gets irritated, never realising who is really to blame.

An even more distressing confusion can occur if the adult uses words which are in direct contradiction to the silent signals being used. For instance, a parent scolding a toddler may unwittingly combine harsh words with affectionate body talk.

"You are being wicked," says an angry mother. But her posture and gestures convey soothing affection. Alternatively, soft words can unknowingly be combined with hard signals.

"I love you," the father assures his small child. But his body talk is snarling a threat.

For the infant, this is like being offered candy and getting clobbered at the same time. The anxiety which would anyhow have been generated by angry signals—whether verbal or non-verbal—is intensified by the *double bind* situation created through the direct contradiction in the messages. If this happens frequently it may trigger behaviour changes in the infant, resulting in a rise of aggressive or fearful responses, something which happens far more frequently than most parents realise.

To illustrate how we can be so wrong about infant body language let me describe three incidents from my own recent observations.

"I'm a leader!"—"He's a bully!"

Two-year-old Nicky and three-year-old Jamie were playing with some coloured bricks in the nursery school when four-year-old Anthony arrived on the scene. Five minutes later he had taken over the game. With all the bricks collected around him he was building a garage for his toy cars, while the other children watched. Now and then one of them handed him a brick. Sometimes they copied his actions as he carefully laid the blocks on top of each other. Nicky's mother, who had been watching Anthony's take-over, commented disapprovingly: "He's a proper little bully. He bosses the others around something terrible, and always takes their toys."

These comments were not only unfair to the boy, but clearly showed that she had misread the exchange of body signals. Anthony had not bullied his way into the game. He gained the bricks through persuasion and consent. His body talk told Nicky and Jamie something like this: "If you let me play, you will have lots more fun. I know how to build very exciting things with bricks, and you can both help me. But, of course, if you don't want me to play then I'll go away".

By using this softly, softly approach Anthony had eased himself into their company and taken over the blocks without risking protests, tears and an appeal for help to that ultimate authority of the infant's world, the nearest adult. While approaching them he was sending out messages of reassurance. As he squatted down by the bricks he continued to soothe their anxieties. He made it clear that no threat was intended. He would not use his greater size and superior strength to snatch the toys from them. Nicky and Jamie, recognising the true nature of his intentions, remained relaxed and co-operative. To the other children Anthony was a leader. To Nicky's mother he appeared a pint-sized dictator.

In Chapter five I will describe the language of domination and explain how you can distinguish between the leader and the lout.

"I'm being good."—"She's being naughty!"

At sixteen months, Karen was a bold explorer. So much so that she had already given her mother a few grey hairs by her fearless expeditions away from the apron strings. Taken into a new park for the first time, she eagerly investigated the novel surroundings while her mother watched carefully from a bench. About thirty yards away was a shallow and deserted paddling pool. Soon after they arrived, Karen had toddled inquisitively towards the pool and been hastily called back. After playing quite close to her mother for some time, Karen suddenly walked away from the bench at right angles to the pool. When she was about twenty feet from her mother she stopped, turned and pointed purposefully towards the water while staring in that direction. At once the woman got to her feet and went quickly over to the toddler. Grasping her wrist firmly, she said in a scolding voice: "No, Karen. I told you not to go over there. You are a naughty girl."

But it was very unlikely that Karen ever intended to go towards the pool, even though her gesture and gaze seemed to indicate a move in that direction. A more probable interpretation of the signals was: "I am going to return to you. Stay there." Since the pointing finger and the child's glance were directed away from the bench and towards the shimmering water, her mother's misunderstanding was not surprising. But it must have come as an unpleasant shock to the child to be scolded, when she had no intention of doing anything naughty. It might even have encouraged her to disobey on future occasions. After all, if you are going to be punished it might as well be for something as for nothing! Certainly the child must have felt that adults are unjust and unfathomable creatures. In Chapter seven I will explain the ways in which children attempt to communicate with adults, and describe the signals they use.

"I want you!"—"I reject you!"

Philip's mother was a large, friendly woman. Philip was a slightly built and usually unfriendly three-year-old. He refused to join in games at the day nursery, and spent most of the time in a quiet corner playing by himself with toys which none of the other children wanted. If one of the others came over and grabbed a plaything, Philip surrendered it without protest. In the infant pecking order he was definitely a non-starter.

"I can't understand why Philip doesn't make friends more easily, when his mother is so out-going and friendly," commented one of the other parents. An understanding of the secret language might have suggested at least a possible explanation.

When she came to collect him at the end of the day, Philip's mother gave everybody the impression of being impatient and preoccupied. This was not entirely her fault. She did a full-time job and had to hurry home to prepare a meal for the family. While other infants were warmly greeted and often affectionately held or cuddled as their mothers chatted, Philip was snatched out of the room after only the briefest of greetings. He clearly needed more time and greater contact with his mother. But the situation was made worse by the body signals which this tired and over-stressed woman unintentionally sent out at their almost daily reunions. While her spoken words, although brief, were warm enough, her silent speech was extremely hostile. The message she was sending Philip was one of rejection and dislike. Of course the woman had no idea this was happening, and was horrified when it was gently pointed out to her. But for Philip every afternoon brought a confirmation that his mother did not really want him at all.

I am not suggesting that this confusion, disturbing though it must have been for the child, was the sole case of his constant anxiety and isolation. Such an explanation would be simplistic in the extreme. But there can be little doubt that his mother's insensitivity to her body language contributed to his social difficulties. This is shown by the fact that when the problem of her unintentional silent signals was explained, and she was shown how to change them to those signifying warmth and welcome—at the same time she was also persuaded to pay rather more attention to the boy at home each evening—Philip's behaviour underwent a dramatic change. He became far more assertive, self-confident and friendly.

There is clearly a close link between the development of a proficiency in body language and the mastering of social skills. Not that such a connection is really so remarkable. All social behaviours including the ability to make friends, to assert oneself, and to express needs or desires, are learned responses. Communication is a prime requirement for any type of learning. So it is hardly surprising that children who are fluent on body talk are much more likely to be confident and articulate after the age of four when the spoken word takes over as the dominant means of communication and self-expression. Because they can relate to other infants easily and naturally, such children are able to learn a repertoire of social behaviour which stands them in good stead in later childhood, adolescence and adulthood. Those who for some reason never master body talk, whose signals are weak or inappropriate during the years before verbal speech, may find it far more difficult to develop satisfactory relationships later in life.

I must emphasise that the evidence is by no means conclusive, and the outcomes I have described are certainly not inevitable. But the findings are clear enough to make us realise that we underestimate the significance of infant body talk at our peril.

This clearly raises an extremely puzzling question about the language of infancy. If it is as important as I have suggested, how did it ever become to be a secret?

Contained within this query there are really three basic questions about infant body talk.

First of all, why has it taken so long for the scientific penny to drop? Children have been the subject of serious investigation by doctors, psychologists, psychiatrists and educationalists for more than a century. Library shelves are filled with volumes on every aspect of their growth. A recent international bibliography of the literature on infant development, lists more than two thousand studies, ranging from investigations into the eye reflexes in babies to the mechanisms of early feeding. It is certainly not a complete list, since the rate of research and publication inevitably outdates any bibliography even before it can be printed. Scientific interest has ranged from the study of very small pieces of behaviour, such as thumb sucking in two-week-old babies, to explorations of major areas of change like the effects on mental growth of inadequate mother love. Yet, despite all this interest and concentrated expertise, the whole area of non-verbal communication remained a closed subject until fairly recently.

No less remarkable is the apparent blindness of those in an even better position to watch the everyday habits and behaviour of the very young, namely parents themselves. How have they remained so seemingly blind to a system of communication which is widely used and readily understood by infants? Finally how is it that, as adults, we seem to have forgotten a language we once knew well and used fluently?

Bees, Birds and Body Talk

For centuries mankind's sweet tooth was satisfied by honey, and bee-keeping must rank as one of the oldest agricultural skills. The first hives were probably constructed not long after the first houses. During this long stretch of time, hundreds of thousands of people tended bees and observed their habits. Many of them will certainly have noticed that bees returning to the hive frequently perform a strange "dance" on the honeycomb. Their movements, which are always accompanied by a vigorous wagging of the abdomen, sometimes trace out the shape of a figure eight. At other times they make two peach shaped outlines. Probably some of those who saw the strange movements were puzzled by them. But nobody even seems to have wondered if they meant anything. Like the movements of infants they appear to have been dismissed as being random behaviour without any particular significance. It was not until late in this century that the German naturalist Von Frisch realised the strange "dances" were not the disorganised activities they at first seemed, but a highly organised system of communication. By careful observation and simple experiment, Von Frisch demonstrated that the shape of the outline followed by returning workers varied according to the distance and direction of the best nectar-gathering fields.

The "dance" of the bees was there for everybody to see and once its purpose had been revealed many naturalists must have kicked themselves for being so blind! It is much the same with body language. When you realise that such a system of non-verbal communication exists, you see human movements in an entirely new way. Changes of expression, gestures and postures, which you would probably have taken for granted before, all at once assume a considerable significance. A good example of the way in which body signals can easily be seen—once they have been pointed out—occurred during a recent conference at which a number of papers dealing with non-verbal communication had been presented. One of the speakers, the anthropologist Professor Eibl-Eibesfeldt of the Max Planck Institute in Germany, had told delegates about the "eye-brow flash" which is used as a greeting gesture. This is probably one of the most universally used signals in body language. It has been observed amongst such diverse peoples as Europeans, Balinese, Papuans and Waika Indians. When we see a familiar face coming towards us we send a greetings message by raising our eyebrows very briefly, the movement lasts about one fifth of a second. Until the signal had been pointed out to them, none of the delegates had been aware that they used such a body movement. After Professor Eibl-Eibesfeldt's speech, all that was changed. One of the delegates, Professor Robert Hinde of Cambridge, describes the effect of that revelation: "Suddenly the members of the conference were made conscious of a gesture which they were using many times a day without realising it. From that moment on it became impossible to greet a colleague without a momentary mutual embarrassment as each realised that he had used this commonplace gesture without meaning to."

The study of body language, or kinesics as it has been labelled, originated in observations of non-verbal communication amongst such diverse species as insects and birds, domestic animals and African lions. As naturalists studied the courtship dances of mating birds, and watched the ritualised combats of the big cats, they realised that non-verbal communication played a vital role in the social life of the wilderness. It took students of human behaviour rather longer to apply the same disciplines of observation and analysis to their own species. The first book on the subject appeared as long ago as 1872, when Charles Darwin published *Expressions of the Emotions in man and animals,* which described and analysed many of the signals that are now called body language. But it was not until almost a hundred years later that serious attempts were made to investigate the subject. It soon became clear that the importance of silence speech had been seriously underestimated. We now know that movements of the face and body are as vital to effective communication as words themselves. As one researcher has commented: "We speak with our vocal cords, but we converse with our whole body."

But while researchers quickly realised that adult body language would provide a fruitful and fascinating subject for investigation, their interest seems to have stopped short of infants. The social encounters of infants appeared to most adults to be disorganised and lacking in any significance. The infants apparently possessed as little body language as they did verbal speech, and many observers concluded that everything which two infants could say to one another during even the lengthiest exchange might be written on a postage stamp with room to spare!

It was only when slow motion film techniques and video-recording cameras were used to monitor exchanges between the very young that scientists began to realise how wrong they had been. Infants without words were not lacking in language. They could and did communicate with one another. They were not the unsociable, self-centred beings of popular judgement and belief. Taking a leaf out of the bird-watcher's book, some psychologists constructed hides in day nurseries in order to watch their young subjects without being seen. Other investigators fitted up their laboratories with two-way mirrors, high chairs and soft toys so that they could observe and record the very young in action.

But the photography is only the starting point. Once the films and tapes have been made, they must be painstakingly analysed, often one frame at a time. It is not unusual for a researcher to spend twenty hours or more examining two minutes of film. But this laborious work has paid off. Although our knowledge of infant silent speech is still at the early stages, a number of important discoveries have been made, and many new and intriguing avenues for future investigation have been opened up.

Movements which seemed random and idiosyncratic before such analysis, were frequently found to have a clear rhythm and purpose. The infants were not only well aware of each other but they interacted in a way which closely resembled verbal exchanges between adults. Just like a polite grown-up dialogue, their silent speech had a beginning, a middle and an end. They did not all try to communicate at once, but took it in turns to send and receive signals, which were almost always carefully formed and correctly interpreted. More and more signals were identified and examined. Today we are slowly building up an extensive vocabulary of silent speech. In time the full repertoire of body movements will probably have been recorded, described and interpreted.

Scientists failed to appreciate the significance of body-language in humans for much the same reason that naturalists and countrymen were able to observe the behaviour of wild animals, birds and social insects for centuries without realising they were watching an intricate system of communication in action.

When you do not know that something does exist it may not occur to you that it *could* exist. Blinkered by this larger ignorance, the signals of body talk remained as effectively hidden as if they had been deliberately concealed. Everybody saw them but nobody noticed them!

Looking Without Seeing—Observing Without Noticing

"I watch my baby son very attentively," protested an indignant mother, when I suggested that parents might not spot body signals because they did not look for them in the right way. "I see every move he makes."

I am sure that she *did* look closely at her little boy on many occasions, and honestly felt that she saw all there was to see. But she was mistaken. Even parents who feel sure that infants are not the egocentric, anti-social and uncommunicative little creatures which many experts have labelled them, will find it impossible to spot all the signals of silent speech—unless they know what to watch out for. The problem arises because a number of psychological barriers come between the loving adult and the child. These make it very difficult to view infant exchanges in the correct way, so as to see the silent language in action.

When grown-ups watch their children, it is usually for a number of very good reasons which have nothing to do with looking out for body language. It may be that they are worried in case the child gets hurt, becomes a nuisance to somebody, or does some damage. They may be worried about the mess a toddler is making. They may be regarding the infant with pride or thinking how sturdy and good looking the infant is, or just noticing resemblances to the infant's parents. They may be absorbing all the details of some special moment, such as feeding the park ducks for the first time or cutting a birthday cake, so that they can preserve the scene in their memories. All perfectly valid reasons for keeping a close eye on the infant but none of them conducive to noticing body language. To see that, as I will explain in the next chapter, you have to adopt an objective outlook and watch for the right things. Otherwise it is as if an ornithologist were to focus exclusively on the colour of a bird's plumage, or a naturalist's sole concern was for the safety of some newborn cubs. Both might be sound reasons for mounting a watch, but neither could be expected to contribute anything of interest to our knowledge of how, when, where and why non-verbal communication in the wild occurs.

The second psychological barrier arises as a result of adult familiarity with the behaviour of children. Teachers, and nursery supervisors, in fact anybody who spends a lot of time with the very young, will see the majority of silent speech signals scores of times each day. When we become that used to anything we tend not to see it any longer. This is the reason why strangers to a town often notice things which long term residents will overlook. Psychologists call this type of response a *set*, and sometimes illustrate it by asking people to read the phrase: Paris In The Spring.

Did you look at those words without really seeing them? If you thought there was nothing odd about the well-known message then re-read it. You have just had a good illustration of the way in which our expectations can prevent us from believing the evidence of our own eyes.

Until you are aware that such a thing as the secret language exists, it is virtually impossible to see it in action. Remember how it was impossible for generations of bee-keepers to spot the fact that their hives were simply buzzing with informed conversation!

How Silent Speech Is Simply Lost For Words

Parents often ask me: "How did we come to forget the secret language? What caused the knowledge to be lost as we grew up?" It may seem paradoxical but if the language had been forgotten, it would probably have been remembered decades ago. If we had ever really lost silent speech there would have been far less difficulty in finding it again.

Suppose that due to neurological changes in the developing brain that part which dealt with silent speech disappeared at around the age of about five when verbal speech took over. It seems at least possible that some people would be more seriously hit by this selective amnesia than others. After all, every brain is a unique biological mechanism which works in a highly individual manner. So it is not too far fetched to assume that the loss of memory would affect some people, or certain races, worse than others. Those who retained a memory of silent speech, however slight, would soon regain their missing knowledge by observing infants interacting. They would start from the favourable position which we have only recently attained. They would know that such a system of communication exists. Within a short space of time, the lost language would have been regained.

But this can never happen, because while we can no longer recall a time when we used silent speech as our sole method of communication, we never forget the signals. In fact we use them everyday of our lives. What has happened is that they have been driven underground, deep into the recesses of our unconscious mind, by an artificial but extremely efficient system of self-expression and social exchange. That is, by man-made languages of the world. Once a verbal communication has taken possession of our reasoning processes and filled our memory-banks with sounds, it can never be exorcised. However much we try to recapture a time without words, the fact that we have to use words to make that attempt ensures our defeat. It seems no more possible to think in non-verbal terms than it is to think of nothing at all. If you disbelieve me, just try it.

Learning a language is one of the most difficult things we have to do. Research has shown that human beings have a unique sensitivity to the rhythm of the spoken word, something which I will talk about in greater detail in Chapter Three. It also seems likely that our ability to master the complex vocabulary, syntax and grammar of language is to a large extent innate. Certainly brain power, rather than any special vocal apparatus, is what distinguishes word-using man from the other primates. A chimpanzee has a voice box and throat muscles which are perfectly capable of producing human speech, but none of the attempts to teach them to talk has been very successful. In one painstaking experiment, a house-reared chimp was finally taught to say a few words. But at six, when a human child's vocabulary is around 2,000 words, the chimpanzee had still only learned seven.

By the age of about six months, the baby will have started to babble and imitate vocal sounds. But while the baby's verbal abilities remain slight, and are likely to stay that way for another four or five months, non-verbal communications skills will be well established. Within a few weeks of birth the baby starts to use several signals, especially the smile, in a way that is essentially social. Provided the infant is given the chance to practise these body movements, the secret language will develop rapidly.

At one year old the infant can manage many of the vowels and consonants of human speech and uses a number of specific sounds. But effective communication using this system remains a still distant goal. Body language, on the other hand, is well established. The child can use silent signals to communicate with other infants, and enjoys these exchanges.

Most children have grasped the essentials of spoken language sufficiently well, between the ages of eighteen months and two years, to understand and use a limited number of words. A lot of these words will consist of family jargon, which often only their parents or other children can make head or tail of. But the child's repertoire of silent speech signals will be extensive, and body language will start to become integrated with the spoken word.

Both verbal and non-verbal vocabularies increase

considerably between the ages of two and three. Less jargon words are used. "Wannum neetie mum-ah" starts to reappear as: "I want a sweet, mummy". As verbal language increases, some of the silent speech signals are phased out, while others are used more frequently. Which will decline and which will increase depends to a great extent on how they are received by others. The integration of facial expression and body movement with the spoken word continues as more words are mastered and sentences of greater complexity are achieved. During exchanges with other infants the child will often use words in addition to gestures and facial expressions, in order to make its meaning clear.

Such words are, however, mainly used to emphasise messages which have been sent by silent speech signals. For example, a child who wants another toddler to hand over a toy will start by making the appropriate secret language supplication movements. If this combination of posture, gesture and expression fails to have the desired effect, the infant may add abruptly: "Give me . . ." or plead: "I wan' it . . ." In moments of anger or fear, very clear signals of aggression or anxiety may be accompanied by a loud and abrupt use of such words as "No . . .", "Go away . . .", "Stop!" Small children are also quite likely to use both verbal and non-verbal communication when addressing an adult. But this is only because their silent signals are so often ignored or misunderstood. For example, on one occasion I was watching a group of three-year-olds at play when an aggressive older boy came and snatched a toy. After a number of half-hearted attempts to recover it, one of the boys nervously approached an adult who had been talking to a friend and not paying any attention to the children. For a full thirty seconds the little boy sent out clear silent speech signals for help, pointing to the older boy and the stolen plaything. When this failed to make any impression on the grown-up, the child added plaintively, "Toy . . . get toy for me." But this clarification failed to help, because the adult had no idea what had happened or what toy he was talking about. Eventually the crestfallen youngster crept away with his friends in search of a new game.

After the age of five, most children are fluent in their mother tongue and find it by far the easiest and most direct method of communicating with the outside world, although for another year or two they will continue to be adept at silent speech when playing with much younger children. I remember on one occasion my five-year-old nephew was having tea with his two-year-old sister when the little girl made some utterance which left the grown-ups baffled: "What did she say, Sam?" the boy was asked, and he interpreted effortlessly. "How on earth did you understand that?" his father inquired. "I don't know..." he replied. "I just did." And he had understood perfectly correctly. It is almost certain that the body language of the two-year-old, and not her garbled words, had provided him with the answer.

From the age of five onwards, body language attains its more or less adult status, and is used either in conjunction with the spoken word or as a means of expressing feelings which are too profound for verbal speech. A woman, grieving after a bereavement, will often communicate her intense misery more by body language than by tears or words. She clasps her face with her hands and rocks silently with despair. In the West, a man who has been infuriated to a point where words seem inadequate to convey his anger or disgust may make a series of complex face, hand and arm movements. His right fist clenches, his right arm bends at the elbow and then thrusts sharply upwards. As it rises, his left hand slaps firmly down on his right bicep. At the same time, his face assumes an aggressive expression, the lips are drawn back from the teeth and the eyes stare. It is an inherently meaningless gesture which would probably baffle anybody raised in a different culture. Yet few Americans or Europeans would be left in any doubt about the message being sent!

Once a spoken language has become firmly established, our thoughts run on verbal rails. The extent of this influence on our ability to reason is a matter of deep philosophical debate and psychological speculation. If we are all truly prisoners of language then, as the Austrian philosopher Ludwig Wittgenstein put it: "The limits of my language mean the limits of my world." There are grounds for supposing the language barrier to be less than absolute, but these are complex debating points which need not concern us here. It is sufficient to realise that once we can talk in words, silent speech loses its initial role as a system of communication in its own right. The signals still have a vital part to play in our use of verbal language, but we are no longer aware of them as separate entities. Can word-dominated adults ever hope to think and communicate, as infants do, in terms of pure movement? Some people are specially trained to achieve this, and by their achievement enable us, for a short time, to see again through the eyes of the very young. As we watch a great dancer in action, or see a consumate mime artist at work, the shadows may briefly lighten so that we catch a glimpse of ideas liberated from language and of thoughts without words. But the verbal curtain soon comes down again. Like lost innocence, such perceptions can only be evoked—never recaptured. Body talk does not vanish from neglect or become forgotten through indifference. It just gets lost for words.

2 Learning the First Language of Life

There are hundreds of signals in the secret language, and dozens of different ways of combining them into a smooth and fluent dialogue. Mastering body talk is certainly not as complicated as learning to speak a man-made language. All the same, acquiring the necessary signals and finding out when and how to use them correctly would seem to be a formidable task at any age. How does the infant manage to do it so quickly and, usually, so well?

Some of the signals develop from reflexes which are programmed into the baby's genetic make-up. The most socially important of these innate movements is the smile, whose story will be told in Chapter Four. Other very early signals, such as touching, stroking, grasping, sucking and making eye-contact, are initially used by the infant in order to explore the surrounding world.

As the child develops they are modified by learning and become signals in silent speech. For example, a reaching and grasping movement begins by providing the baby with valuable tactile information about objects close by. Later the grasping action will become a much more complex and sophisticated movement. The speed and confidence with which it is made, the position of the hand and arm before and after the grabbing attempt, together with the infant's expression and posture, combine to produce a wide variety of signals. These range from a firm but polite request for something which the toddler

23

believes is his by rights, to an agressive grab at the property of another child.

Many of the exploratory movements, while not as rigid as reflexes, owe a great deal to the way in which the human brain and nervous system are designed. Not surprisingly, these have evolved with a predisposition to work in a way which will give us the best chance of survival. We are selectively programmed to hear, see and respond to some forms of sensory stimulation better than others. For instance, it will clearly be more valuable for a baby to notice animate things in its immediate environment rather than inanimate ones. Moving objects are more likely to threaten or aid survival. So right from birth we all have a bias towards movement. We pay more attention to it, and it catches our eyes more readily. This is a preference we retain all our lives. In an otherwise static landscape, any movement, however small, will draw our attention as surely as a magnet pulls iron. But the infant's gaze is not just pretuned to action, it is selectively programmed to pay maximum attention to the human face. I will discuss this innate preference in Chapter Three. Here I will just make the point that this enables the baby to learn that the face is a major area for sending and receiving body language messages in the shortest possible time. The baby is also able to discover early on that the eyes have a special potency. By using eye-contact correctly, the baby finds it is able to attract and hold the attention of the adults on whom life depends.

All these movements and responses are drastically shaped by the culture into which the child has been born. Infants are plastic creatures. They can be readily moulded into any behaviour patterns which the conventions of a particular society demands. This is largely achieved in two ways—by offering the infant body language signals which it can copy, and through a system of rewards for the movements which are regarded as correct. Some signals are encouraged in this way, by praise, games, attention, a smile or a caress. Others are more critically received, and so wither. The smile, for example, begins as a fairly tentative movement of the lips. But because it is so warmly received the signal rapidly develops. More face muscles are brought into play, and the movements become increasingly frequent and positive. Biting, on the other hand, is regarded unsympathetically by adults and older children. It starts as an exploratory movement, with the baby putting things into the mouth as part of a general investigation into the shape, feel, and taste of objects around it. Later it becomes a playful or aggressive signal. But most adults firmly discourage the bite for either of these purposes, and by the age of two it has usually vanished from the vocabulary of silent speech. Biting may, however, occur both during very aggressive fights, and also in the quite friendly, but no less uninhibited, rough-and-tumble play of the under-fives. In either of these situations girls are more likely to bite than boys. I will be describing both types of interactions in Chapter Six.

Signals Large and Small

A child of three or four probably has a secret language vocabulary containing many hundreds of body movements. So far we have been able to observe and analyse only a small proportion of them.

Some of the signals are so brief that they are almost impossible to detect without the aid of slow-motion filming. These have been labelled *micro-movements*. Others, termed *macro-movements*, are easily seen and appear to contain unambiguous messages. For instance, most adults would claim they understand exactly what a child means when laughing, smiling, frowning, crying or grimacing. Often the immediate impression a *macro-movement* conveys will be correct. But accepting such a signal at face, and body, value can lead to misinterpretations.

Although *micro-movements* are brief, they should not

be dismissed as being of no importance. They can affect the whole sense of the message, in exactly the same way that a very small change of inflection can completely alter the meaning of a spoken sentence. For instance if I say: "He's a *good* boy" and place a slight stress on "good", it will be clear I am stating what I consider to be a fact. But a rising inflection on the last two words changes an opinion into an inquiry. During a conversation I will also underline my true meaning by using body language. The statement may be accompanied by a smile and a nod, the query by raising the eye-brows and slightly tilting the head. But even without these visual clues, if I make the comment over the telephone for example, my listener should be left in no doubt about my views. Yet the change of intonation will have lasted only a tiny fraction of a second.

Now let me show you how similarly small variations in body language can have the same profound effect on the way a message is received. Look at the photographs below and decide which you prefer.

The chances are that you picked the photograph on the right, although there is no immediately obvious difference between them and you may not be able to give a reason for your choice.

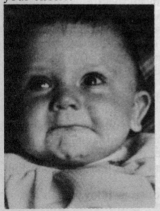 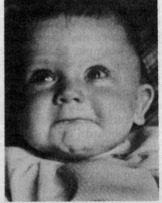

The answer is that the eyes on the right hand photograph have been retouched so that the pupils are fractionally enlarged. A widening of the pupils is normally associated with greater interest, and the majority of people respond to this signal without realising what has triggered their preference.

Macro-movements, as I have already explained, are easy to see; and in this ease of observation lies the major pitfall for the unwary. We notice them so readily and so frequently that they get taken for granted. When we do make a special effort to watch them, our immediate response is likely to be "so what?" The child is smiling, that means she's happy. If the child is frowning that means she is cross. The child is wearing a sad expression, that means she's miserable.

Yet it can be as risky to seize on these easily identifiable expressions and interpret them in isolation, as it would be to try and translate a long exchange in a foreign language on the basis of one or two familiar words. An amusing way of illustrating the hidden danger of the obvious body signal was suggested to me by a member of my audience during a recent lecture on infant language. The person in question was a well-known television actor who had learned his trade in the provincial theatre. He explained that highly critical reviews in the press could often be turned into glowing front-of-house testimonials by some judicious editing on the part of the theatre management. As an example, he mentioned one play of which a critic commented: "The boredom I endured was one of the most profound experiences of my critical career.... It has all the tension, excitement and entertainment value one could expect from watching paint dry." When this less than enthusiastic notice had been suitably modified for the bill-boards, the critic found himself saying: ". . . one of the most profound experiences of my critical career. . . . It has all the tension, excitement and entertainment value one could expect."

You can be fooled by the obvious body signals just as

badly as those theatre-goers were being misled by the edited review extracts!

As with any language, it is as important to know the context in which the signals have been used as it is to understand their content. During a lengthy exchange, the more familiar body movements can be combined with much less obvious signals which change the message. I can best illustrate this by describing an interaction between two boys at a play group. John, aged three years seven months when the observations were made, was a dominant and occasionally aggressive little boy who usually managed to get his own way in the group. Andrew, two months older than John, was a self-confident child who, while not at the top of the group's pecking order, still managed to stand up for himself in most disputes.

John was rearranging the furnishings in a doll's house, when Andrew walked over to him. After a moment, John turned and gave him a brief smile. Andrew returned the smile and watched for a few seconds. Then he reached out and took a wooden bed from the items scattered around the house. John looked at him hard for a moment and smiled again. Andrew half turned as if to carry the bed away. John reached out and touched his arm. Andrew handed him the bed and watched him for a little longer. Then he took a book from a pile near the house, and showed John a coloured picture. John glanced briefly at it, then looked away again. Andrew smiled rather uncertainly, and then replaced the book as John turned back to the doll's house. Andrew watched him for a few moments and finally wandered away. When Andrew had gone, John looked around and suddenly stamped his foot hard on the ground.

A casual observer of that exchange might have concluded that it was reasonably friendly. The boys smiled at one another, and Andrew showed John a picture. There were no blows or obvious threats. Yet to a person trained in infant body talk the interaction appeared very different. The boys were in conflict, and barely masked aggression lay just beneath the surface. What had really happened was this.

As Andrew approached, John gave him a smile which was actually a warning. (In Chapter Four I will explain how an apparently friendly body signal can be a mask for distinctly unfriendly feelings.) John was saying to Andrew: "You are invading my territory. Be careful!"

Andrew's smile was an acknowledgement of that warning and a plea not to be attacked. He was appeasing John by telling him: "OK. I am not going to harm your interests in any way. Just let me stay and watch."

Partially satisfied, John turned back to the doll's house. But his posture had changed. From being relaxed he was now tense and on his guard. Previously he had leaned right into the house to arrange the furniture, now he only put his head partly inside so that he could keep an eye on Andrew. After watching for about ten seconds Andrew picked up the bed. It was a gesture of self-assertion; "I am not really afraid of you," he was saying. "These toys are not yours. They belong to me just as much as you". But even as he took this bold stand Andrew offered John a face-saver. Instead of trying to grab something from inside the house, he chose an item of furniture which had been discarded by John and lay some distance from him. His choice was intended to tell the other boy: "I don't want to fight. I am not doing anything against your interests by standing up for my rights."

But John was not to be placated by this manoeuvre. He stared hard at Andrew, his body tense. His fists began to clench and his arms grew taut, although they did not move. In body talk he was telling the other boy: "Are you crazy? Don't you realise what a chance you are taking by trying my patience like this? Put it back!"

His arms, which had been hanging at his side, bent slightly at the elbow. He leaned forward. Then he smiled again. As I will explain in Chapter Six, all the movements leading up to that smile had been clear threatening signals. The smile itself was a menacing full-stop to that message of impending attack.

Andrew, still attempting to assert himself, partly turned away. In terms of the secret language the exchange could be translated as follows:

"Unless you put it back right now, things are going to become very unpleasant. I'm warning you."

"I don't care about your threats. I'm going."

At that point John reached out and touched Andrew's arm. It was not a blow or a grasping action. It did not physically hurt or restrain the boy. What it did was say: "I mean it . . . now do you really want trouble?" Andrew did not, and backed down at once. But he refused to run off immediately. By staying, he was telling John: "All right, if you feel that strongly about it. But that doesn't mean I am afraid of you."

After six seconds Andrew decided to try and win John's companionship for a game. He picked up a picture book and opened it at random. Neither the book itself nor the chosen picture was important. What mattered was the act of offering the other boy something with a smile. These formed a solicitation message: "Let's be friends. Look, here's something interesting I want to give you." But John was not to be tempted. After a brief glance at the book he looked away again. This was a clear rejection. So Andrew decided that he had tried all he could to be friendly, and went in search of a more agreeable companion. John's foot-stamp could be interpreted as irritation with himself for not having been more aggressive. His position at the top of the play group pecking order had been threatened and he had not defended it strongly enough. It was a bit like an adult saying: "I should have been tougher. These people think they can walk all over me." By stamping his foot, he was able to work off a little of the tension which had built up during the exchange. But not all the anger had been drained out of him. A few seconds later he ran over and pushed a small and very dominated two-year-old girl. There was no reason for the attack, except to demonstrate to the others that he was a tough guy. This type of redirected aggression is common with under-fives. So too is the offering of gifts, toys, objects picked up from the ground, sweets, books and so on, to other children and to adults. Both these traits follow us through into adult life. The man who has been bawled out by his boss is likely to storm home and take it out on his wife. The woman who has had a row with her husband may shout at the children. Gift-giving or requesting is a frequent social ploy for breaking the ice and starting a conversation. The proffering of, or request for, a cigarette, a light, a drink, or even the correct time, are all relationship-establishing manoeuvres rooted in our infancy. At least part of the popularity of smoking may lie in the fact that it provides a low cost, easily portable and socially acceptable form of casual gift. Even a handshake contains a strong element of giving. Not only is the other person saying: "Look, I am unarmed and my hand is flat in greeting, not clenched in a threat," he is also extending part of his own body as a symbolic gift. The difference between Andrew offering John a coloured picture and a nervous business man trying to placate a superior by handing him a fat cigar is merely one of degree.

The need to observe the flow of body language is as important to a correct understanding as it is with any verbal system of communication. Just as words blend into phrases and sentences so that we become caught up in the rhythm of speech, so too do the gestures, expressions, movements, postures and positions of silent speech blend effortlessly into one another. Unlike a spoken language, however, there is no occasion when non-verbal communication ceases completely. Even during sleep, both adults and children betray something about their personalities, feelings and attitudes from the way they lie in bed. By studying the amount of tension or relaxation in face, body and limbs, and noting the sleeper's posture, a trained observer can discover, amongst other things, whether that person is dominant or fearful, aggressive or anxiety-ridden.

How You Can Learn The Secret Language

Silent speech is learned like any other language, by memorising the more important words and phrases, in this case the body signals, and then by watching, rather than listening to, these signals in action. With practice you should find that you can understand a flow of signals without having to "translate" them into words. When this happens you are starting to use body talk in the natural way which infants use it.

In many ways silent speech is much easier to learn than a verbal language. For a start its range and scope, although perfectly adequate for the social needs of infants, is obviously far more limited than any spoken tongue. Secondly, the context in which the exchanges take place frequently provides a clear indication of the kind of dialogue which can be expected. Finally, though this is not always the advantage it may appear, most infant exchanges are shorter than the majority of adult conversations. But there are also some special problems. If for instance you decide to learn German, or Russian, you start with your ears already tuned in to the spoken word. No initial training is required to enable you to hear the sounds. When you start to look out for silent speech signals, you have to teach yourself to see beyond the psychological barriers which I described in Chapter One. Becoming sufficiently objective about infant body talk can prove tricky. Then there is the speed of delivery. A foreign language teacher not only slows down sentences to a fraction of normal speaking rate to help out the beginner, but also repeats difficult words or phrases over and over again. If at the end of all this you have still failed to understand what has been said, you can always ask for a translation. Obviously none of these helpful procedures is available to the student of silent speech. Scientists have got round the speed of delivery problem by using photographic and video-recording equipment to play back body movements at a snail's pace. In the absence of such elaborate apparatus one must train the eyes and the brain to observe what would otherwise be missed.

Despite these differences, the way in which the secret language is learned does have some similarities with learning a spoken language. Imagine that you are eavesdropping on a conversation between two native-born speakers in a language of which you know only a few phrases. Most of their dialogue is likely to remain incomprehensible, no matter how attentively you listen. But now and then familiar words are used, and for a few moments you can follow what is being said. Then comes another torrent of unknown words and you lose your grip on the meaning. When the conversation is finished, you try to piece together what was said by thinking about those words you understood.

As you observe an exchange in body language, you notice expressions or gestures whose meaning seems clear and unambiguous. You are confident that you know what the soundless conversation is all about. Then something goes wrong. One of the children responds in an unexpected way, and the signals suddenly lose their pattern. Instead of having a clear purpose, the exchange seems to break down into a series of unrelated and disorganised body movements.

Do not become discouraged, there is usually a reason for every piece of body language no matter how purposeless it may seem at the time. Be persistent and patient. Carry out your observations according to the basic rules below, and use the information given in this book to help you.

By learning the secret language, you will not only be able to understand exchanges between the very young, but you will also start to understand the children themselves more deeply. With these new insights, you should be able to respond more effectively to their needs and relate more easily to their anxieties.

Six Rules For Successful Child-Watching

1: At first, it is usually better to look at other people's children. In order to observe body signals accurately it is essential to remain a detached objective onlooker. This will be much easier if you are not worried about what the youngsters are getting up to. When watching your own children the psychological barriers which I discussed in the last chapter will make your task far more difficult.

2: Try to make your observations even more objective by pretending you are looking not at young humans but at a strange new species about which you know nothing. Some parents may retort that this is exactly how they regard their children already! If this is really the case, then they have a head start. But most adults need to try quite hard to become sufficiently dispassionate. One approach, which I suggest to mothers who are being taught silent speech, is to pretend that they have just stepped off a flying saucer from Mars and are watching the human animal for the first time. You will find this much easier to do if you concentrate on looking out for body signals. After all, in the past your motives for wanting to look closely at young children will have been many and varied but they will not have included watching for a secret language. Keep in mind exactly *why* you are making your observations, and the novelty of what you are trying to notice should help you to see the exchanges through fresh eyes.

3: At the start limit yourself to no more than three minutes of observation. Even this short period will provide you with far more information than can easily be absorbed or analysed.

4: To begin with only watch interactions between two children, again to restrict the amount of body language which you have to notice and interpret.

5: Try and become in tune with the rhythmic flow of the

language. Do not allow the obvious macro-signals to blind you to the smaller but no less significant micro-signals.

6: You will find it easier to see everything that happens if you train yourself to watch each exchange in a methodical way. Instead of flicking your gaze randomly over the children follow the critical path shown in the illustration opposite.

Start With: Surroundings. Make this observation quickly. During the exchange watch out for changes, such as the arrival of other children, adults etc. which may affect the interaction. Now move on to...

Position of Infants: Check the following points. Sitting or standing? Tense or relaxed? Proximity, note any changes as they occur. Do they become more tense or more at ease? Do they move closer or apart? Abrupt changes of position can be important. Try and see what triggered them. Now move on to...

Stance and Posture: Check the following points. Leaning towards or away from each other? Facing or sideway on to one another? Note changes, especially abrupt ones. Now move on to...

Position of Hands and Arms: Check whether they are stiff or relaxed. Fingers clenched or open? Held close to body or away from sides? Moving vigorously, lethargically or not at all? Holding parts of body or clothes? Palms turned in to body or outwards? Now move on to...

Position of Head: Check whether straight or angled. Note direction of tilt, sideways, upwards or downwards. See if held stiffly or relaxed. Take note of abrupt changes in head position. Now move on to...

Expressions: Look at the mouth, lips, muscles of the forehead and around the eyes. Check direction of gaze and note how long one child looks at the other and whether the break, when it comes, is to their left or the right? Notice eye-contact between the children. Now move on to...

Differences and Similarities: This final observation in the cycle brings you back to a more general view. Are both children relaxed or both tense? Is one more relaxed than the other? Do their postures appear to mimic one another? Note differences or similarities in expression, gaze and head position. Now check on any changes in overall position and surroundings, then proceed through the check list all over again.

Looking at exchanges in this way means zooming in from a general view to a close-up, and then out again. First you observe the whole situation, and then you focus in on smaller and smaller details of the interaction. While doing this you must be constantly be on the look-out for changes of position or expression, expecially abrupt ones. When something like this happens try and remember anything which could have triggered the change.

Clearly there is a great deal to be seen in any exchange, however simple it may seem at first glance. But do not worry about the apparent complexity of silent speech. As I explained in the introduction, any perceptive adult who has experience of small children, which must include almost every reader of a book like this, already has a good grasp of infant body language.

You may not realise it, but you already know most of the signals and what they mean. All it requires is practise in observation in order to overcome those subjective, psychological barriers which I discussed earlier.

Before very long you will find out what others have discovered before you.

The secret language may not make a sound. But its messages come over loud and clear.

3   Baby Talk—And What
It Means

A baby begins to talk at the very moment of birth. Before
the first gasp of air is sucked into the newborn lungs and
the first cry uttered, the naked infant has spoken urgently
and powerfully to the world. The message sent out is one
of the most primitive and potent found in nature. It is also
amongst the most crucial.

"I am helpless and at your mercy," says the baby.
"Unless you love, care and protect me I will die." This
heart-rending plea is intended to evoke an intense
response from the adult world. Usually it works perfectly
and ensures that the full resources of the parents are
mobilised to safeguard the infant.

Within a few weeks of life, the baby will have acquired
a basic repertoire of silent speech signals and be able to
make its feelings and needs known by means of gesture
and expression. At birth these are almost completely
lacking. The few signals which the baby does possess are
embryonic and largely unco-ordinated. Yet even when it
is denied that most fundamental of body signals, the
smile, the baby still manages to make its meaning clear.
This is achieved not by anything the baby does, but by
what it is—a baby! The human infant, like the newborn of
many animals, provides a perfect example of Marshall
McLuhan's famous dictum: 'The medium is the message.'

One of the first scientists to realise the existence of this
message was the great anthropologist Konrad Lorenz.

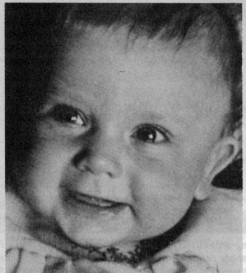

The baby is the message. Research has shown that the special features which make up babyishness form a powerful biological signal that releases a special response in adults.

After studying the young of many species, Dr. Lorenz put forward the idea that the physical qualities we describe by the general term "babyishness" had a special significance. He believed that the special physical characteristics of the new-born constituted a biological signal whose effect is to trigger the "mothering" responses in adult animals. He labelled this signal a "releaser" because its purpose, and usual effect, is to release a whole series of complex rearing behaviours. This "releaser" clearly works at a very basic, biological level. It is primarily an inborn response, rather than a learned one; although learning does play an important part in its development.

All animals, and especially the female of the species, whose young need care and protection during the early stages of life, have a biological predisposition to raise

Young animals as different as a human baby and a lion cub share certain similarities of shape which help ensure their survival during the dangerous and vulnerable first months of life.

their young. And it is the young themselves who trigger off this response!

However strange, and perhaps offensive, this proposition may strike you, there is a good deal of hard scientific evidence in support of Dr. Lorenz. Human babies, like the young of many other mammals, *do* possess particular physical qualities which provoke a unique response amongst adults.

To try and find out how such a "releaser" might work, psychologists have devised a number of experiments. One of the earliest was carried out by Dr. M. A. Cann at the University of Chicago during the early 'fifties. He used drawings of 53 different kinds of animals, including humans, which depicted them as youngsters and adults. Each pair of illustrations was shown to a wide cross-section of the population; married and single women, husbands and bachelors, couples with and

...ess is another nonverbal message that
animals will often respond to. An animal's need to nurse the
other species. This breed dong of these of orphaned
orphaned lion cubs.

...al expression

...without ...ses ...ly ...th
elderly. The ...and ...that
preferred ...ble to ...ly, ...e
...ere ...only ...
...preferred for ...w...
strength of their face ...when ...
where ...were married or single children mothers.
If they had children or were expecting, ...
preference for the baby pictures tended ...
stronger. Men, although generally photo...
the baby pictures also varied in their choices ...
...men, single men and the teenage boys...
...ho...worried, expectant wives we...
...at the strongest baby preference ...was
...owed was for the preference. Young, ...
...plified. Try this fascinating experiment for ...
using the drawings on page 42.

Babyishness is such a powerful message that adult animals will often respond to the signals when sent by other species. This great dane, for example, mothered orphaned lion cubs without protest—despite her mournful expression.

without children, young adults, the middle-aged and the elderly. They were asked which of the two drawings they preferred, and invited to comment on their choice. The results were intriguing. All the women tested showed a marked preference for drawings of baby animals, but the strength of their interest varied slightly according to whether they were married or single, childless or mothers. If they had children, or were expecting them, their preference for the baby pictures tended to be a lot stronger. Men, although generally showing less interest in the baby pictures, also varied in their choice according to marital status. Single men had the least bias towards the baby drawings. Men whose wives were expecting their first child were much more interested, while fathers showed the greatest preference. You may care to try out a simplified form of this fascinating experiment for yourself using the drawings on page 42.

Illustrations also formed the basis for a series of tests carried out in the mid-'Sixties by another American researcher Dr. Eckhard Hess. Instead of asking his subjects to express a preference for one or other of the drawings, he made a more objective evaluation of their responses by measuring something over which they had no direct control, changes in pupil size.

As I explained in Chapter Two, these tell-tale changes occur whenever we see something of special interest, and there is nothing we can do about it. Market researchers use this technique to assess the effectiveness of advertisements, psychologists to determine a clients sexual orientation, and criminologists to discover if a particular face or location has a special significance for a suspect.

Dr Hess made his volunteers look into a box in which pictures, similar to those used by Dr Cann, were being projected. Using a mirror, an infra-red light source—which is invisible to the naked-eye—and a movie camera, he was able to record changes in pupil size. His results confirmed those of the earlier experiments. Interest in pictures of human babies and young animals varied according to sex, marital status, and the subject's own involvement with children. But women were always more interested in the very young than men.

What Makes Babies So Special?

Dogs, cats, sheep, and lions may not seem to have much in common. But, as youngsters, they did share many similar features. Baby animals are not scaled-down versions of their parents, any more than a human infant is a manikin. They are a special kind of creature with unique, physical features. Take a long, hard look at puppies, kittens, lambs, or lion cubs, and some of these look-alike characteristics will become apparent.

Their limbs are short and heavy, their abdomens bulge, and most strikingly of all their heads are out of proportion to their bodies. They have plump cheeks, large bulbous foreheads and prominent eyes, which owing to the size of the forehead can be located as far down as the middle of the face.

These features not only distinguish them from adults, they serve to *release* the maternal response in grown-up animals. And not only amongst their own species. A dog's reaction to a kitten will be very different from its reaction to an adult cat. And as the illustration on page 43 shows, a bitch can even be persuaded to rear orphaned lion cubs. The human response to the young of many species is equally selective and warm. The usual reaction, especially amongst women, to kittens, puppies or lambs, is to want to hold, stroke, caress and generally "mother" them. Lap dogs, which are often given such lavish attention by elderly, single women, frequently keep some of the basic babyish features even in their adult form. The most popular toy breeds, the pekinese, chihuahua, pug and pomeranian, all have flattish faces and big round eyes.

We all tend to regard cruelty to animals which still retain "baby" characteristics as being worse than similar acts of violence against the adult animal. Kicking a kitten or beating a puppy is likely to provoke a far stronger feeling of revulsion in most people than inflicting the same treatment on a cat or dog. As most adult animals are just as defenceless as young ones, the reaction is clearly more emotional than rational.

As the animal grows out of its "baby looks", attitudes change. Farmers' wives apart, the majority of women would probably agree that lambs are pretty but sheep look stupid, calves are adorable but cows unattractive.

Plump human babies, with features which most closely match the idealised concept of what a baby should look like, are usually seen as more attractive than thin ones. Doctors and nutritionists constantly warn that overfeeding small children is unhealthy, but many mothers—and baby show judges—continue to show a marked preference for the chubby, wide-eyed baby.

All these responses can be attributed to the powerful

maternal feelings which are spontaneously released by the special physical characteristics of the human baby and young animal.

By emphasising these qualities, strong emotions can be deliberately generated for commercial gain. Toy manufacturers have always designed their dolls to incorporate all the basic "releaser" signals. The faces are made large and round, the cheeks bulge, the eyes are prominent, the torsos' plump and the limbs pudgy. By building in these distortions they ensure that small girls feel strongly attracted by their products. Interestingly, one of the most spectacularly successful new dolls in recent years, *Action Man*, was designed with boys in mind. This series, whose sales run into millions, avoids all the releaser features found in dolls for girls. The manikin's face is lean, his body spare and muscular.

Perhaps the most successful exploiter of the built-in "releaser" was Walt Disney. All his most popular cartoon characters, from the Seven Dwarfs to the Three Little Pigs, are drawn so as to maximise the "babyishness" of their features. Disney cartoon villains, from the Wicked Witch to the Big Bad Wolf, are uniformly lean and scrawny.

Mickey Mouse, the best liked character in the history of the cartoon film, is a perfect example of releaser signals put to commercial use. His forehead is large, and his big round eyes are the major feature of a head which is out of proportion to the plump body. In 1928 when Mickey first appeared before the public (he was known as Mortimer Mouse in those days) nobody had any idea that such a thing as a biological releaser existed. Disney, either by luck or intuition, knew how to stylise his creation so that it evoked a deep and positive response from his audiences. This is not just speculation. Using the "pupil size" measure for interest as in his earlier experiments, Dr Hess later tested the response to different types of drawings. These ranged from naturalistic pictures of the human and animal features, to Disney-type representations of the same subjects. The more Disneylike the illustrations, the greater the pupil response they produced.

I have said that the "babyishness" of babies is the first signal of the secret language. But an even earlier act of communication may occur, although here the message is not sent directly by the infant but *by the act of giving birth itself*. Adults who see a baby delivered usually feel that they have witnessed a very special and deeply moving event. Husbands who were allowed to stay with their wives during childbirth have frequently told me that any fears they had that it might upset them disappeared as soon as the baby started to arrive. Afterwards the majority felt that it had been one of the most moving and important experiences of their lives. Even doctors and midwives who have attended hundreds of deliveries often report that each birth is special and means something to them.

These powerful and positive feelings were experienced and discussed by delegates attending a recent symposium on parent-infant relationships, which had been organised in London by the CIBA Foundation. After a film showing childbirth in American hospitals and homes had been projected, one member of the audience commented that the infectious excitement evoked by witnessing deliveries even spread to those watching the event on film.

Dr J. S. Rosenblatt of Rutgers University, New Jersey, agreed with this view and added: "One of the two photographers who came to film a birth in California said afterwards that he felt he loved the woman more than he loved his wife. Both photographers felt very involved with the family."

Dr A. Bentovim, of the Hospital For Sick Children in London, mentioned the effect that the film had exerted on the audience of doctors and psychologists: "There was a moment of excitement in the group here," he commented. "The boundaries between each of us seemed to dissolve with the shared feeling. The potential for ecstasy therefore seems to be universally present, particularly in those with a vested interest in infancy!"

That a baby's special shape acts as a signal which

releases maternal behaviours in adult animals can no longer be doubted. But this fact neither diminishes the value of a human mother's love, nor undermines its uniqueness. The mothering response of a female rat may be triggered by the same type of genetic programming which forms the basis of a human mother's immediate and intense attraction to her baby. But beyond that starting point the comparison ends. As it happens, rats make excellent and painstaking parents. But to say that their behaviour is the same as ours is absurdly inaccurate. We now know that many of our most important social acts are deeply rooted in biology. A whole new area of study called Sociobiology has grown up around this realisation. But while we can recognise man's true place in nature more clearly than at any time in our history, we are not, despite what some experts would have us believe, naked apes at large in a human zoo. We have language, and the ability to consider such abstract concepts as love and the inherent rights of the individual. We learn, not merely by direct experience, but from our knowledge of language and our powers of reasoning. Our societies have, as a result, created strong moral, ethical and legal codes, which would seem to safeguard the very young. Even if the parents fail, the community will feel obliged to take over the rearing of the infant. Why then should the primitive biological "releaser" have survived? Surely nature can trust us to feed and protect our young without any need for a biological primer? It is important to remember that in terms of evolution our present structure is no more than a blink in the eye of time. It is sometimes said that if the entire history of the world was compressed into just twelve hours, then civilisation would only start at one minute to midnight. For the human species to survive the thousands of years before moral codes and social constraints were developed, some powerful biological mechanism was clearly essential. However, while it is easy to believe that Neanderthal man was not exactly flowing with the milk of human kindness when it came to child rearing, it comes as a shock to discover that our own great-great-grandsires were probably not all that much better as parents.

The whole idea of caring for children, and the cultural pressures on parents to do so correctly, are of surprisingly recent origin. "Good mothering" is an invention of modernisation, as Professor Edward Shorter graphically illustrates in his book *The Making of the Modern Family*. He comments: 'In traditional society mothers viewed the development and happiness of infants younger than two with indifference."

That is an under-statement. Before they had even learned to walk, children could expect to have been savagely ill-treated, neglected and starved. Even babies in the cradle were subjected to horrendous treatment. If they cried excessively, they ran the risk of being knocked unconscious or rocked so violently they became insensible. Such horror stories were by no means confined to the poorer and less educated classes. A peasant's baby might be left out as food for the wild animals, but a merchant's child was likely to receive brutal punishments for the slightest offence, while an aristocrat's off-spring might even be thrashed to death for disturbing his illustrious parents. Sometimes not even royal blood could save them. One of the entertainments with which European courtiers used to while away their time was to throw tightly swaddled babies from one palace window to the next. An infant brother of Henri IV of France was being used as a human ball in this way when he was dropped and fell to his death on the cobble stones below. The American historian Lloyd de Mause sums up the situation in his book *The History of Childhood* when he remarks that "Childhood is a nightmare from which we have only recently begun to awaken."

Does this litany of horror mean that the first message of life usually falls on deaf ears? Fortunately not. Even in the most primitive and brutish societies, the "releaser" succeeds frequently enough for the population levels to be maintained. My point is that had nature relied on the pious hope that a mother would love her child simply because she had given birth to it, and that a father would protect the baby simply because he had helped to conceive it, then the human race would have become extinct long ago.

The Touch Of Love

The baby sends its message of helplessness. It pleads with the world to be allowed to survive. How does the mother signal her response, and reassure the infant that it will receive that essential love and protection? Curiously enough the precise nature of the mother's first message seems to depend on when and where the baby was born. An intensive study carried out by Dr M. H. Klaus, of the Department of Pediatrics of America's Case Western Reserve University, has shown that while all mothers send generally similar signals to their newborn babies, small but possibly very significant variations do occur. These depend on whether the baby was full-term or premature and whether the birth took place at home or in hospital. The method of communication is one of touch. The mother strokes the infant with her fingers and hands and she does so in a very methodical way. Dr Klaus reports: "The same sequence of behaviour was observed in all the mothers of full-term infants when they first interacted with them. Every woman began with fingertip-touching on the infant's extremities and proceeded within the first four to eight minutes to massaging and encompassing palm contact on the trunk."

These soothing movements started with the mother gently touching the toes and hands of the baby with her fingertips. She then transferred to the infant's face and body, stroking her fingers lightly against the soft skin. After a while she began to use the whole of her hand to perform the massage, rubbing the child with her palm. As she did this the mother became increasingly excited and then progressively more relaxed. After her arousal had passed a peak she sometimes fell asleep.

Dr Klaus and his assistants accurately measured the amount of time each mother spent caressing her child, and compared the duration of fingertip-touching to palm massage. They found that mothers always began by making fingertip contact, usually on the baby's hands or feet, and only then proceeded to palm massage of the face and trunk. In his report Dr Klaus notes that "fingertip contact decreased from 52 per cent of the first three minutes of contact to 26 per cent of the last three minutes, while palm contact increased from 38 per cent to 62 per cent. Every mother made this changeover."

For this sequence of movements to be followed, however, the researchers found that certain conditions had to be assured. The infants in their study were always given naked to the mother. In an earlier series of observations, where the baby was kept wrapped in a blanket, it required many more sessions for the palm touching and close contact behaviour to occur. The second condition was that the mother and child had privacy. Observations were made discreetly through a small window. If a stranger was present in the room then the mother's pattern of caresses would change.

The total amount of time a mother spent touching her baby increased markedly between the first and third period of their time together. During their first ten minute session of close contact, the mothers actually touched the baby for about two minutes, and mostly concentrated on fingertip stroking of the hands and feet. There was only a small amount of palm massage or touching of the face and body. By the third visit, they were touching the child for around five minutes and dividing their caresses more or less evenly between fingertip-touching and palm massage, while concentrating their attention more on the face and body.

The mothers of full-term infants were given their babies as early as one hour after birth. Mothers of premature babies had to wait between one and three days for their first long period of contact. Then when the naked baby was placed on the bed beside them they would first only touch them with their fingertips and for a shorter amount of time than full-term mothers. They always took longer to make the change over from fingertip stroking to palm massages.

Mothers who gave birth at home had a slightly different pattern of communication to mothers whose babies were born in hospital. Instead of starting by fingertip-touching the hands and feet of their infants, home mothers immediately started to caress the baby's face with their fingers, making a gentle stroking movement. After only a few moments they would switch to palm massage of the face and body. Not only was touching of the face and body begun far earlier, and the changeover from fingertips to palms made far more rapidly, but there was more overall contact during the early sessions. Dr Klaus believes that these differences can be accounted for by the fact that the home mothers were given their babies far sooner after birth. Often they would be nursing the infant before the delivery of the placenta. The mother also had more say over her surroundings. Dr Klaus comments: "In sharp contrast to the woman who gives birth in hospital, the woman who delivers at her own home appears to be in control of the process. She chooses the room in the house and the location within the room for her birth, as well as guests who will be present. She is an active participant during her labour and delivery rather than a passive patient."

Under these conditions the baby is in a quiet and alert state when first placed in the mother's arms, rather than in the sleepy condition in which hospital mothers often received them.

There is some evidence to suggest that this very early contact between mother and baby is highly beneficial to the infant. But it would be quite wrong to assume because of this that home births are always better than hospital deliveries. This is a subject which I will be discussing in detail in Chapter Nine, when I explain how mothers can make use of their new knowledge of the secret language.

It is clear that these stroking and massaging movements are body language signals. In response to the baby's silent cry: "Help me..." the fingertip touch of love says gently: "I am here. Don't be afraid any more." And feeling the soft warmth of the baby's body beneath her slowly moving fingers, the mother too receives a signal of reassurance. "I am vibrant with life," the infant's body tells her. The palm massage has a more soothing message. It helps to relax and calm the child by its firm pressure, smoothing away whatever phantoms of dread may disturb the baby's mind. And the mother, feeling her child intensely through the larger area of body contact, has her own anxieties eased.

Beyond these certainties, there is at present only ignorance about these signals. We do not know why the mother of a full-term baby touches his body in a different way from the mother of a premature baby. There are theories, but little clear evidence to support them. We are not certain why mothers whose babies are delivered in a hospital should approach them more cautiously than those whose babies are born at home. Again there are theories, but no firm conclusions. Finally we do not yet know how, if at all, these changes in touching and massaging alter the message which the fingers and hands convey. All these mysterious areas of early body language still remain to be explored.

Reflecting The Rhythm Of Speech

Some of the most frequent and intriguing body movements can only be detected by means of slow-motion recording techniques. These are the small, quick responses we all make as a result of the rhythm of language. If you strike a tuning fork any other fork in the vicinity, which is tuned to the same pitch, will immediately start to vibrate. The human brain has a similar sensitivity to the vibrations of the human voice. We are born with the ability to respond to the rise and fall of man-made speech, and translate pace, pause and intonation into body language. This unique awareness of the rhythm of human speech has been detected in babies only a few days old. It is almost certainly present at birth.

In the film industry the term "lip synch" means that pictures and sound track have been adjusted so that people on the screen will seem to talk naturally. If the track ever gets out of "synch", then it is immediately apparent and very distracting. Largely through the work of Dr William Condon of Boston, we now know that it is not only in films that people have to be in lip synch. Effective communication depends on it! Dr Condon discovered many microscopic body movements by taking miles of cine film and then painstakingly going through every frame of it dozens of time. The footage in his film library looks ordinary enough until he slows it down, runs it backwards and forwards and explains what is really happening. Then the commonplace events he has recorded become quite extraordinary. One short piece of film, for instance, shows a man and a woman talking together in an office. Even at normal running speed it is clear they are moving around while speaking, and many of these movements are recognisable body language signals. They shift in their seats, fiddle with their hands, turn their heads and alter their positions slightly. When analysed, these can be seen as highly organised and mutually synchronised movements which reflect the rise and fall of the conversation. They are dancing together to the rhythm of their words. Everybody does this, but it takes the slow motion camera to reveal the fact to us. "The body of a speaker moves in a precise synchrony with his own speech," explains Dr Condon. "This occurs all the time. It indicates a unified human being. In further studying this we began to see that a listener also moves in precise synchrony with a speaker."

Babies too take part in this sort of rhythmic dance, their bodies making small but definite movements in response to the rise and fall of words flowing around them. They do this not only when being spoken to directly, but also when adults are talking to each other in their hearing. An infant lying in his cot while the grown-ups are chatting will be making almost imperceptible but perfectly synchronised movements of the body and limbs.

This built-in sensitivity to man-made sounds enables the baby to learn, from the moment of birth, that human speech has a unique rhythm: In order to speak correctly, whether in silent speech or using both body language and the spoken word, this rhythm must be acquired. It is as important for the child to get the pace and intonation right as it is for him to learn the body talk signals and the words of his native language. When the mastery is inadequate the child will still be able to communicate, but much less efficiently. Children who are born deaf can never acquire the rhythm of speech. They may be highly articulate, but their fluency will always be of a different order to that of the hearing child. As soon as they begin to talk, rhythmic speakers realise that something is not quite right. They are out of "lip synch." The same thing happens to a greater or lesser extent when a person speaks in a foreign language. To be mistaken for a national they must not only pronounce the words correctly and use the right body language, but they must also match the natural rhythm of that particular form of speech.

A similar break-down in communication can occur if, usually because of brain damage, a child cannot synchronise his body movements to his own or other people's speech patterns. This can be so disturbing that it may make relaxed communication almost impossible. In one case, the mother of a baby who suffered from cerebral palsy found herself quite unable to form any bond with the baby, even though she loved him dearly. The jerky movements resulting from the brain damage made it impossible for the mother to synchronise with him. Communications were restored, and the relationship established, only after a therapist had taught the mother to move in the same way as her little son. By copying the child's abrupt actions she achieved perfect synchronisation.

Breaking The Silence Barrier

Silence may not be a word which most parents readily associate with babies. Anybody whose nights have been made sleepless by unending bawling can be forgiven for assuming that the very young are extremely vocal. Yet in a very real sense babies have been imprisoned behind a wall of silence throughout mankind's history. Indeed it is only in the past five or six years that the barriers have started to come down.

However much a baby rends the air with loud cries, there is little or no social content to their sobs. They may be telling the world that they are hungry, thirsty, soiled or generally unhappy about life. But this is only communication at the most basic level. Infants, we now know, are capable of far more than that. Given the opportunity, a baby of even a few days old is a precociously sociable little creature, who wants and needs to interact with other human beings.

For centuries the silence barrier was as much physical as perceptual. Tightly swaddled in yard upon yard of bandage the newborn child, unable to move either arms or legs, was rendered incapable of reaching out to grasp and explore its surroundings. Swaddling died out in Europe around the middle of the nineteenth century, and today would quite rightly be regarded as a barbarity. Yet even now babies can remain as effectively isolated from the outside world as if they were still being transformed into miniature mummies. They are tucked firmly into high-sided prams or cots, covered with blankets so that only their head and occasionally their arms can be seen, and left for hours on end with nothing more stimulating than a dangling toy for company. Newborn babies do, of course, spend sixteen hours out of twenty-four asleep. But the periods of sleep are scattered during the day, and in their waking moments babies need the stimulation and learning experience of social exchanges as keenly as food and drink.

As the baby gets older, the need for sleep diminishes. By six months, it is down to about fourteen hours a day, and consequently the importance of these interactions becomes all the greater. How is this need normally met?

Sometimes a baby is taken up and held against his mother, placed on her knee or supported on one arm in a more or less upright position very close to her body. On other occasions the baby will be "talked to" whilst lying in the pram or cot. Under these conditions it is hardly surprising if the infant finds it hard to communicate effectively. Put yourself in the baby's position and imagine how difficult it would be to hold an intelligent conversation if you were being tightly clasped, your legs restrained and your arms held against your sides, only a few inches from the other person! Or consider the problems facing a baby lying flat on its back staring up at the large, almost bodiless adult faces looming over it, from a few inches away. Being sociable under these conditions must be like trying to hold a serious conversation while lying flat on your back in a sick bed. And anybody who has ever had to attempt that will know how awkward and restricting it soon becomes.

The human animal is designed by nature to communicate most effectively when in a more or less upright position, with the whole body in view so that all the non-verbal signals can clearly be seen. Faces, those critical areas for sending and receiving messages, should be almost level with one another with both heads held vertically. The distance between the two parties involved should be close enough for the exchange to be easy and comfortable, yet not so close that either person feels intimidated or overwhelmed by the other. In adults, proximity varies according to the nature of their relationship. With intimates, about eighteen inches is the preferred distance. In this way, bodily contact can easily be achieved, and it is possible to speak in whispers. The usual distance between close but not intimate friends is between eighteen inches and four feet, while more formal social discussions, for example between an employer and a subordinate, normally take place at between nine and twelve feet. As a general rule small children like to be much closer when talking or playing. Even infants meeting for the first time will stand or squat within three feet of one another. But at its closest the distance small children like to keep around them when communicating is greater than adults normally allow. The grown-up will typically press the toddler close or hold a baby within a few inches of her face when attempting to communicate. Under these conditions an effective two-way dialogue is impossible.

How To Talk To Your Baby

To ensure the best possible social exchange, make the conditions as near perfect as you can by following the six guidelines listed below:

1: The baby must be placed in a comfortable, secure seat which holds him safely while allowing the arms and legs complete freedom of movement.

2: The seat should support the back, neck and head firmly. Babies aged less than six to eight weeks have a tendency to curl up. This is not because their spines are weak, but through an instinctive need to find warmth and comfort, something which is achieved by curling up in a bed or against the mother's body.

3: The baby should be as near upright as possible. Again, babies of less than eight weeks find this an uncomfortable position, and their chairs should be angled as much as is necessary to ensure their complete relaxation.

4: Position the chair so that you can bring your face level with the baby's. This can usually be arranged by placing the baby seat on an arm chair, thus raising the infant three or four feet above the ground.

5: Make certain that the baby can see your hands, arms

and trunk. Do not let them become obscured from view, by the arm of a chair for instance.

6: Remain relaxed. Never try to force the pace of the exchange. Let the dialogue flow naturally and easily.

With the baby in position, you can start a dialogue. What kind of signals will the infant use, and what kind of things ought you to be on the look out for during exchanges?

It will immediately be obvious that the baby uses a number of face and body movements. The arms and legs will waggle or kick with varying degrees of vigour and excitement. The infant's head will turn, his eyes will gaze into yours and then look away again, his mouth may form different expressions. None of this will come as any great surprise, for you will have seen most of the signals before. At first, they are unlikely to appear any more significant or organised than they did when the baby was lying flat on his back in the pram. But there are some important differences which careful observation will soon reveal. These lie in the sequence of the movements and the cycle of activity which gradually becomes clear to the watchful eye.

What Every Baby Must Learn

To be successful, any form of communication must follow one simple rule. An agreement to take turns. Whether you are sending a message in morse or by heliograph, using English or Esperanto, signalling in body language or semaphore, the exchange will only work if those concerned agree to a system of give and take.

The fact that people must take turns to send and receive information seems so obvious that it is sometimes a little difficult to realise that we ever had to learn how to do it. Yet without an understanding and general acceptance of that fundamental law, the kind of bedlam that can occur during a heated political debate, a family row or an office argument, would be a permanent feature of language.

Let us look at a typical conversation between two adults to see how the law of give and take applies to both verbal and non-verbal signals.

They recognise one another at some distance, but it is not until they are close enough for their body talk to be clearly seen that they silently acknowledge each other. They make eye-contact, smile, nod and exchange small waves of greeting, then stop three or four feet from one another, and shake hands. One of them takes the initiative and says:

"Hello, nice to see you. How are things going?" The speaker then stops, having indicated in a number of ways that he has now ceased sending his message and awaits a response. He will probably break eye contact, and look away quickly. He might also incline his head slightly and raise his eye-brows to match the rising inflexion on the last words of the phrase which emphasised the question. If the adults in question are socially skilled, the signals sent by the first will be unambiguous, and the second man will be left in no doubt that the speaker has now reverted to the role of listener. He, in turn, will come in smoothly with an appropriate response.

"Just great, thanks. I was sorry to hear that your wife has been ill. How is she doing?" At this point the man stops and indicates that it is now his turn to become a "receiver" of information. So the conversation proceeds, with each taking it in turns to offer or accept information. When one or both parties decides to end the exchange, signals are sent to make this clear. It will be done both verbally and non-verbally, with one of the speakers again taking the initiative:

"Well, it's been great talking to you. Look after yourself."

"You too, see you around," acknowledges the other person, and they finally break eye-contact and move away from one another.

We normally do this so many dozens of times a day

that what is actually an extremely complicated piece of behaviour involving scores of non-verbal signals gets completely taken for granted. The next time you hold such a conversation, try to notice the different ways in which the moment of change-over is signalled. That point in the exchange when either you or your companion relinquishes one role and adopts another. You will probably find that a number of integrated signals are involved in making a smooth switch from speaker to listener or receiver to sender. But one of the most frequent and powerful ways of switching off as a speaker is to stop talking and immediately break eye-contact with the other person. They will invariably assume you have stopped talking and want them to take over. Even if you stop in the middle of a sentence and look firmly away, they are likely to respond by stepping into the role of the speaker, although they may do so only to demand what is wrong with you!

This breaking of eye-contact occurs during exchanges between infants and adults. It is, in fact, the key body signal which gives the dialogue a structure. Grown-ups respond to it in the same way that they react to a break in eye-contact during an exchange between adults. But, although it will achieve this social status in time, when the baby first uses the signal there is no intention to communicate anything at all. The infant looks away because of the special needs of its developing brain.

In Chapter Two I explained that babies have an inbuilt preference for the human face. They not only seek them out, but they observe them in a special way. A baby offered a new toy will probably study it intently for some moments, and then turn abruptly away and start looking at something else. When looking at people, the child goes through a fairly elaborate cycle of behaviour, before glancing away. It may then return to gazing at the person and repeat the cycle of movements. If the other person is talking and gesticulating in the infant's direction, these watchful periods are likely to be frequent and the baby will respond in a positive way.

Dr Barry Brazelton, one of the pioneers of the study of mother-infant exchanges, considers that these different ways of looking at life are caused by the baby's need to process the information which it receives. A static object offers less information than an animate one, so the infant gives it a long hard stare, and then glances away while his brain sorts out all the details which his eyes have absorbed. Human exchanges provide far greater and much more complex information, which the baby's limited brain-power can only handle provided there are breaks when less data is taken in. Consequently, the baby looks and participates in an exchange, then takes the initiative of terminating the dialogue briefly while his brain races to organise the mass of new information.

When this happens during a social exchange, the adult behaves as if—by making this break in gaze—the baby had said: "OK, I've finished. Now it's your turn." This shapes the adult's own behaviour, and so imposes a pattern on the interaction which comes close to a dialogue between adults. In this way the baby begins to learn the concept of taking it in turns.

In order to demonstrate how this works, let me describe part of a short exchange between a nine-week old baby girl named Josey, and her young mother.

When her mother came into the room, Josey was sitting in her chair staring towards the window. Her mother said: "Hello . . . Josey . . . Josey . . ." with a rising inflection. The little girl did not respond until her left foot was gently shaken. Then she gazed into her mother's eyes. After a moment she opened her mouth slightly. Her mother lent forward and repeated her greeting. Then she raised her right arm and waggled her fingers saying: "Look up there . . ."

Josey opened her mouth wide, raised her left arm so that it covered her chin and kicked out her feet. Her mother brought down her hand and said: "Pretty girl . . ."

Josey raised her arms and lifted up her legs quickly. She stuck out her tongue. Her mother said: "Yes, you are . . . yes, you are . . ." nodding vigorously as she spoke.

Josey watched her closely. "You're naughty," she was told gently. "Yes you are."

The baby girl clutched at her woollen jacket with her left hand and covered her mouth with the back of her right hand. Then she looked away.

Her mother continued to talk and smile animatedly for the few seconds it took for Josey to return her gaze. They looked at each other intently. Then Josey moved her mouth quickly and stuck out her tongue. "Very naughty..." said her mother with a smile. Josey smiled back and her legs moved excitedly. She raised her left hand and held her jacket. Then she looked firmly away for the second time.

To a casual onlooker, it might not appear that much of

Electrically operated cameras took simultaneous pictures of a young mother and her nine week old baby Josey. They show the main phases in the cycle of body language which makes up baby talk.

Josey's mother attracts her attention by calling. The baby who had been looking away eye-contacted her mother. A conversation had been initiated and the orientation phase begun.

Josey's mother smiles a greeting and the baby responds, looking pleased and alert. In body talk she is saying: "Let's have a chat!"

During the play-dialogue stage of their conversation Josey is able to learn a lot about the way body talk works. Like most mothers, hers deliberately exaggerates expressions and gestures so as to make them easier to see and follow. Here Josey mimics her mother's mouth movements. They maintain eye-contact throughout the dialogue.

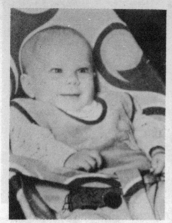

Again Josey tries to copy her mother's mouth movements. She is alert and clearly enjoying their exchange.

Their conversation has now lasted twenty-five seconds. But Josey shows no sign of wanting to bring it to an end. She is still giving her mother eye-contact and looking interested.

*After forty seconds Josey breaks eye-contact and closes
that particular play-dialogue. This is probably due to her
need to process all the information she has received
during the exchange. Her mother continues to talk,
however, and after six seconds Josey looks back at her
and a second play-dialogue takes place. In this way the
mother shapes the exchange but the baby still plays an
active social role.*

a conversation had taken place. But a more careful
analysis reveals that mother and daughter were in fact
having an animated and mutually rewarding dialogue. In
her first two months of life, Josey had already mastered
some of the ground rules of silent speech. Let me expand
on some of the details of the exchange to show more
clearly what happened.

Josey was still sleepy when her mother came in. She
had just been woken up from an afternoon nap, and like
anybody aroused from a peaceful slumber probably did
not feel too much like talking.

Her mother took the initiative by calling out and gently

touching her foot. At this Josey made eye-contact with her mother and stared at her rather seriously for about five seconds, before rousing herself and deciding that it might be fun to talk with Mum. Her movements became more vigorous. She watched her mother intently, and very accurately copied the arms raised movement which was made to attract her attention. As her mother's hand went up, Josey lifted her own left hand towards her mouth, bringing it down again at the exact moment her mother lowered her own arm.

Josey's mother said: "Pretty girlie..." splitting the words into four clear syllables. On each of those stresses, Josey moved a part of her body in synchrony with the sounds. As her mother said "*Pret*..." Josey's right hand came up towards her face. Her left knee bent and started to come upwards. Her mouth opened. She looked delighted. On the second syllable... "*tey*" her feet both came up. On the stress of "*Girl*..." her legs started to move down and her right hand came in towards her body, as if she was conducting the word like an orchestra leader. On the final syllable... "*lee*" both hands came together so that the fingers touched, and the legs went down in a quick almost explosive movement. Josey and her mother had now gone through four of the five phases of mother-infant exchanges which have been identified by Dr Brazelton. These he has labelled: *Initiation; Mutual Orientation; Greetings; Play Dialogue* and *Disengagement*.

The dialogue had been initiated by Josey's mother shaking her foot gently. But this could have been achieved by either of them and in a number of ways. For example the mother could simply have smiled at Josey, or the baby girl might have started the exchange going by smiling herself or making a noise to attract the mother's attention.

Then came six seconds of eye-contact. During such mutual orientation the mother can be talking or smiling, the baby can be looking bright or glum. At the end of this phase Josey acknowledged her mother and agreed to play, signalling her interest by returning the smile and brightening considerably. Play-dialogue followed with Josey responding delightedly to her mother's words and gestures. This lasted twenty-four seconds and was terminated by Josey breaking eye-contact and turning away to the left. She had disengaged, and the first exchange was at an end so far as the baby was concerned. But her mother reacted as though she had been handed the role of speaker, and increased her verbal and non-verbal signals. After six seconds Josey looked back at her mother. They made eye-contact for three seconds, then she signalled a greeting with her mouth and tongue. These lip and mouth activities, during which the tongue can protrude partly or entirely, are very early pre-speech movements. The baby is taking the first, tentative steps towards training all parts of the vocal apparatus in the formation of words. Sometimes these movements are imitations of the mother's own expression, just as many of the infant hand and arm actions are a copy of the adult's gesticulations.

When grown-ups, especially mothers, talk to babies they do so in a very special way. Their own body movements are slowed down and elaborated. They repeat simple words and phrases many times and, as Josey's mother did on several occasions during the exchange I have described, they accompany the words with elaborate silent speech signals. These convey the rhythm of the phrase as much as emphasising the words: "Yes, you are . . ." says Josey's mother, and each word is drawn out, accompanied by an exaggerated nodding which starts with her chin tucked into her neck and ends with the head tilted right back. The slow and deliberate hand and arm movements used during these dialogues remind me of a person trying to communicate with somebody in a foreign language. There is the same careful enunciation of body talk. It is as though the silent speech volume control had been turned up. Such elaboration is not only necessary, but essential, if the baby is to learn the complex range of signals that will so soon be needed.

It is sometimes claimed by scientists who study

mother-baby interactions that their exchanges are not genuine conversations but pseudo-dialogues. "There is no real communication," they insist. "But the mother acts as if there is, and so imposes a pattern on the interaction." This seems to me a debatable point. In one sense, and it is an important one, they are correct. The adult does have to take the initiative. But, at the same time, both adult and baby get something out of the exchange. The baby learns a great deal about the way conversations are put together. It is given the chance to watch a number of body signals sent slowly and deliberately so as to make them as easy as possible to imitate. By copying these movements, and receiving feedback from the grown-up in the form of praise and delight when the copy is a good one, a repertoire of body signals is quickly built up.

The adult too gains a great deal. Most people find it is pleasurable to be able to amuse and stimulate a baby. The smiles and gurgles which result are considered very rewarding.

So we have a situation in which information is exchanged and a lot of pleasure is generated. This seems to me to be the essence of any good conversation.

How much of all these movements can one hope to see with the unaided eye? The answer is quite a lot, when you know what to watch out for.

Look especially for imitations of your own actions, particularly movements of the hands and mouth. Remember to send your own signals in an exaggerated manner—most mothers do this naturally—so that the baby can see them clearly and have the best chance of copying them. Smiling is an important piece of mimicry, and you should read the next chapter to find out how this valuable social signal develops.

Notice the five phases of each interaction. The *initiation: orientation* or mututal eye contact: *greetings; play dialogue* and *disengagement*. Observe how the dialogues are initiated. Do you start them or does the baby? When *orientation* occurs, see how rapidly it is transformed into *greetings* and *play dialogue*. If you are a mother yourself, it will probably be easier at first to watch another mother with her baby. When you are attempting to keep your own baby amused and interested, it can become very difficult to notice everything that happens.

It is impossible to convey in words the smooth flowing rhythm of these exchanges. Study them for yourself and you will quickly appreciate the perfect rhythm of a dialogue dance between an alert baby and a sensitive mother.

Writers of romantic fiction and the makers of television commercials designed to sell baby products, tend to portray child-rearing as an easy, enjoyable and rather glamorous occupation. Their world is filled with sun-warmed nurseries, docile babies and immaculately turned-out mothers. Real life, as you will probably not need reminding, is hardly ever like that! However rewarding, the task of bringing up a family is very hard work. Often the demands made by the new born are so unending and exhausting that even the most caring mother, begins to look on her baby as a burden.

One of the problems during the first few months of life is that the baby appears to be a sort of emotional sponge, who soaks up all the love and attention his parents provide, without giving very much in return. But babies do not ask to be cast in this role of passive recipients. As we have seen, they are born with a hunger for social experiences. By sharing and enjoying play dialogues, mother and child can increase mutual responsiveness with tremendous benefits to them both. The baby is helped to develop more rapidly and confidently. The mother finds that her baby has become the kind of person they both most keenly desire him to be: an active partner in the exciting business of learning what life is all about.

4   How To Read A Smile

Children smile so frequently and spontaneously that we tend to take this most commonplace of social signals for granted. Questions about when and why infants smile are usually greeted with surprise or scorn. To most parents the answer is self-evident. They smile for the same reasons as adults. Because they are happy, pleased, excited or friendly. Those who have studied the smile are a lot less confident that popular theory provides more than a small part of the truth. Although smiles can result from feelings of happiness and pleasure, they are also produced by far less agreeable emotions. The child may smile in order to cover up anger, conceal aggression, hide anxiety or cloak misery. The smile can indicate fearful uncertainty just as easily as it can convey delighted self-assurance. In fact, the more we discover about this apparently simple movement of the lips the more complex it becomes.

"Almost as soon as I started to study 'smiling' I found myself in a mass of contradictions," admits Professor Ray Birdwhistell, of the University of Pennsylvania, in his book *Kinesics and Context*. "From the outset the signal value of the smile proved debatable. Even the most preliminary procedures provided data which were difficult to rationalise."

The precise origins of the smile are still something of a mystery. There are a number of theories, which I will describe in a moment, but no conclusive answers. What can be said for certain is that learning to use the smile correctly is a complicated business. For the youngster, as for the adult, it is not just a question of being able to smile, but also of knowing when and where to do so. Smiling in the wrong place and at the wrong time can be as socially inept as failing to produce a smile when it is expected.

During an investigation of the smile, which took in almost every State of the Union, Professor Birdwhistell found that smiling behaviour which was perfectly acceptable in one region of America produced a very different response in another.

It was considered normal and friendly for a young woman to smile at strangers on Peachtree Street in Atlanta, but extremely inappropriate on Main Street in Buffalo, New York. "In one part of the country, an unsmiling individual might be queried as to whether he was 'angry about something', while in another, the smiling individual might be asked, 'What's funny?'," comments Professor Birdwhistell. The interpretation which other people put on a smile varied from "pleasure" and "friendliness" in one area, to implying "doubt" or "ridicule" in others.

There were also considerable variations in the amount of smiling which went on from one State to the next. By going out onto the streets of scores of towns and cities, Ray Birdwhistell discovered that the middle-classes in Ohio, Indiana and Illinois, smiled more often than people from the same social background who lived in Massachusetts, New Hampshire and Maine, but they in turn smiled more than western New Yorkers. The greatest incidence of smiling occurred in Atlanta, Louisville, Memphis and Nashville. But even within States, variations could occur. By crossing a mountain range or travelling a few hundred miles down the highway, you could move from an area where smiling was commonplace to low smile regions. These differences are due to localised social traditions whose origins may have been lost generations ago.

Genes, attitudes and opinions are not the only things which parents give their children. Whether they smile frequently or very little, is also due largely to family outlook. Children who smile a great deal usually come from homes where the parents smile a lot. Glum, serious faced children, on the other hand, are very often the product of homes where smiles are seldom seen. When these children marry and bring up sons and daughters of their own, the smiling habits they learned during infancy tend to be passed on.

So far as I am aware, no such surveys have been carried out in Britain. But if and when they are, it is very likely the same kind of regional differences will be found.

A Smile Is Born

The smile is a uniquely human response. No other animal uses it. Some apes, especially chimpanzees, appear to grin on occasions, but their teeth-baring is actually a grimace which signals a threat or an appeasement.

The smile is an enigmatic signal—which may be why Leonardo da Vinci painted the Mona Lisa as he did—but there can be no denying its potency. Smiling is not only the most universal social signal—Charles Darwin commented that he had seen smiling babies in every culture with which he had come into contact—it is also amongst the most direct and powerful. A straight line is only the shortest distance between two points. But curve that same line into an arc and you have a potential grin. Show the curve to a dozen adults at random and more than half of them will identify it as a smile without any further clues. Place it within a circle and the verdict will be unanimous.

Smiles, like yawns, tend to be infectious. As the old song says: "When you're smiling, the whole world smiles at you." Professor Birdwhistell's research, and our own experience, shows that this is not always true; but generally we do prefer to be in the presence of somebody who smiles frequently. Time after time adults will comment that a child is "wonderful company, always so bright and smiling." Given the choice, any parent would prefer to have a houseful of smiling children than serious-faced infants.

What is it that makes the smile so popular and forceful? At least part of the answer is that we have an inborn attraction for this particular kind of expression. In the last chapter I described how the physical shape of babies serves to release maternal behaviour in adult animals. In much the same way, grown-ups appear to act as a trigger which produces smiles in human infants. The newborn baby, as we have seen, finds the face an area of special attraction. It seeks out, and pays careful attention to it, within a few hours of birth. At first a crude representation of the face—a circle with dots for eyes and lines for the nose and mouth—will prove sufficient to attract the baby's attention. But soon it takes a much more accurate drawing to hold its interest. As the baby grows older and even more discriminating, smiles become more frequent and more selective. From birth, the infant will have made movements of the lips which we sometimes take—or mistake—for smiles. Because these occur spontaneously and not as a result of anything they have said or done, most parents ignore them. It is only when the baby makes similar lip movements in response to stimulation by the parents that they are confidently identified as smiles. But is this correct? Does the baby smile socially within a few weeks of birth, or is the child simply making random lip-movement which over-eager parents invest with a significance they do not deserve?

Until the early 'sixties the general opinion amongst the experts was that smiles in very small babies were like mirages in the desert. The mere fact that some mothers claimed to see them clearly, was no proof of their existence. The baby was regarded as a self-centred, antisocial little animal who lacked the ability to produce anything as sophisticated as the smile. A more reasonable explanation, it was thought, was that the movements of the lips were burping actions. Parents who wanted their infants to express themselves in a more grown-up way misinterpreted these expulsions of gas as genuine smiles. After many weeks the baby discovered that by making these particular movements of the lips it could produce a very pleasant response from the grown-up world. Just by turning up the edges of the mouth it could encourage adults to cuddle it, smile and talk excitedly. All this attention rewarded the baby, and so made it more likely that the smiling movements would be repeated. According to this theory then, a burp is an egg which incubates into a smile in the warmth of a misguided parental reaction.

The difficulty about this idea is that babies who are born blind, deaf and dumb, smile just like physically normal infants. Even thalidomide children, born so terribly handicapped that they can neither see, hear nor respond to touching, are still able to smile. It is hard to see how these children could learn to smile in the way this theory suggests.

In the opinion of many modern researchers, a more probable explanation is that the smile is an innate response which only occurs in man. Learning does have an important part to play. The fact that smiles are well received by grown-ups means that a baby quickly discovers it can be well worth while to smile. But even without this reinforcement, the social smile rapidly develops. According to this idea, the early lip movements are genuine smiles which reflect the mental rather than the digestive state of the child.

The view is supported by studies of apes and monkeys who produce a wide variety of lip and mouth movements, all of which have a special social meaning. They can be used to greet one another, to appease an aggressor, or as a threat. The human smile can signal all of these, but in marked contrast to the apes we are also able to use the smile to express inner states of happiness, or to reflect our pleasure and amusement.

What makes a baby smile for the first time? Some psychologists believe it is initially used not to indicate pleasure but fury. According to their theory, the trauma of being expelled from a warm womb into a cold world makes a baby so angry that it snarls in fury! Certainly, being cast from the comfort and security of the mother's body into a noisy and frightening new environment cannot be very pleasant, but none of the parents I have ever interviewed was willing to accept this theory. Most thought it ridiculous. They believed, I think correctly, that a baby's first smile is friendly and sociable. It mirrors contentment and pleasure, not some immense internal hatred.

It seems more likely that the smile started life as an appeasement signal amongst our hair-covered ancestors. For primitive man, life was very much a case of nature red in tooth and jaw. The mouth was just as much a weapon of attack as the hands and feet. So when a couple of friendly Stone Age neighbours met one another, they liked to make their non-hostility clear. They signalled this, to a great extent, by producing the same kind of specialised movements with their mouths which other primates still use. They lifted their lips in a relaxed manner to reveal that their teeth were still closed. The message sent was: "Look at my mouth! I am not about to bite you. I am not threatening you." This reassuring signal gradually became ritualised into the smile, in much the same way that indicating non-hostility by offering an open weapon-free hand evolved into the handshake.

Anything that makes us feel less anxious is always well received. Smiles helped to reduce levels of tension, so they became popular. They developed a strong social importance which they still possess today. We smile when a meeting is friendly, and tend to withhold our smiles if a hostile encounter is anticipated. We smile to break the ice and reduce levels of mutual tension when meeting strangers. A smiling baby soothes parental anxieties by appearing well and contented. Since most mothers and fathers very much want their children to be healthy and happy, such smiles provide a welcome reassurance. A smiling baby is more attractive than a glum-faced child, and certainly a great deal nicer to be with than a bawling one. So parents encourage the infant to smile by behaving very positively each time smiling occurs. These responses speed up the development of the smile as a silent signal.

Smile Watching

Any serious attempt to understand the secret language must involve smile watching. By this I do not just mean casual recognition of the fact that a child has smiled, but careful observations which will help you to answer the questions why, when, where and, especially, how the smile was produced.

The smile, as I have suggested, is one of the most powerful signals in the vocabulary of silent speech. But in order to interpret it accurately, some key points must be kept in mind.

First of all, the smile can only be properly understood when seen in the context of other silent speech signals, especially gaze, posture and proximity. Where a child is looking, and how he is standing when the smile occurs, tell us a great deal about the true nature of the signal. Even small differences in the movement of the eyes, and subtle changes in the degree of tension or relaxation in the face and other muscles, can considerably alter the meaning of the smile.

Then the smile must be seen within the flow of body signals. No piece of silent speech occurs in isolation. However spontaneous or eccentric a particular message may appear, it is no more unconnected with what has gone before than one carriage on a long railway train. Only by noting what movements preceded the smile, and watching to see what happens after the smile has been made, can an accurate picture of the overall message be constructed.

The smile itself should be studied very exactly. If you ask the average person to describe what happens when somebody is smiling, they will probably say: "The edges of the mouth are turned up. The mouth opens sometimes. You can see the teeth." This is perfectly true, and quite satisfactory as an everyday description. But for a correct interpretation every smile must be seen and analysed in far more detail. For example, you must notice the way in which the teeth are uncovered, and observe whether the top or bottom row is more exposed. Then you must note the length of the smile, and spot when and why it stops.

The intensity of the smile is determined by a number of simultaneous signals. Normally one automatically assesses this intensity without having to break down the message into its individual components of gaze, posture and so on. We know without having to think about it when somebody is giving a warm spontaneous smile, or merely a polite one.

For the purposes of interpreting the secret language correctly, however, it is useful to notice and take into account the main elements of body talk which determine the intensity, or otherwise of a smile. These are the duration and direction of gaze; the extent of lip and mouth movements; the duration of the smile; and especially changes in the muscles around the eyes. The influence of the eyes over the type of smile produced is considerable.

There may seem a great deal to watch out for. But it is far less difficult in practice than it sounds in theory. Mainly it is a matter of perfecting ones powers of observation. A famous artist once told me that his skill lay not in his hands but in his eyes: "Anybody can paint," he commented. "It is not a question of training the hands to obey, but teaching the eyes to see."

It is exactly the same with smile watching.

There Are Smiles—And Smiles!

The descriptions which follow should be regarded as Identikit pictures of smiles, rather than universal

portraits. They are intended to help you identify and
interpret smiles correctly, and for the most part will do
just that. But remember that no two smiles are exactly
alike. There are so many permutations of body signals
which can subtly alter the smile's message that it is
impossible to place a final meaning on any one of them.
They are as unique as the children producing them. All
one can safely say is that most of the time a certain smile is
most likely to be expressing one particular kind of
emotion, or sending out one specific type of message.

The smiles listed below are arranged according to
intensity. That is, by the strength of meaning behind
them. The more intense a smile, the more powerfully the
message is sent. But changes of intensity, brought about
by switching from one type of smile to another, do not
simply mean that the same message is being sent at an
increased or reduced power. It is more likely to indicate
that the content of the message has changed. For
example, a small boy with a low intensity *simple smile*
may be conveying anxiety. If he then changes to a high
intensity *broad smile*, a shift from nervousness to
amusement is indicated, not increased anxiety. Major
changes in intensity are produced by quite obvious
alterations in expression, especially of the lips and the
muscles around the eyes. But within each type of smile,
intensity can be varied by small movements of the face
which do not drastically alter the expression. These
variations do indicate a turning up or down of the secret
language volume-control. The same message is being sent
out only with increased or reduced urgency.

Early Smiles: In the first few weeks of life, babies smile
only when drowsy or during periods of irregular sleep.
The smile reflects the infant's inner state, and is not made
in response to any specific sight or sound in its
surroundings. The movements of the lips are often very
tentative, and may not even be recognised as smiles at all.
These are the mouthings which some psychologists
believe are the result of a baby breaking wind. Others, as I

explained earlier, see them as the first indications of a built-in social response. After each smile there is an interval of at least five minutes before the next one is produced. This seems to be a period of recoupment. It is as if psychic tension slowly builds up, is released in the smile, and then gradually increases again to the point where another smile occurs. The interval is greatest during the first ten days of life.

Croissant Smiles: First seen around five weeks, but may not develop fully until the baby is four months old. The smile is produced by pulling back the edges of the mouth and forming a small aperture at the centre of the lips. There is a slight upturn at each corner, and its appearance rather resembles the French pastry, which gives the smile its name. Babies make croissant smiles during exchanges with adults. They can be used to signal greetings and an intention to take part in a play-dialogue. They are also used during the subsequent play-dialogues. Croissant smiles express pleasure and excitement at being involved with another human being. The secret language message they contain is: "This is fun . . . I am enjoying myself. How thrilling life is!"

Simple Smiles: Develop from the croissant smile. They are usually present by the age of six months, but can sometimes be seen, in a slightly weaker form, as early as twelve weeks. Because simple smiles are much more positive and "smile-like" than the often hesitant croissant smile, parents are especially pleased with them. The infant has, in fact, mastered the first grown-up signal. The croissant smile vanishes during early babyhood, but this smile will be used throughout childhood and adult life.

Simple smiles are used during greetings and play-dialogues with adults, and when interacting with other children. They express pleasure, delight and a general happiness at what is going on. The smile is also evoked by anything unexpected but pleasantly exciting. For example a game of peek-a-boo, or the "hiding" and sudden "discovery" of a toy by a grown-up. Simple smiles are also seen during games with objects, but usually only in infants of eight months or older.

The simple smile is produced by drawing back and raising the edges of the mouth. The amount of upturn varies according to the intensity of the smile, but need not be very great to produce a warm, compelling expression, provided the eyes also mirror the smile. Unlike the croissant smile, no small central aperture is formed; but the lips may part along their entire length to reveal a little of the top row of teeth. The exposure of the teeth is minimal in the simple smile. As more of them are revealed it changes its form to that of an upper smile or a broad smile (see below).

It is only when the child is able to crawl vigorously and starts to interact with other infants that the simple smile fully comes into its own as a social signal. The smile is used between small children during greetings and between infants and adults in the same way. It normally expresses either pleasure or a polite welcome. But the intensity of the smile can be varied to produce two very different types of message. This is done less by variations in the movement of the lips than by the duration of the smile, and the way in which it is framed by other body movements. In its low intensity form, the simple smile indicates uncertainty. When used as a high intensity signal its message is one of pleasurable anticipation and general self-confidence.

Simple Smiles—Low Intensity

The key message conveyed by this use of the simple smile is one of hesitation, and a lack of confidence. It is often seen for example on the lips of a shy toddler who is watching other infants at play. Children who hang back from group games during their first few sessions at a day

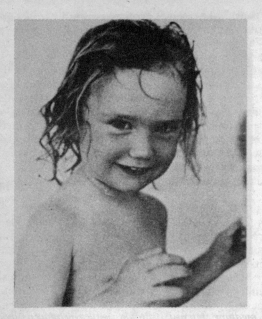

A low intensity simple smile. This two-year-old is being friendly but uncertain. Posture and the duration of the smile as much as the movement of the lips distinguish this signal.

nursery frequently have low intensity simple smiles. They want to be friendly and join in, but lack the necessary nerve to make the first move. The same signal may be sent by otherwise confident infants when meeting strange adults. A toddler being introduced to an unfamiliar nursery supervisor, or a new teacher, will use this type of smile to indicate a friendly intent coupled to an uncertainty about how they are expected to respond or what will happen next.

The movement of the lips are almost the same as for a medium or high intensity simple smile, although there may be less upturn at the edges. The main differences are

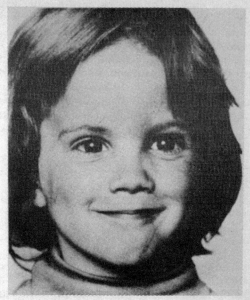

A medium intensity simple smile produced by a four-year-old boy as a friendly but not overenthusiastic greeting. The lips are drawn back but the teeth remain covered.

to be found in the length of the smile, the posture and the way the child looks at others. The smile usually flickers like a dying lightbulb, and so does the gaze. The child may watch other children or adults intently so long as no one is returning the stare. But if somebody does glance in his direction, the child will probably assume a serious expression and look, or even move, away. Low intensity simple smiles do not indicate real fear, or even a high level of anxiety. But they do suggest that the child is uncomfortable about the situation in some way. This type of body talk is more likely to be a reflection of inner feelings, rather than a deliberate act of communication when it is not directed at any one person in particular. It becomes an intentional piece of silent speech, however, when combined with brief eye-contact aimed at an adult, older child or an aggressive infant of the same age. In this situation the low intensity simple smile, combined with the appropriate body movements (see Chapter Six) forms an appeasement signal. The infant is saying: "You don't have to worry about me ... I am not going to cause you any trouble. I am no threat. I just want to be left alone."

Simple Smiles—High Intensity

While the uncertain simple smile flickers nervously, the high intensity simple smile of the confident, happy infant shines like a beacon. You can see it on the faces of children who are happily playing on their own or watching others with every intention of joining in at any moment. There may be a rather more pronounced retraction of the sides of the mouth and greater upturn at the edges. The lips may be more separated, while both the expression and the gaze will remain steady. The child's posture is relaxed but alert. It is pleasurably watching all that happens and feels no anxiety about its surroundings. When used as a greeting to familiar adults, the warmth is increased by a slight narrowing of the gaze as eye-contact is made. You can see smiles like this on the faces of infants running to greet their mothers at the end of a morning at play school, or when saying hello to a favourite relative.

When combined with a widening of the eyes and an eyebrow raise, the simple smile conveys delighted surprise or pleasurable anticipation. "Guess what I've brought you?" asks Dad on his return from a trip. As the gift is produced and unwrapped, the child may give a simple smile, open his eyes wide and arch the eye-brows. When the present is actually revealed, the mouth may open wider to make an upper or broad smile, which indicates a much higher level of excitement and happiness.

A high intensity simple smile on the face of an assertive and self-confident three-year-old as he watches other children playing and debates whether or not to join in.

This change from a high intensity simple smile to the even stronger upper or broad smile also frequently occurs at the moment when an infant who has been watching other children playing decides to join in. As the child moves forward a rise in overall tension can be observed. The shoulders may be drawn back, loose arms flexed and open hands clenched into half fists. The infant is like a high diver keying up every part of the system before leaping from the top board.

Compressed Smiles

These smiles are very similar to simple smiles. There is just as much if not more retraction of the corners of the mouth. But the lips appear thinner because they are pressed tightly together. Compressed smiles are the silent speech equivalent of the verbal: "Oh my goodness..." They indicate repressed amusement at the antics of an adult, and arise in situations where a grown-up has suffered some misfortune. The child would really like to laugh aloud, but is inhibited by the possible social consequences. Compressed smiles are more often seen in older infants, that is children aged at least four or five, who have learned that an open expression of mirth in such circumstances is often badly received. The girl who was smacked because she grinned when the teacher tripped and dropped all her books, or the little boy who received a scolding after he laughed at daddy sitting down on the cat, are both likely to use compressed smiles in the future. The amusement which leads to a repression of the smile is usually provoked by adult dignity being punctured, or by something which strikes the child as ridiculous. In many instances the compressed smile is quickly hidden behind a raised hand or by a turn of the head. Infants aged four or five will also use the compressed smile to cloak their embarrassment when talking to adults about what they regard as delicate subjects. "I can see Mary's bare bum," announced a four-year-old boy as the infants changed to go home. Other children giggled, but the boy—who had addressed one of the supervisors directly—only gave a compressed smile.

There is nothing unusual about a child using compressed smiles. But if they occur more frequently than uninhibited smiles, and are linked to some of the anxiety signals which I will describe in Chapter Six, it may mean that the infant finds it difficult to express feelings openly. Such a reaction normally indicates that open amusement

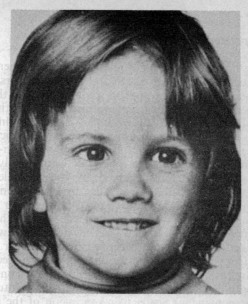

Doubt is expressed by curling the bottom lip over the lower teeth. Resting the upper teeth on the lip increases the intensity of the doubt. The direction of the gaze and the position of the eye-brows are also important components of the silent speech message.

is discouraged by the parents or teachers. It may be regarded as ill-mannered, impertinent or inappropriate for social, religious or other reasons. Since this type of emotional constipation can be harmful to an infant's development, you should try to discover the reasons for it. Most of the time, however, compressed smiles are to the grin what the snigger is to the laugh.

Upper Smiles

Are so called because the top lip is drawn back far enough to uncover the upper row of teeth. However the real significance of this signal is not that the top teeth can be seen, but that the bottom row of teeth remain hidden. When an ape wants to threaten attack, it bares its lower teeth. This message means simply: "Watch out. I am going to bite!" Children too make this menacing movement of the lower lip to signal aggression. The upper smile, by emphasising that the bottom teeth are being kept hidden, assures the other people that the smiler's intentions are friendly and non-hostile. It is rather like the gunfighter in a Western keeping his six-shooters in their holsters. No weapons—no war.

Although the meaning of the upper smile can vary according to the exact position of the lips and the framework of other secret language which surrounds it, the most commonly sent message is a greeting: "I am happy to see you. I am friendly."

When used in this way, the smile is produced by retracting the lips, turning them slightly upwards at the edges, and partly opening the mouth. In a low-intensity upper smile the teeth remain touching, and only the top part of the upper teeth is made visible. When used together with strong eye-contact, the message sent is one of friendship. The infant uses it when meeting a friend or greeting an adult they are pleased, but not over-whelmingly delighted, to see. It might be used, for example, when a child meets a fond relative or a familiar and well-liked family friend. Normally when infants greet people with whom they are more intimate, for instance their mothers, a far more intense form of the smile is produced. But be careful when watching upper smiles. Even when the comparatively undevious infant uses them they can be false. That is, produced not in response to a genuine emotion, but as a result of an adult's command.

A rather artificial upper smile produced on request. The position of the lips remains the same as for a genuine upper smile but there is little expression in the rest of the face. Compare this picture with the much more enthusiastic upper smile on page 90.

This type of artificial upper smile might be termed the "frozen cheese" grimace. It is as cold as ice and often made in obedience to the photographer's command to "say cheese".

The "frozen cheese" can be seen on the faces of bored or tired children who have been sternly commanded to "look happy." Parents who have organised an outing which is not being received by the child with what they regard as sufficient enthusiasm may snap: "At least look as if you are enjoying yourself, for God's sake! If you only knew what this is costing me!"

The absence of a smile in what adults regard as the appropriate social circumstances can lead to a similar sort of instruction, and exactly the same kind of "frozen cheese" response: "Look pleased when Auntie talks to you," hisses an embarrassed mother. The infant obeys. But no one with any knowledge of the secret language would be fooled for a second.

The "frozen cheese" smile is stiff and lifeless. It might have been painted on to an otherwise expressionless mask. The lips are drawn back and the upper teeth revealed. But the rest of the face remains unmoved. Literally motionless. The eyes will give only brief glances and remain mostly downcast. Other silent speech signals

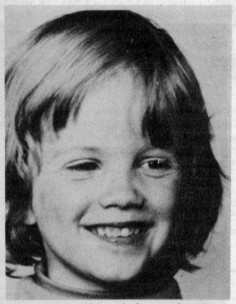

A warm upper smile. Although the mouth is not as open as in the picture on page 89 there is still far more intensity because of the changes in muscles around the eyes. The gaze has been narrowed and small folds of flesh have formed beneath each eye. These are a sure sign of a genuine smile.

may indicate weariness, frustration, anger or indifference. These will be described in Chapter Six.

But the greatest give-away is to be found in a small piece of body movement which we are all powerless to influence directly.

Under each eye there are a number of very small muscles which swell out to form a wrinkle when we are genuinely amused or happy about something. These muscles are not under our voluntary control, so while there is no difficulty in moving our lips whenever we smile

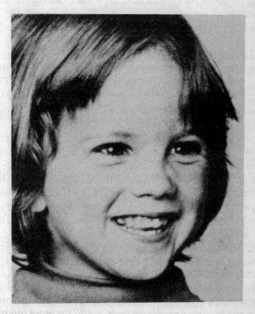

An upper smile which is on the borderline of being a broad smile. The top row of teeth are fully uncovered but the bottom teeth remain partly concealed. Narrowing of the gaze and a slight lift to the eye-brows adds warmth to the expression. Note the little folds of skin under each eye.

without meaning it, we can do nothing about these tell-tale swellings. One such way of telling whether the smile of a child, or an adult, is a true reflection of their feelings is to see whether or not these folds are present.

When the upper smile is genuine and being used as a greeting, it will often be preceded by the brief eye-brow "flash" which I described in Chapter One. The rapid raising and lowering of the brows, has the effect of drawing the other person's attention to this area of the face. We usually take notice of the movement, without even being consciously aware of the fact, as we lock our eyes onto the other person's. By doing so we make sure that face signals are clearly seen. Children use the brow raise when meeting friendly adults or friends of their own age.

The intensity of the smile can be increased by uncovering more of the teeth, opening the mouth slightly, and narrowing the gaze by partly closing the lids. The far greater warmth of expression which these small and simple movements produce can clearly be seen in photographs on pages 90 and 91. Upper smiles can also be used to signal good-natured doubt or amused astonishment. This is achieved by keeping the lower teeth covered and curling the lower lip over them. Slight uncertainty in a relaxed and friendly situation will be signalled by the infant making this open-mouthed lip curling movement without any changes in the muscles around the eyes. A child who has stopped playing one game and is thinking about what to do next may send out this message.

Greater surprise or doubt is expressed by resting the top row of teeth on the curled-over lower lip, and raising the eye-brows while opening the eyes wide. To increase the intensity of the expression still further, the mouth is opened while the eye-brows raise and wide-eyed look become even more pronounced.

By making small changes in the positions of the eye-brows, eye-lids and lower lip, messages ranging from polite doubt to open scepticism can be produced. There is often an element of anxiety about this type of upper smile.

You can see them on the faces of children watching circus clowns or pantomime knockabout men in action. These supposed figures of fun frequently send very ambiguous messages to the small child because their antics are so grotesque and often violent. The infant may watch wide-eyed, mouth set in a doubtful upper smile as the excitement grows. The slow build-up to the moment when a custard pie lands fair and square on the clown's face, for instance, generates growing levels of stress. As the pie lands and the tension collapses, the explosion of mirth is all the greater.

The doubt or disbelief expressed by this type of smile is good-humoured and polite. The infant is saying: "I don't think so, but I am willing to be convinced." Not: "That's a damned lie!" It is an amused and friendly query, rather than an aggressive challenge. Because these doubtful smiles come and go so rapidly, one needs to keep a careful watch for them at times when some anxiety may be generated by an otherwise pleasurable event. Their importance lies in the fact that they provide a valuable insight into an infant's true feelings. This becomes even more helpful in understanding the youngster after the age of four or five. By this time, many children have become socially skilled enough to conceal attitudes or emotions which they feel might not be well received. A small boy who has been sternly told that it is babyish to cry, for instance, may continue to smile even though he feels anxious and miserable. "Of course he wants to ride on the giant dipper," insists a proud father. "He's not a baby any more. Look at him smiling!" It may be that the smile is a signal of doubt rather than enjoyment. This is not to say, of course, that the boy should not be taken for the dipper ride or that he will not be thrilled by it. But it is still very helpful to be aware of what is actually going on in the infant's mind.

Lower Smiles

Unlike upper smiles in which the bottom teeth remain completely covered by the lower lip, the upper teeth are never entirely hidden during a lower smile. The difference between this and the broad smile (see below), in which both sets of teeth are exposed, is merely one of degree. There is usually more opening of the mouth and a greater retraction of the lips in a broad smile. But it is the body talk which accompanies these often similar types of smile which removes any doubt about the content of the message.

The lower smile is a gift-wrapped threat. It is the smile on the face of a tiger who has eaten recently but can feel the pangs of hunger stirring again. It is not a pouting snarl, or the lip-curled attacking signal of an angry child who is about to fight and bite others. The lip positions are sometimes very similar, but posture, stance and the rest of the facial expression clearly distinguish such naked aggressions.

Translated, this silent speech signal means: "I demand it ... please!" The child is determined to get his or her own way, but feels the matter can still be negotiated. The only stipulation is that the decision must go in their favour! It is a signal used by dominant children determined to stay at the top of the group pecking-order. Only occasionally can it be seen on the face of a more submissive child goaded beyond endurance by some injustice. Usually such infants react by bursts of blind rage, kicking and striking out with little or no warning. By declaring, through the use of a lower smile, that they are determined to be assertive, the infant is nailing its colours to the mast. Only a child who is confident enough to issue such an ultimate will risk using the signal. The remainder tend to go to war without warning.

The lower smile is produced by uncovering the bottom

*An aggressive lower smile. By uncovering the bottom row
of teeth the infant is sending out a threat. Note the steady
gaze and the horizontal line of the eye-brows.*

teeth more than the top set and fixing the other child with
a long, hard stare. The eyes are wide open and the
eye-brows remain level. Sometimes the bottom jaw is
thrust forward. The posture is tense and the body inclined
towards the intended victim.

Less dominant infants usually respond to the lower
smile by giving up whatever the other child wants and by
offering appeasement signals in an attempt to defuse the
aggression. Those who are equally dominant may decide
to back down and get their revenge at a more appropriate
time, or to stand their ground. When this happens a short
tussle or skirmish normally occurs. If a child uses the

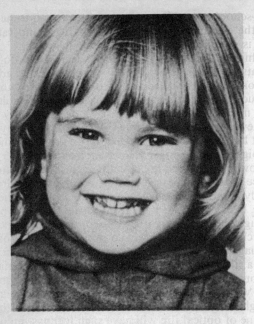

The lower smile is transformed into a broad smile and the message changes from aggression to pleasure. The top teeth are now uncovered and the gaze has narrowed slightly. But this type of broad smile still contains an element of aggressiveness. Compare it with the upper smiles on pages 90–91 and the much warmer broad smile on page 98.

signal against a more dominant infant, the response will be indifference or an attack. However, once a pecking order has been established, less dominant children seldom assert themselves strongly against the more aggressive members of the group. The main time that this is likely to happen is when strange children get together to play either informally, or during the first few sessions of a new play-school term. Then the signals are used to help sort out the dominants from the submissives, and establish who is going to be allowed to peck at whom.

This type of smile can also be seen when dominant infants are either being ordered or persuaded by adults to do something they dislike. "Eat up all your cabbage," instructs a mother. The child looks at her and smiles. But it is not necessarily a submissive or a friendly smile, whatever the mother thinks. The child may be saying: "I don't like you at all for making me do this. But since you are bigger and stronger than I am you win."

Lower smiles, coupled with aggressive posture and stance, can also be seen when dominant children are simply standing and watching others at play. Then it is more likely to be an indication of the thoughts passing through their minds, rather than direct communication. Any child in the vicinity who notices this type of body language, however, is likely to respond to it as though it were a silent signal directed specifically towards him. The anxious ones may become more fearful, the confident ones watchful. If this smile is accompanied by a long, thoughtful gaze in any particular direction then those in the line of optical fire will have such feelings intensified. As with all facial expressions, the lower smile acquires a much greater power and significance when accompanied by direct eye-contact.

Broad Smiles

At their most intense, these express the highest intensity of pleasure or excitement of which the smile alone is capable. Beyond this lies laughter, which is basically a broad smile set to music, or the relaxed play-face seen during uninhibited infant games.

In a broad smile the lips are full retracted so that both upper and lower teeth are exposed. These may be together, in the low intensity form of the smile, or well

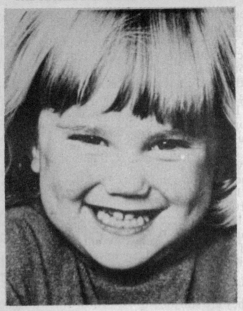

This is clearly a more friendly and intense smile than that pictured above. But can you say exactly why? What small changes of expression have occurred to alter our feelings about it? By observing subtle shifts of expression and body movement like this you can discover the true meanings of a smile.

separated to indicate the greatest possible amusement.

Broad smiles, the ultimate in non-hostility signals, are mainly used in situations which combine good fun with relaxed companionship. An extensive piece of research carried out by two British psychologists, Tony Chapman and Hugh Foot, has shown that children produce broad smiles much more frequently when with other children or adults than they do on their own. By showing cartoon films to a wide range of youngsters, the investigators discovered that children who watched on their own laughed and smiled much less often than those who saw the films in company. But there were some significant, and as yet unexplained, sex differences. Boys laughed just as much whether they were watching the films with a girl or another boy. Girls found the cartoons more amusing when they had a boy sitting beside them rather than a girl.

The broad smile is one of the most infectious types of smile. Infants are prepared to use it, and to laugh aloud, far more readily if other children are already doing so. If an adult smiles and laughs, then they have no hesitation about doing so. In fact a smiling grown-up is the most effective way of producing smiling infants.

When used in pleasurable situations, the broad smile says: "I am having fun—and I don't care who knows it." As part of a greeting message, the broad smile expresses unqualified delight. Combined with firm eye-contact and a slight narrowing of the gaze, it is the warmest possible way of saying: "Hello."

Smiles, as you can see, are not the simple, spontaneous signals which popular theory would have us believe. While they are never more than a component of body talk, they are still amongst the most important signals in the vocabulary of silent speech. Never is their importance greater than during social encounters where there is going to be a winner and a loser. As I will explain in the next chapter, the infant who can use smiles effectively almost always has a great deal to smile about.

5 The Language of Leadership

Alan and Tony are only three years old, but they have already found ways of getting what they want out of life. If they monopolise a popular toy, take first place on the slide, or occupy the most coveted seat at the painting table, the other children hardly ever protest. In the pecking order of the under-fives, Alan and Tony rule the roost.

But there the similarity between them ends. While both boys have discovered how to dominate, the methods they use are entirely different. So too are the responses of their companions and each boy's status in the group. One is well liked and has a great many friends. The other is disliked and isolated. Alan is a leader. Tony is a bully.

Tony gets what he wants by bossing the others around. He is an aggressive little boy who shoves and pushes, often for no apparent reason. He only asks once for what he wants. Sometimes he dispenses with even that brief formality before making a grab. Several times each day he is the centre of a scuffle or a tussle, which usually ends with another smaller child in tears. It is hardly surprising, therefore, that the other infants are wary of him. They seldom ask to share his toys or join in his games. He only occasionally takes part in a group activity. Much of the time he plays alone.

Alan smooth-talks his way to social success. He does this not with words—he is a slow learner when it comes to verbal communication—but by means of a wide repertoire of fluently performed silent speech signals. He rarely has to put up a fight to get what he wants, or defend what he has. Alan's chosen methods are persuasion and placation. He appeases the other children so that they let him have his own way willingly. He is friendly, sociable and well-liked. He makes spontaneous offerings of his own toys or sweets. He initiates games, organises noisy romps, and invents new playthings out of anything from empty boxes to discarded plastic bottles. He is frequently imitated and cheerfully followed.

The world of infancy is in many ways a microcosm of adult society. Not only does it have leaders and the led, but there is remarkable similarity in the methods used to achieve and retain status within the group. In fact, it seems very likely that whether we are dominant or submissive, competitive or retiring, may to a large extent be due to the lessons learned during early childhood. Clearly this is an area of considerable interest and great potential importance. Yet, surprisingly, it has only been extensively studied in the last few years.

One of the pioneer investigators of infant leadership is Professor Hubert Montagner of the University at Besançon in Eastern France. A biologist by training, Professor Montagner first became interested in non-verbal communication while studying dominance behaviour in social insects. When he decided to switch from bee hives to the nursery, Hubert Montagner found that living in Besançon offered certain advantages for his work. Because the city is a fast-growing industrial centre it has a large population of working mothers with young children. To allow the mothers to stay in employment, the municipal council have set up a number of crèches where infants can be left all day. They are accepted from a few months old to the age of three, after which most go on to a nursery school. The crèches are well-equipped and professionally supervised. In one of these centres, Professor Montagner found all the raw material necessary for his very extensive researches: co-operative adults and dozens of infants.

In the early seventies he moved out of the laboratory

and into the crèche, taking with him 16mm cine cameras, research assistants and almost endless patience. Professor Montagner's plan was to make film records of exchanges between the children, and then analyse them frame by frame. In order to conceal the cameras and observers, a special hide was constructed at one end of the play room. This was designed to double as a puppet theatre, in order to disguise its true purpose from the inquisitive youngsters. Between shows, Professor Montagner watched and filmed through one-way mirrors. Today, some twenty miles of film later, the research is still not completed. But Professor Montagner has been able to define six different categories of dominance and domination into which all the children in his studies can be placed. These detailed behavioral profiles range from the dominant sociable child to the isolated and fearful child. The profiles are of course based on studies amongst French children, but my own observations carried out in Britain, Europe and five North American States, has satisfied me that these psychological portraits have a much wider application.

Profiles In The Pecking Order

Dominant Leaders
Leadership children, like Alan, stay on top without throwing their weight about. They are the centre of attention for others in the group, and take the initiative in organising games, playing with toys and discovering fresh ways of amusing themselves and their companions. They are just as likely to be girls as boys.

Dominant Aggressives
Like Tony they tend to be bullies. They grab, push and elbow their way through nursery life. They are seldom imitated, and only rarely start a game which the others want to follow. Their aggression is often spontaneous and directed not against some child who has upset them but towards an innocent third party—almost always a child

from one of the four dominated groups described below. Dominant aggressives are much more likely to be boys than girls.

Dominated Leaders

These are children who sometimes display leadership qualities. They may initiate the occasional game or take the lead when playing with new toys. But when it comes to a fierce contest for some eagerly contested object or position in the nursery, they lose out. However much they may want to sit at a favourite place during mid-morning break, scramble to the top of a climbing frame, or pedal around in a coveted toy car, the *Dominant Leaders* and the *Dominant Aggressives* beat them to it. *Dominated Leaders* can be either boys or girls.

Dominated Aggressives

Dominated Aggressive children are willing to resort to violence and strong-arm tactics to get their own way. But unlike *Dominant Aggressives*, who use such methods with at least short-term success, the dominated but aggressive child is neither determined enough nor sufficiently self-assured to carry it through. They can bully the fearful children, who make up the two remaining categories, but are outclassed by both *Dominant Leaders* and *Dominant Aggressive* children. They are more likely to be boys than girls.

Dominated Frightened

These children strike me as accidents looking for somewhere to happen! Not only are they frequently the direct victims of attacks, by both *Dominant* and *Dominated Aggressives*, but quite often become innocent by-standers caught up in a clash between more violent children. They are very submissive infants who make frequent appeasement gestures in an attempt to placate the others. *Dominated Frightened* children can be either boys or girls.

There seems to be a link between the speed at which a

child learns how to talk, and his or her place in the nursery pecking order. Professor Montagner has found that children who master verbal communication before their companions are often amongst those in the *dominated* or *frightened* groups. This may be because, while they are busy developing their spoken word vocabularies, they fall behind in the use of silent speech signals. This makes it easier for them to communicate with adults and older children, but far harder for them to deal with social situations where silent speech signals are still the main language.

Isolated Infants

Many children when they are first introduced to the group at a play school, day nursery or crèche, find the new environment both bewildering and terrifying. They cling to their mothers, sob in anguish when left, and spend much of the day on their own in the quietest corner of the room, either crying or looking extremely rejected and miserable. I will describe the kind of anxiety signals which such children produce in the next chapter. But early fears and tears usually give way to more settled behaviour after only a few days' exposure to the group. The child is gradually accepted, and finds his or her way into the social structure. Some, however, remain isolated and frightened for much longer periods of the time. These children are often kindly treated by the *Dominant Leaders*. They are looked after, defended and offered toys and other gifts. Thanks to this patronage, they frequently get priority in playing with toys which have been discarded by more dominant children.

How The Analysis Helps Us

This kind of behavioural analysis provides a valuable insight into the social structure of the young child's world. But it would be a mistake to see these profiles, or indeed any type of psychological labelling, as providing rigid compartments into which every child can be neatly pigeon-holed.

A particular profile may fit one child accurately for several days or weeks, and then suddenly become completely inappropriate. A *Dominant Leader* may grow more aggressive, an aggressive child start using appeasement gestures typical of a leader; a dominated child may develop dominant behaviour, an isolated child become more sociable.

For example, John, the boy whose picture appears in the next chapter, changed his behaviour radically over the twelve months in which my observations were made. At the start of the year he was a *Dominant Aggressive*. Ten months later he had developed into a *Dominant Leader*.

Gradual changes in social status almost always take place as the child gets older. *Dominated Frightened* and *Isolated* infants are more often found amongst those aged two and younger. As they grow up and become physically stronger, self-confidence increases. They also master a much wider range of appeasement and solicitation gestures, which enable them, if they wish, to develop into *Dominant Leaders*. Yet, as we have seen, not all children make this choice. Some appear unable to dominate except by means of aggression. Furthermore, changes in behaviour are not entirely related to age. Abrupt shifts and puzzling fluctuations are sometimes observed. A once confident leader will suddenly become aggressive, and abandon appeasement in favour of bullying. Equally, a previously aggressive child may begin to use leadership signals for no apparent reason. These variations can be attributed to something which we normally associate with adults rather than the very young—changes in levels of stress.

The ambitious executive on the way to a second ulcer and the dominant child may not seem to have much in common so far as the strains of everyday life are concerned. Yet it is now clear that even in the nursery world the rat-race takes its toll. A youngster is unlikely to produce the kind of distress symptoms seen in the much less resilient body of a middle-aged man or woman. But their physiological response to excessive stress will be identical. The same kind of nervous arousal is going to take place, similar hormones will be involved, and the system will tense up in exactly the same way. Increases of stress amongst the very young can be produced by many of the situations and circumstances which put additional strain on adults: rows or tension in the family, harsh treatment, a lack of affection, rejection, changes caused by a move to a new neighbourhood, or a different group of companions, aggression either witnessed or suffered. These and many other external events are responsible for internal changes in the body chemistry. A major part in this stress response is played by the hormone adrenalin.

The Chemistry of Stress

Adrenalin is produced by the adrenals glands which are located above each kidney. It is often termed the "fight or flight" hormone, because one of its main functions is to help the body survive a physical threat. When a surge of adrenalin enters the blood-stream, important physiological changes occur which are designed to give an individual the best possible chance of fighting and winning, or fleeing and escaping. Breathing becomes more rapid and extra glucose is released from the liver. This ensures that adequate supplies of richly-oxygenated, energy-laden blood are available to the limbs and brain. The digestion stops, causing the familiar dry mouth and churning stomach sensation of anxiety, which everybody experiences at some time or another. Since these responses are triggered by a part of the central nervous system which is not under the direct command of the "thinking" brain, differences in the hormone levels caused by stress cannot normally be adjusted at will. This means that the more adrenalin there is in the blood-stream at any one time, the greater the stress being experienced.

After circulating in the body, the waste-products of the adrenal glands are filtered through the kidneys into the bladder and eventually passed out in the urine. A convenient method of measuring the level of this hormone, therefore, is to see how much there is in a urine sample. This is the procedure which Professor Montagner decided to adopt when he began to investigate the link between stress and an infant's behavioural profile.

He decided to look for just one adrenal product, a steroid with the lengthy chemical name of 17-hydroxycorticosteroid. Samples of the urine from dozens of infants were collected at home and in the crèche seven times each day, starting first thing in the morning and ending at eight o'clock every night. The samples were placed inside code numbered bottles and sent to the Faculty of Medicine in Besançon for analysis. This safeguard meant that the biochemists making the measurements worked blind. They did not know which children had provided any particular sample, nor the time of day it had been taken. The quantity of the steroid present in the urine was calculated using an absorbtion spectrometer. This sensitive equipment allows very small changes in hormone secretion to be accurately determined.

The results were significant. They showed a clear relationship between what is happening in a child's body and the type of behaviour being carried out. During the weekdays, most of the children produced the maximum amount of steroid at two fixed times during the day, eleven o'clock in the morning and three o'clock in the afternoon following the lunch-time rest period.

When the rise and fall in the hormone levels of each child was plotted on a graph, the majority were found to be in synchrony. These regular, tide-like variations in hormone production are perfectly normal and form part of a cycle of physiological activity called the circadian rhythm. The word means "around the day", and as its name implies this rhythmic pattern is repeated once every twenty-four hours. These biorhythms have a tremendous effect on the way we feel. Whether we are alert or sluggish, energetic or lethargic, at any particular moment depends to a great extent on where we are in our biological timetable. The major cycles of each day, the periods of waking and sleeping, eating and working, are mirrored by activities going on inside the body. Certain cells are more active at one period than during others, the secretion of hormones increases and decreases according to a clearly laid down programme. When we upset this delicate internal clock by working night shifts or flying through time-zones, the upheaval which results can be extremely disturbing.

So there was nothing especially strange in the fact that the infants' production of a stress-related hormone rose and fell. Nor were the times at which production peaked surprising. By eleven o'clock, early morning sloth had been shaken off and the crèche was loud with noisy games and excited shouts. With a high level of stimulation in the environment and a large number of potentially stressful exchanges going on, it was reasonable to expect most of the infants to react in the same physiological manner. The afternoon peak was in contrast to a fall in steroid excretion by lunch and a siesta.

The key points were not that most of the graph lines were neatly synchronised, but that marked variations did occur. First of all there was a difference between the peaks found on Monday and those recorded on Friday. Secondly there were important variations between some individuals and the rest of the group.

By Friday the main peak in hormone production occurred in most of the infants at eleven o'clock. The three o'clock peak was never as high as the morning maximum. But at the start of the week this situation was reversed. Samples taken on Monday showed that the children were producing more hormone in the afternoon than in the morning. It was only after a day or so back at the crèche that the majority switched over to a morning peak.

Professor Montagner had a hunch that the afternoon peaks in the children would match those of at least one, perhaps both, of the parents. It was most likely, he thought, to fit that of the mother. During the morning she would be kept busy cleaning the house and preparing lunch. By the early afternoon she would be freed to play with the child. To check this theory he asked entire families to provide urine samples. All the samples were taken at the same time, so that it would be possible to establish whether or not a relationship existed between adult hormone peaks and those of the children. The measurements showed that such a link did exist between the mother and the infant, but not between the father's levels of hormone production and those of his child. During the week this clear synchrony disappeared as infants matched their hormonal rhythms to those of the group. The resetting of the body clock normally took no more than twenty-four hours. By Tuesday most of the infants were in hormonal tune with one another. But there were exceptions. A marked lack of synchronisation was detected in two groups of children—those whose behavioural profiles showed them to be aggressive, and those classed as isolated and fearful. These groups were very slow to reset their body clocks. It could be Thursday before they were more or less back in synchronisation with the rest of the group. But even then the graphs of these infants were still easy to detect. They tended to peak higher, and vary from one day to the next, much more wildly than the smooth rhythmic lines of the leader children. Professor Montagner comments:

"The *Dominant Aggressive* children who mainly express themselves through aggression and have very fluctuating behaviour also show many fluctuations in the daily curves of excretion of adrenal hormones. These children are amongst the most vulnerable to stresses in the outside world and also amongst the most vulnerable to disease. Leaders who express themselves through appeasement develop complex social behaviour and show regular daily curves. These children are among those who are rarely ill."

There is more than a hint of the chicken and egg problem in the relationship between stress and body language, bodily response and social behaviour. *Dominant Leaders* enjoy better interpersonal relations because they are adept at silent speech. Since life is easier in the nursery they are more relaxed and less stressed. Their nervous systems are not so highly aroused and they respond to situations in a more equitable and balanced manner. This makes it easier for them to get what they want without struggling. And so the positive cycle is repeated. Aggressive children, on the other hand, are much less successful in personal exchanges. Their body language is abrupt and unpredictable, so they experience more antagonism, conflicts and rejections. This makes them anxious and steps up their level of physical arousal. As there is a well-established connection between constantly high stress and disease it comes as no surprise that they are more vulnerable to childhood ailments. The resulting absences from play-groups and nursery schools only make it harder for them to fit in with others. They never learn those secret language signals which are the essential ingredients of leadership.

But which comes first? The stress egg or the aggressive chicken?

Certainly the connection between what a person is doing and what is happening inside his or her body is an intimate and complicated one.

The probability is that social responses shape the hormonal reaction, which then helps to sustain a particular behavioural profile. This is certainly suggested by the effects of the social conditions in which a child is being brought up. As I will explain in Chapter Eight, it is possible for a mother to influence dramatically the behaviour of a young child by her own attitude. In one case, carefully documented by Professor Montagner, an *Aggressive Dominant* boy was transformed into a leader after his mother was able to spend more time with him and show her affection more powerfully. As the boy's behaviour in the group changed, so too did his production of stress hormones.

So far we have seen that children behave in different

ways in the group, and achieve a variety of social positions through this behaviour. It seems likely that this behaviour influences and is influenced in turn by the way in which the body is working at that time. But what kind of body talk distinguishes the leader from the led, and the bully from the appeaser? In the next chapter I will describe in detail the body language of aggression, and the signals of anxieties they generate. Here I want to concentrate on the positive messages which the leaders use.

Winning Ways

Dominant Aggressives attack, *Dominant Leaders* appease; the bullying infant strikes blows, the placating one solicits help. The main purpose of the actions and body talk of the aggressive child is to scare others into agreement. The aim of the dominant leader is to persuade other infants to do what he wants but in their own way.

We can compare these different approaches most dramatically by translating silent speech signals into the spoken word, and transporting exchanges from the play room to the board room. Turning the clock forty years on, let us look at middle-aged versions of Tony and Alan, the boys whose styles of command were discussed at the start of this chapter.

Tony the tough-minded toddler has become Anthony the blunt business executive. His methods may allow him to influence people, but they are unlikely to win him friends. He believes strongly in the iron hand in the iron glove. He is a difficult and aggressive man to deal with. He never backs down, delights in a head-on confrontation, and prefers the weapons of threat and bluster. His speciality is brow-beating others into submission. He will storm, rage and thump desks. If really provoked he may even strike people. His world will be dominated by the assumption that his might is right. His moods will be unpredictable and he may lash out for no apparent reason. Nobody will much enjoy working for him. But in certain situations he may be highly effective. Echoing the nursery response of infants, many of the grown-ups he encounters will let him get his own way, rather than provoke aggression.

Alan's approach will be entirely different, and probably far more successful in the long term. His ambition to win in any given situation is no less powerful than Tony's, but he believes in stealth rather than intimidation. His wheeling and dealing will be done by finding out what people need to keep them happy, and then if possible providing it, while taking what he wants almost by default. In Alan's world, an unsuccessful negotiation will be one which results in an obvious loser. His aim in any exchange will be to make the other person feel they have won a victory, even when he has taken them to the financial cleaners. Alan wants the people who work for him and with him to be happy. He will go out of his way to notice their efforts, and reward them. Those who praise his business acumen and negotiating skill will probably never realise that the seeds of his success were planted half a century earlier amongst coloured building blocks and toy cars.

Returning to Alan in short pants, let us look at one of his exchanges to see how he uses this basic technique of keeping other children happy in order to get what he wants.

Mary, aged four, is playing on the day school rocking horse. Her three-year-old friend Jane is pushing her energetically. Both the girls are laughing and obviously having a lot of fun. Alan has been watching enviously for a few minutes while seeming to play with a garage. Suddenly he gets up and runs towards them. Both girls glance in his direction. Mary's grip on the reins tightens. She suspects, correctly, that Alan wants to take her place. She is equally determined not to let him have a go.

But Alan, on reaching the horse, makes no attempt to grab either the reins or the horse. Instead, he smiles broadly, while looking hard at Mary. She relaxes and smiles more widely. Both girls respond to his interest by playing even more vigorously and laughing loudly. Mary, clinging joyfully to the wildly rocking horse, throws back her head, her mouth opening in a relaxed play-face. Alan starts to rock the horse with Jane. To help him get a good grip, she moves from the right to the left side of the animal. Alan at once jumps onto the rocker, placing his feet each side of the back leg and leaning across the hind quarters. As Jane swings them both backwards and forwards the boy laughs even more excitedly. Jane, thinking that this looks more fun than pushing the horse, clambers onto the other rocker. Mary is still smiling, and as the rocking motion slows down under their combined weight, she clambers off, clearly wanting to try out this unusual way of playing with the horse. From Alan's reaction, it seems to be much more enjoyable than simply sitting in the saddle. No sooner has she climbed down than Alan scrambles onto the horse. They are all smiling and enjoying themselves. Mary pushes the horse and swings for a time on the rocker. But this game no longer appears to offer as much fun as when Alan was doing it. After only a few rocks she gets down and runs towards the slide. Jane follows her, and Alan is left as the undisputed owner of a coveted toy.

An aggressive boy, lacking Alan's guile and patience, would probably have tried to force Mary off the horse. With some children, threats and a few shoves might have been successful. But the girl was also a dominant leader in the group, and rarely allowed herself to be bossed around. So any pushing or grabbing would have provoked a struggle and the possible intervention of an adult. The outcome was almost certain to be failure.

Perhaps you feel that I am crediting a three-year-old with an astonishing amount of calculation, or an alarming amount of cunning! A more likely interpretation, you may feel, is that none of the events was really planned. It just seemed that way to an adult mind. Alan pushed Mary because he wanted to join in the game. He climbed onto the rocker because it was not possible for him to get onto the horse's back. The girl eventually got down because she thought Alan was doing something interesting, and he took the opportunity to claim the horse. It was fortunate for him, but not in any way the result of a carefully laid plot!

Were that an isolated example of the way leader children behave, you would probably be right. But similar sequences occur time and again in infant exchanges. To dismiss them all as random events resulting in a lucky outcome, is to fall into the trap of adult elitism. We see nothing remarkable in older children, adolescents and ourselves behaving in a carefully structured manner in order to achieve a certain goal. Yet because infants cannot express their desires in words, and use silent speech to gain their ends, we are inclined to rule out any idea of premeditation. This underrates both the power of the secret language and the social skills of the pre-verbal child.

In order to gain control of the rocking horse, Alan smiled and laughed, so as to increase the amusement of the other children. As I explained in the previous chapter, all youngsters, and especially girls, will smile and laugh more readily in company. An ability to produce an amused or excited response in others is the basic function of all types of appeasement and solicitation behaviour. In fact, we can define such manoeuvres as any body signals which produce smiles or laughter. They include caresses, pats, embraces, mutual co-operation in a game, the removal of a threat, or the prevention of aggression. An appeasing child leader may offer another infant a gift, such as a toy or a sweet, take his hand or touch his shoulders. So long as the result is a smile or a laugh, the child making the signals will have either appeased or solicited the other in a positive way. Very often these body messages trigger off a chain of offerings. A leader child will hand a toy to an infant, who may then hand it—or another toy—on to a third. Frequently the pattern of responses started by a leader involves close copying by the other children. For instance, a small boy making pastry at a crowded play-group table starts to bang with his wooden rolling pin. As he does so, he smiles broadly at the girl beside him. She takes up her own rolling pin and begins to copy his beating movements. Soon, half a dozen children are all drumming away and smiling broadly at one another as they do so.

It's not just an enjoyment of the noise they are making, though this is very pleasurable, but the chance to join in a group activity and share a common excitement. Imitative acts like this should never be seen simply in terms of the activity itself. Chain responses starting with one of the dominant leaders, and eventually encompassing a number of infants, have a strong social significance within the group.

The end result of a successful appeasement or solicitation signal is a smile, so it is not surprising that the key element in any such message is also a smile. No matter what other gestures or body movements are involved, the starting point will always be a smile. The more intense the smile, the more powerful the message.

The sequence of behaviour followed is usually the same, whether the final gesture is the offering of a gift, a caress, or the invitation to join a game. The child sending the signal will attract the others' attention, bring their faces level, by sitting or squatting if necessary, and move to within a foot or eighteen inches. Eye-contact will be established and there may be an eye-brow raise for additional emphasis.

Nina, a bright four-year-old leader, wants a toy iron which Hilary is playing with on the floor. She squats down beside her and stares hard at the iron for about fifteen seconds. Then she raises her gaze to Hilary's face and smiles in a slightly exaggerated manner. She slowly extends her hand towards the iron. After a moment, Hilary picks it up and hands it to her, without a murmur of protest. This type of solicitation is common and effective amongst infant leaders. An even more certain method of persuading another child to co-operate, or spontaneously offer something, is to combine the steady smile with a special posture of the trunk and head.

Philip, aged five, wants to play with a clockwork train which is being monopolised by four-year-old Adrian. He crouches down directly in front of the boy and inclines his head to the right. At the same time, he bends his body slightly in the same direction. After Philip has held this position and continued to smile for ten seconds, Adrian picks up the train and hands it to him with a cheerful grin.

This combination of a smile, an inclined head, and the outstretched hand, produces one of the most powerful messages in silent speech. It not only works between infants, but also between adults and small children. A mother who is having difficulty in persuading a toddler to eat his food should find that the proffered spoonfuls are taken without protest if this solicitation gesture is made at the same time. A play-group supervisor trying to cheer up a miserable new-comer will make the infant far more responsive to her soothing words if they are combined with a warm smile and head tilt.

Professor Montagner, who was the first to identify this extremely important signal, found that in 80 per cent of all observed cases an infant handed over a prized possession after this body signal had been sent. The delay between sending out the message and evoking a response was usually between 10-15 seconds. This period is in line with the reaction periods which I have observed in England and America. When an attempt was made to take a toy or some other object without using this signal, a refusal or a struggle followed in 80 per cent of observed cases.

To test the strength of these wordless messages, Professor Montagner filmed crèche supervisors making them while wearing dark glasses, which completely hid their eyes. Even without the powerful influence of gaze, the solicitation gesture worked in the majority of cases. Interestingly, these gestures influence not only the infants to whom they have been specifically directed, but also any children close enough to see the signal clearly. These children will often come over to offer the adult a toy, embrace her or sit close to her.

The head tilt message is also used by leader children to start a lengthy exchange of signals, including imitation and mimicry. Tom is sitting with a group of others rolling out modelling clay. He makes a long sausage shape, and then triumphantly holds it up for the little girl at his right to see. As he does so, four-year-old Tom tilts his head to the right and smiles. The girl immediately returns his grin and rolls a similar shape from her own clay. She holds this up in exactly the same way and they both laugh. A five-year-old on her right copies their behaviour. Soon every child at the model making table is busy rolling out lengths of clay and holding them up. As in the previous example of imitation, the table drumming, this sequence of behaviour has a social and communicative meaning. It reinforces the pattern of leadership within the group, and simultaneously binds them together in mutual pleasure at a shared activity.

In a different play group, but a similar situation, two-year-old Hilary sticks a ball of dough onto the end of her pencil. She shows it to four-year-old Barry sitting beside her, and smiles quickly. Hilary looks at the other children, waving her creation eagerly. They glance at it and look away. If Hilary had combined her offering with solicitation movements, it is almost certain some of the infants would have copied her. But had she been able to manage this, she would not have been amongst the ranks of the dominated.

Appeasing children make spontaneous offerings to others. They may thrust out a bar of toffee for another infant to take a bite, hand over a toy, or proffer some modelling material. But it is not sufficient merely to push the gift in front of the other child. Unless the appropriate face and body signals are present, the gift is more than likely to be refused.

Leader children not only persuade others to imitate them, but they also co-operate with one another to achieve a desired goal. This is in marked contrast to the

In this sequence of four still pictures taken from the original video-tape the aim of Robert and Barry (right of picture) is to take Hilary's place on the slide ladder. Barry makes a noise to attract Hilary's attention. As she looks around, Robert starts to slip in front of her.

lone wolf behaviour of many dominant aggressive infants.

Hilary, the rather anxious little girl mentioned above, became the victim of such a "mutual benefit" operation when she was waiting patiently for her turn to go down the play-group slide. She was standing by the frame, with one hand firmly holding an upright, when three-year-old Robert came running up. He had just been down the slide and was impatient for another go. Coming up behind Hilary, he grasped her around the waist. A moment later, Barry also came past, having just had his turn on the slide. Both boys were dominant leaders, and they immediately collaborated to steal Hilary's place. The sequence of photographs on pages 118–121 shows how this was achieved. It involved maximum co-operation between the

Robert makes a solicitation, gesture by tilting his head. Hilary keeps her eyes fixed on Barry who begins to move around to her right.

boys, and no aggression against the girl. First Barry attracted Hilary's attention by making a loud cry. She turned sharply, and kept her eyes on him as he took his place behind Robert. He held her gaze by smiling and giving her eye-contact. As she did so, Robert eased himself to her right, and tilted his head in a solicitation gesture. Hilary moved back slightly, still keeping her left hand on the frame upright. Robert then squeezed in front of her. By the time Hilary looked back at him, her place had been forfeited. While she looked at Robert in dismay, Barry wriggled in behind his friend. He then gently pushed at her hand, and she let go the slide. Hilary took a step backwards as Robert began to climb the frame. Barry followed him swiftly, and brushed Hilary lightly off with his left hand. The takeover bid was completed.

Hilary moves back and Robert squeezes in front of her.
Hilary now looks at him in dismay. As she does so Barry
eases himself in behind Robert.

The language of leadership involves more acts of
appeasement and solicitation than of aggression. But this
does not mean that Dominant *Leaders* are never
aggressive, or that *Dominant Aggressives* never make
appeasement gestures. All young children at the top of the
nursery pecking order will use violence and threats at
times. However, a leader child's aggression is usually
restrained, infrequent and ritualised. It is also, normally,
far more specific. The leader will resort to violence in
self-defence, or to protect a dominated child, but only
occasionally produces spontaneous aggression as the
result of temper or frustration. *Dominant Aggressive*
children not only make spontaneous acts of violence, they
also redirect their attacks against uninvolved but more

As Robert climbs to the top of the slide, Barry gently fends Hilary off with his right hand. By claiming her place in this non-aggressive way the boys were able to demonstrate their higher status in the group without provoking tears and adult intervention. The whole exchange took only a few seconds.

dominated infants. Yet they may also appease and solicit to get their own way. Their body language is rarely limited to threats and blows.

Because of this mixing of behaviour and silent speech signals by both types of dominant children, it is unwise to reach any firm judgement on the basis of only a brief observation. What you see during one or two short exchanges may not be at all typical of a particular child's normal behaviour. It might easily happen that, for a short time, a child who was a *Dominant Leader* used aggressive behaviour, while a usually pugnacious infant was very appeasing and sociable. A snap verdict formed from this kind of limited information could easily be wrong. Yet it is often in this casual way that infants do get labelled as "nasty little bullies" or "friendly and sociable." This kind of cursory tagging can sometimes have lasting social consequences for the infant.

To make an accurate assessment of a particular child, exchanges with other infants must be closely watched for at least an hour. During these interactions every gesture of appeasement or solicitation, and all acts of spontaneous aggression, have to be noted down. With this information a behavioural profile can be drawn up using a simple calculation devised by Professor Montagner.

What matters, when it comes to determining the nature of a child's dominant behaviour, is not whether there were any incidents of spontaneous aggression or frequent acts of appeasement, but the relationship between the total numbers of both kinds of behaviour. To produce a mathematical value from his careful observations, Professor Montagner divides the acts of appeasement and solicitation by the incidents of spontaneous aggression.

If the result of this division is *more than ONE*, the child can be classed as a *Dominant Leader*.

If the result of the division is *less than ONE*, then the child comes into the caetgory of *Dominant Aggressive*.

The chart below shows the results of an analysis of the behaviour of Tony and Alan, recorded during two hours at play school.

	Acts of Spontaneous Aggression	Acts of Appeasement And Solicitation
Alan	12	36
Tony	25	9

Acts of Appeasement and Solicitation   =Alan $\frac{36}{12} = 3$

f Aggression   = Tony $\frac{9}{25} = 0.36$

Behavioural Profiles: Alan (3) = *Dominant Leader*.
Tony (0.36) = *Dominant
Aggressive*.

In everyday life, this kind of scientific precision is quite unnecessary. I am not suggesting that you go around watching children with a notebook in one hand and a pocket calculator in the other, so as to decide whether little Billy is a bossy brat or a potential diplomat. The point which does emerge from these detailed studies is that making up your mind about whether a child is the group bully or not, is not something to be done quickly and casually. If you arrive at a conclusion on the basis of a few haphazard observations, you could be committing a grave injustice. Nor should parents whose children never seem to hit back with physical violence automatically assume that their children are less confident or capable of standing up for themselves than the obviously pugnacious child. It may well be that they have found far more satisfactory methods for dominating their playmates. Remember too that these profiles are fluid. Children's behaviour not only changes as they grow older but, as I have explained earlier, can alter on a much shorter time-scale. An infant who is an aggressive bully may develop into a successful leader within the space of a few weeks. Such rapid changes can nearly always be traced to variations in the amount of stress the child is under. Because stress levels can vary from one environment to another, a child's behavioural profile sometimes alters in different surroundings. A *Dominant Aggressive* in a play group may become a *Dominated Aggressive* or a *Dominated Frightened* child at home, amongst older brothers and sisters. A child who is a leader in a group, however, is unlikely to lose those qualities either at home or when placed in a different group of children.

When looking for the language of leadership, I suggest that the following six key points be kept in mind.
1: Avoid making rapid judgements on the basis of brief or casual observations. Do not label a child in a particular way because you have noticed one or two examples of

either bullying or appeasing behaviour.

2: Remember that behavioural profiles are not pigeon-holes into which a child can be tidily placed. Neither are they static. They can fluctuate according to the environment, and usually change as the child grows older.

3: *Dominant Leaders* use more acts of appeasement and solicitation than other children. These can be defined as any gestures or actions which make other infants smile. They include the offering of toys and sweets, sharing of games, caresses, embraces, hand-holding, patting and stroking. One of the most powerful pieces of body language is the solicitation gesture produced by smiling and tilting the head and sometimes the trunk. This works when used by an adult as well as during exchanges between infants. Spontaneous acts of offering and giving are often preceded by this silent speech signal.

4: *Dominant Aggressives* make use of appeasement and solicitation gestures, but they also use many more acts of spontaneous violence. They grab toys, push and shove others. Sometimes their violence is directed at submissive children who have done nothing to upset them.

5: Leader children are often copied and followed. They initiate games. Aggressive children are seldom imitated or followed. They frequently refuse to join in games.

6: To determine the behavioural profile mathematically, Professor Montagner suggests that the total number of appeasements and solicitations be divided by the number of acts of spontaneous agression. If the result is higher than *one*, a *Dominant Leader* is indicated; if it is less than *one*, the child is a *Dominant Aggressive*.

Being able to place a child in a particular behavioural category does not of itself provide any answers. But, when used intelligently, it does help us to start asking the right kind of questions, and to begin responding in the most appropriate way.

In Chapter Ten I will explain how you can use your knowledge of the secret language to help children safely and effectively.

6 The Language of Aggression and Anxiety

The world of the under-fives is frequently aggressive, but only occasionally violent. It is a play ground far more often than it is a battle ground. Yet while most angry exchanges are made up of ritualised attacks and symbolic demonstrations of rage, the anxiety which these exchanges can generate is far from imaginary. Small children may become extremely fearful in situations which grown-ups—used to the far more brutal realities of adult aggression—look upon as neutral or even friendly. Because we have not seen any actual blows struck, we may be tempted to conclude that the level of antagonism must be negligible. As a result, adults may be inclined to dismiss obvious indications of anxiety—such as sad expressions, sobbing, clinging to mother, and refusals to take part in group activities—as being solely due to timidity and babyishness.

In fact, the response could be a perfectly reasonable reaction to an aggressive and frightening environment. The two groups of infants specified by Professor Montagner as being the most anxious, *Dominated Frighteneds* and *Isolateds,* are likely to show the most extreme response to group aggression. But they are not the only ones affected. Like a stone dropped into a previously tranquil pond, a violent interaction between two infants sends ripples over a wide area. All the children in the vicinity will react in one way or another to the

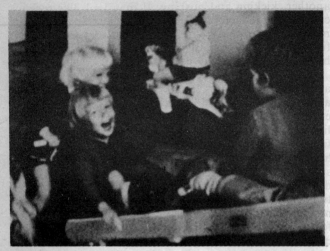

A happy play-face seen during an uninhibited game of rough-and-tumble. The open, relaxed mouth gives an impression of joyful participation.

antagonistic exchange. The dominated ones will react with anxiety, and the dominant infants with a defensive watchfulness.

In order to assess the different levels of fear or violence in any group of under-fives, it is essential to interpret the exchanges correctly. This requires a knowledge of the secret language signals which are used by the very young to express aggression and show anxiety.

Child's Play and Friendly Fights

It is eleven o'clock in the morning, and a group of three and four-year-olds are "fighting" on some big cushions piled up against the nursery wall. With a good deal of shrieking and yelling, they roll around on top of one another, kicking and pushing. It may look like serious combat, but in fact it is all in fun. The children are not the most violent in the group but the least aggressive. Their fights are always friendly, and may actually prevent real battles from being fought.

The difference between this type of amicable wrestling and hostile encounters lies not so much in the way blows are struck, although these are gently delivered, but in the expressions. Angry children have tense, set faces. Their lips, eyes and brows all send out unmistakable signals of fury. Infants indulging in what has been termed 'rough-and-tumble' play have relaxed, joyful faces. They smile and laugh a good deal, and even more frequently display an open-mouthed "play face". In this, the head is tilted back slightly, the teeth are widely separated but remain covered by the lips, and there is no tension in the features. Play faces are one of the key body signals which indicate to other children that, however aggressive the game may seem to outsiders, there is no real hostility between those taking part.

Rough-and-tumble games frequently occur around popular toys which demand a certain amount of vigorous activity, such as the slide and climbing frame. There is often a buildup to the friendly tussle, with the infants chasing one another faster and faster around the frame or down the slide. Increasing bodily contact leads, sometimes by an apparent accident, to the mock combat itself. The cries of excitement and squeals of delight rise to a climax. One of the children falls, either deliberately or by mistake, and others pile on top. They roll over and over, pummel, push, hug and grapple with each other. If there is no adult intervention, the amount of activity slowly declines. The children then move away from one another and often lie down, giggling or laughing as they get their breath back. Letting off steam and fighting with kid gloves in this way indicates that the children involved have controlled rather than excessive levels of aggression. Dr Blurton Jones of the Institute of Child Health in London, who has made a detailed study of this kind of child's play, reports that infants who frequently take part in rough-and-tumble games are much less likely to become involved in real fights. The reason for this is not yet established. One suggestion is that rough-and-tumble play helps those involved to "use up" their aggressive feelings, in much the same way that popular theory supposes adult outbursts of rage to be a kind of safety valve which releases inner tensions. But even where grown-ups are concerned the idea is highly debatable. It is by no means certain that aggression works in the way this theory suggests, or that "blowing one's top" helps get rid of pent-up violence. So far as children are concerned, the proposition seems even more doubtful, because the very young are not so given to spontaneous violence as adults. The under-fives mostly fight about things—toys, games, places and so on. The closest they come to venting rage against a third party is when a *Dominant Aggressive* child redirects his aggression against a more dominated infant.

A second suggestion is that because children who enjoy frequent rough-and-tumble games have less time to play with objects—the prime cause of disputes—they are bound to fight less often. This seems more probable, but it cannot be the whole answer. The children most likely to take part in friendly fights are the *Dominant Leaders*. As is only to be expected, *Dominant Leaders*, and aggressive, frightened and isolated infants, do not normally participate in these friendly tussles. This suggests that it is the personalities of the children who take part in rough-and-tumble games which primarily accounts for their being less involved in actual aggression.

These games are more likely to involve older children, those of four or five, than younger ones. Girls are more often amongst the friendly fighters than boys. This is partly because girls are normally much less aggressive than boys, and usually far more socially sophisticated. They settle into the nursery or play school quicker than their brothers, cry less during initial periods of separation, and tend to possess a wider repertoire of silent speech signals, than boys of the same age. During these games girls appear to avoid the close body contact enjoyed by boys, who wrestle and roll around on one another and clasp each other tightly. Girls push, pull and chase after their companions more frequently than they grasp or hold them.

Adults sometimes try to stop rough-and-tumble games in the mistaken belief that a fight is taking place. A closer look at the facial expressions and body movements of those involved will make the distinction clear. Even when the mock combat is not accompanied by actual laughter, the non-hostile nature of the exchange should be obvious from the way in which the "blows" are delivered and received.

Rage and Ritual

Three-year-old Michael is playing with a toy kettle inside the Wendy house, when four-year-old Arthur bursts in and grabs it from him. Michael hangs on. They shriek at one another. Finally Arthur succeeds in pulling the kettle away. Michael smacks his hands loudly and shouts: "No...no..." Arthur, holding grimly onto his stolen toy, stamps his foot. Michael strikes a blow in the air, swinging his arm far back behind his head and then lashing forward in a violent gesture. Arthur shrieks again and slams the kettle down hard on the door of the Wendy house. Then he turns and walks quickly away.

A fight in which no blow actually landed has just taken place. The combat has been ritualised into a series of symbolic gestures, movements and sounds, all of which are frequently used during aggressive exchanges.

The body talk battle began as soon as Michael had his toy grabbed. While hanging onto it, his body went tense and he leant in towards Arthur. His expression grew angry. His brow furrowed, his chin was thrust forward. He stared hard at the other boy. When forced to release his grip on the kettle, he opened his mouth wide, so that

A menacing expression made during a struggle over the possession of a dolls house by a Dominant Aggressive child. The lower lip is thrust forward and the gaze is intense. The threat is very obvious.

the lips formed an oblong shape which uncovered his teeth. The movement was not unlike that used to produce the broad smile described in Chapter Four. But the framework of other silent speech signals which surrounded the expression left no doubt about its hostile nature. The frown Michael produced was not one of puzzlement but rage. The difference between these two signals is slight yet significant. In the former, the eye-brows usually rise slightly and slope up in the centre. In an aggressive frown, they are drawn down and together at the centre. Such an expression is associated with hitting another child in a violent exchange, or crying when an infant is anxious or miserable.

Instead of striking an actual blow, Michael banged his

hands sharply and noisily together. In reply, Arthur stamped his foot loudly. He too was bending forward at the waist, with his lower jaw thrust out and bottom row of teeth uncovered. All these are hostile signals, indicating a threat of imminent attack. Michael struck a symbolic offensive blow, an important signal in ritualised aggression which I will describe in greater detail in a moment. Their bloodless fight was building to a climax. Arthur shrieked again, conveying his rage and making it clear that he had no intention of backing down or handing over the toy. To emphasise his point he struck the kettle against the woodwork, so that it produced the loudest possible noise. Then he simply walked away. Michael watched him go, and made another striking movement by quickly raising and lowering his right arm. A moment later he turned towards the toy box, picked up a model boat and started to play quite happily again.

This kind of exchange is typical of the majority of infant combat. Time after time in aggressive exchanges between the under-fives one can witness furious disputes where the blows are aimed only at empty air. The combatants may shriek, scream and look menacing, but the sound and fury seldom ends in bruising. It is usually when a *Dominant Aggressive* child is venting his anger against a dominated child, or trying to take something from an equally aggressive infant, that fists make contact and kicks find a human target. The no-holds-barred violence of the football terrace and the bar room punch-up of the adult world is never seen. Even the kind of roughhouse which older boys indulge in rarely occurs in the society of the very young. Why should infants apparently possess so much more self-restraint?

The answer is to be found in the biological mechanisms which produce aggressive arousal. This is triggered by that part of the central nervous system not under the direct control of our thinking brain, which I mentioned briefly in the last chapter. Its function is to take care of all those routine chores, such as pumping blood, breathing and digesting food, on which life depends. Because this part of the nervous system functions rather like the automatic pilot in an aircraft, the rest of our mental processes are left free for more intellectual pursuits.

The autonomic nervous system is divided into two branches. They are designed to produce directly opposite effects on the body. One of them, called the sympathetic branch, speeds things up. It increases heart rate and respiration, and it orders more glucose to be released into the blood stream. The chemical messenger boy which sends these instructions to the appropriate parts of the body is the hormone adrenalin. The opposing branch, the parasympathetic, slows everything down. It lowers heart rate, produces slower, shallower breathing and helps us feel relaxed. Normally these branches are like the opposite ends of a perfectly balanced see-saw. But in times of danger, when we feel under attack, the sympathetic branch gains the upper hand. All its operations are designed to help us survive in the ways I have already outlined. When the danger is past, the parasympathetic branch restores the body to normal running.

This type of fear arousal can be produced by either a real or an imagined threat. A phobic, for example, will become extremely anxious when confronted by his or her dreaded stimulus. But even thinking about the thing they fear can produce a high level of autonomic arousal. A woman having a row with her boss, or a husband arguing with his wife, are likely to become equally aroused.

Where the threat is a physical reality, such as a mugger or a savage dog, the "fight or flight" response produced by sympathetic arousal may be very appropriate. Survival could depend on being able to do battle or escape as efficiently as possible. But arousal in social situations is usually much less helpful. We may not be able to fight or flee. We become trapped between conflicting emotions of rage and fear. Our anger is not so great that we lose control of ourselves and lash out with blows. Our anxiety is not so overwhelming that we can only turn tail and make a dash for the door. It may eventually build up to one of these extremes, but in most social encounters neither course is possible. The conflict results not in anxiety but in ambivalence. The desire to attack and the longing to retreat are more or less equally balanced. This produces mental and physical confusion, as the opposing branches of the autonomic nervous system do battle inside our body. The sympathetic sub-system orders more arousal. The parasympathetic sub-system counters the command. Almost all of us must have experienced the kind of anxiety attack which this indecision creates. Our hearts thump, breathing becomes irregular, our stomach churns, we tremble and go pale, and may even feel so faint that we actually pass out.

During the course of evolution, this fight-flight conflict has led to the creation of numerous signals for ritualised aggression and symbolic submission. In the jungle, seemingly savage fights can take place for territory or dominance in which no real injuries are inflicted. In terms of the survival of a species, this has proved a very beneficial development. If all combats took place with no mercy shown and no quarter given, even the strongest and healthiest animals would run the risk of being injured and weakened. This could only help their rivals in the animal kingdom. If you ever watch two angry dogs squaring up to one another, a considerable number of ritualised aggression signals will usually be seen.

Their hackles rise—this happens in angry or frightened humans as well, but our lack of hair makes it hard to detect—and they crouch facing one another. The dogs circle, snarling, lips curled back, eyes watchful. Now and then one will lunge forward, only to retreat as quickly. Often the encounter will end without any actual contact. Even when they do bury their jaws into one another, no serious damage is normally done. One dog quickly submits, rolling over on its back and exposing its throat for the death lunge which never comes. The fight was about dominance, and a token surrender is considered quite sufficient.

Most adult conflicts follow a similar pattern. We may

shout and storm at one another, strike the table, punch our palms or break things, but blood is more often shed in television soap operas than real life. Our society is actually far less violent than man's potential for violence or newspaper headlines suggest it could be.

So infants are not being more restrained than grown-ups when they limit the majority of their fights to ritualised combats. Indeed, the young child is usually far less inhibited about displaying hostility or making threats. The angry toddler who hits at the air, bangs his toys on the ground, claps his hands, stamps, shrieks, and yells, is showing the same kind of ritualised violence as wild animals and angry adults. He too is torn by conflicting desires to fight and flee.

Signalling Aggression

Steven, aged three, had been monopolising the play group tricycle. Three-year-old Tony, who had only been with the group for six sessions, wanted to have a ride. When Steven abandoned the tricycle Tony seized his chance and grabbed one of the handle bars. (See pictures on pages 135–140.) As he did so, Steven also made a lunge towards the tricycle. Both boys held onto the toy firmly. Then Tony turned and appealed to a supervisor for help. As he did so, Steven quickly clambered into the saddle. The adult knelt down and looked at Steven with a frown of disapproval on her face. She reached out and grasped his left arm just above the wrist.

"It's Tony's turn," she told him. With obvious reluctance Steven surrendered the bike, stepped back to about three feet, and stared at them. As the woman started to remove Tony's plastic painting apron, Steven raised his left hand with the fingers unclenched, brushed at his hair, and continued to lift his arm until his hand was behind his head. Tony watched him closely, and only broke his intense gaze when physically forced to do so by

The video-tape sequence, from which these pictures are taken shows Tony and Steven contesting ownership of a tricycle. John watches from the toy car.

having the apron pulled over his head. At this moment, Steven turned away abruptly and strode off. His arm was still bent back and remained behind his head until he was eight or nine feet away from the tricycle.

This "beating" movement is a commonly used piece of body language amongst young children. It can be used both as an offensive and a defensive signal. In an offensive or threatening pose, the arm is raised with the elbow bent out at the side. The hand remains a few inches from the side of the head, with the palm turned forwards and the fingers unclenched. In a defensive beating movement, the fingers touch the side of the head, brushing against the skin or the hair, and the hand is not usually lifted as high. The hand and arm movement is normally accompanied by a rigid posture and a serious or angry expression. Eye-contact is made with the other child and held. In a

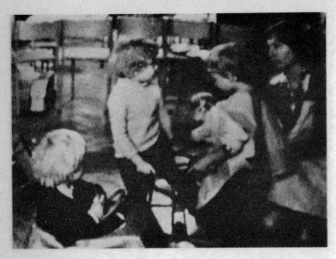

Tony appeals for help and the adult takes his side. As she kneels Steven begins to get onto the tricycle.

defensive situation, the child may retreat, beating the air with a sharp movement. In an offensive stance, the child will advance and again hit at the air, usually bending slightly forward at the same time. The distance at which the signal is sent is a further guide to its true purpose. An aggressive arm raise is usually carried out at closer range than a defensive beating gesture. In the encounter described above, Steven realised he had no hope of keeping the tricycle once an adult had been brought in by his rival. A grown-up is the infant's trump card, which seldom fails to win the day. So, angry but beaten, Steven retreated to a point where the desire to attack and the urge to flee became equally strong. At this distance, ambivalence took over. He transformed the conflicting emotions into a body signal, which by combining elements of defensive and offensive beating perfectly mirrored his

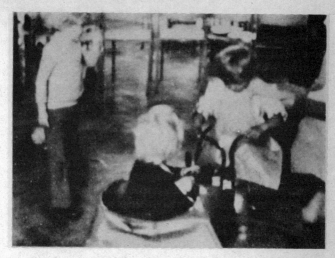

With the help of the adult Tony claims the tricycle. Steven moves about three feet away and watched him closely. His left hand starts to rise in a beating gesture.

confused mental state. If he had made the gesture any closer to Tony, the adult could have interpreted it as a threat, which might have led to a scolding. If he had been any further away, its impact would have been greatly reduced. So the choice of about three feet as the distance to make his stand and indicate his anger was not haphazard decision; it was something clearly determined by his biological response to the situation. This is a good example of the way in which proximity can subtly alter the meaning of a sequence of body signals, and so tell us different things about the child making them.

After the age of five, these beating gestures are modified to make them more socially acceptable. The blatant element of threat gradually declines, until the movement loses any obvious offensive or defensive significance. In adults it is reduced to a touching or

The boys stare at one another as the adult starts to take off Tony's plastic painting apron. John watches the exchange attentively and learns a lesson.

stroking of the back of the head, which is made in situations of doubt or conflict. Like the childish version it is more frequently seen in men than women. A businessman under fire from his colleagues may raise one hand and groom the nape of his neck. To those who can read the signal correctly, it betrays the fact that he cannot decide how to respond, or is frightened to make his true feelings known.

Tony knew exactly what Steven was saying when he sent that silent speech message, and so did John, another three-year-old who had watched the whole incident from a few feet away. John saw how Tony, a dominated boy, managed to win a coveted toy from the much more dominant Steven by bringing about the intervention of an adult. It was a lesson he did not forget, as was demonstrated by an incident which took place a few days

The apron being removed forces Tony to break eye-contact. Steven continues to watch him for a few seconds.

later. What happened is illustrated in the photographs on pages 141–145. This time Tony was sitting on a bus which John wanted. John made a grab for the steering wheel and tried to pull the toy away. But Tony resisted, and while warding off his attacker with the left hand made an exaggerated pointing gesture towards the same adult who had helped him on the previous occasion. As he did so, he glanced briefly in her direction and then gazed hard at John. He too looked towards her, before returning his attention to Tony. The boy smiled broadly and turned his pointing hand slightly to emphasise the gesture. After a few moments hesitation, during which Tony remained gesticulating and smiling, John reluctantly released his grip and wandered away. The meaning of his body talk was clear to both of them: "Do you want me to ask for help again?" Tony was inquiring. "You know what

Steven departs, his left arm still raised in the beating gesture which indicates a conflict between his anger and anxiety over the encounter.

happened last time!" The smile which accompanied the pointing made it clear that he, personally, was not threatening John in any way. As a dominated child addressing a very dominant member of the group, his manner remained defferential, but no less firm because of that. It was rather like a mild but determined adult saying to an unreasonable neighbour: "If you aren't prepared to see sense I shall have to send for the police. Please don't make me do that!"

John, realising that he was bound to lose out, backed away. But it was a tactical withdrawal, not a surrender. A *Dominant Aggressive* child hardly ever lets an infant lower on the pecking order score points against him. It challenges his whole social position and runs entirely contrary to his feelings. A few minutes later, when the

John tries to take a toy bus from Tony a few days after the dispute over the tricycle. Tony, now a more confident member of the group, hangs on and shrieks at him.

protecting adult had moved to a different part of the room, John returned to the attack, grabbed the bus, and this time succeeded in taking it without any trouble. Tony, seeing that he would have to fight his own battle this time, quickly surrendered.

One of the most frequently used methods of signalling aggression is a combination of oblong mouth, bared teeth, threatening gaze, angry frown and loud shrieks. The sudden, sharp sound is intended to confuse or frighten an antagonist, in much the same way that animal combatants produce blood curdling screams and screeches as they move into the attack.

These menacing facial expressions and disorientating sounds are accompanied by overall tension of the body and limbs. The arms may flex at the elbows and fingers

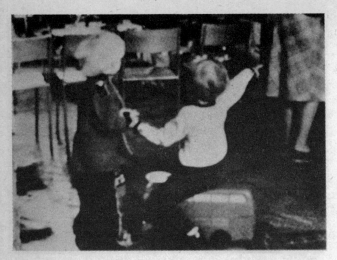

Tony refuses to surrender the bus and points deliberately towards the supervisor who had helped him gain the tricycle from Steven. Both boys look in her direction.

close into a half fist. At the same time the child often bends forward at the waist, itself a very threatening piece of body talk.

Each of these signals on its own contains a large measure of threat. Often they build on one another as the antagonistic exchange develops. The first indication that an aggressive interaction is taking place will be an increase of tension in both children. This is seen as a stiffening of the hands, and arms, back and shoulders.

The infants then stare hard at one another. Even if their expressions remain neutral, the prolonged gaze is highly disturbing, for children as well as adults. As I will explain in the next chapter, it is possible to send out a threat simply by maintaining lengthy eye-contact with another person.

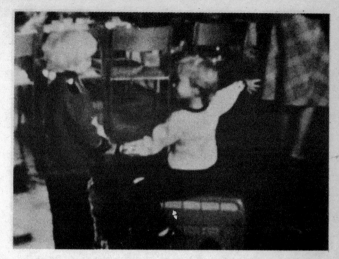

Tony then looks back at John. The boys stare at one another and Tony spreads his fingers to emphasise the gesture.

By this stage of the exchange, although there has been no sign of any gesture, or movement which most adults would regard as menacing, a high level of hostility may be present. If at this point one of the children turns and walks away, only the most observant grown-up will have realised that an aggressive interaction has occurred. Yet the defeated infant may have been made very anxious by the experience.

If the encounter continues, the threatening signals will intensify, as more and more elements of menacing body talk are added—such as the shriek, the oblong mouth and exposed teeth, and the eye-brows drawn together in an angry frown. The next development is usually closer proximity and symbolic blows. The infants may clap their hands, strike a toy against the wall or floor, make beating

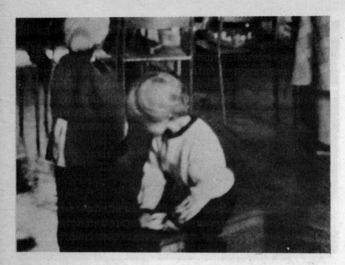

John retreats knowing that an adult intervention will give the more dominated boy a victory. But it is a tactical withdrawal, not a surrender...

gestures in the air, stamp or kick the ground. Provided that there is no adult intervention, the final outcome depends very much on the behavioural profiles of the children involved. When a *Dominant Aggressive* child is exchanging threats with a *Dominated Aggressive* or, less frequently, a *Dominated Frightened* infant, actual blows may be struck. It normally only takes one or two hits to the body to end the fight. The beaten child starts to cry and makes other submissive gestures, such as curling up, looking abjectly downwards, and covering his or her face. The victor then moves away satisfied.

When a *Dominant Aggressive* infant comes up against an equally dominant and aggressive child, real blows are very likely to result. If both back away from an actual fight, as they often do, then their anger is frequently redirected against submissive infants in the group. What

... a few minutes later, when the adult has gone, John returns to the attack and manages to snatch the bus from Tony.

may happen is that two pugnacious children square up to one another and go through the ritual of shrieking, stamping, teeth baring and frowning. They slap their hands together, stamp their feet and generally produce as much symbolic menace as possible. Beyond the climax of these signals, there lies either a resort to blows, which both realise will be equally painful, or retreat. But neither can afford to back down first. The result must be stalemate, not surrender, if the pecking order is to remain intact. So the two boys simultaneously move away from one another. One goes across the room and kicks over a brick house which a dominated child has just finished building. Then, shouting loudly he runs over to the slide and elbows his way up the ladder. The second boy stands still for a few moments, then walks over to an isolated infant and pushes her roughly to the ground.

When *Dominant Leaders* or leader and an aggressive child confront one another, the outcome seldom involves blows. Usually the *Dominant Leader* will either make an appeasing signal, by smiling, tilting the head, breaking gaze, offering a toy, or frequently just shrug and walk away from the scene. When this happens, the aggressive child may again redirect his violence against a third party. If no suitably submissive infants are to be found, some very energetic piece of behavior will frequently follow. The still angry *Dominant Aggressive* may run shrieking around the room, stamp noisily, or hammer a toy loudly against the floor or table.

An exchange which involves three dominant children and provides an interesting example of redirected aggression, is illustrated in the video-sequence on pages 147–154. In this eleven second exchange, John and Robert, both dominant children, contested a seat at the end of the modelling table. The third child, Barry aged four, a *Dominant Leader*, did not appear to be taking any part in their encounter at the time. But analysis of the recording shows that he *was* interacting with the others, and taking care to safeguard his own interests in case the violence between them should spill over to him. In this case an actual fight might have followed, but for the intervention of one of the play group supervisors. Notice especially the direction of Barry's gaze, and the movement of his right hand.

Picture One

John tries to sit down on the only free seat left at the table. But Robert is just about to take that place, as the supervisor ties an apron around him. He immediately tenses, frowns and strikes the table hard with his wooden roller. This is the equivalent of firing a warning shot across John's bows. All the children around the table look towards the roller.

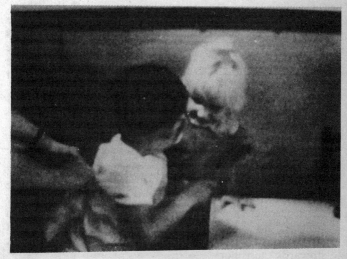

Picture Two

Determined to get the seat, and unimpressed by the symbolic blow, John pushes Robert hard in a vigorous attempt to dislodge him from the seat. Notice the aggressive expression on John's face. His lips form an oblong mouth, and the posture of the chin intensifies the threat. Robert turns to confront him, and raises his roller (which has blurred on the photograph because it was moving upwards so fast.) Barry, seated on John's left, looks towards Robert. His right hand, fingers extended in a grasping action, hovers over his own roller.

Picture Three

John's powerful shove has unseated Robert, who leans over to his right. Robert's arm is coming up with the roller

held in a striking position. Barry has kept his eyes on Robert, and closed his fingers around his own roller. He clearly regards Robert, who has a weapon, as a greater threat than John, even though John is being more overtly aggressive at the moment. Notice that the supervisor is still trying to tie an apron on Robert. This shows that although the interaction is obviously aggressive when broken up into frozen segments, it did not appear that way at the time to the only grown-up present.

Picture Four

John has almost won the seat as he pushes Robert further away from the table. Barry still keeps his eyes fixed on the boy with the roller, and takes an even firmer grip on his own.

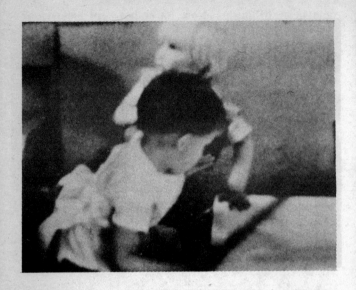

Picture Five

At the very moment when victory is within his grasp, John's attention is distracted by the adult calling out to him: "Stop shoving." As he looks quickly away, Robert makes an immediate come-back, his roller raised as he pushes John away with his left hand. At the exact moment that Robert starts to lift the stick, Barry does the same with his own roller. He is still closely watching Robert.

Picture Six

John is on the defensive. Robert is coming towards him with an aggressive posture and the intimidating roller. Barry holds his own stick in readiness for any attack directed against him.

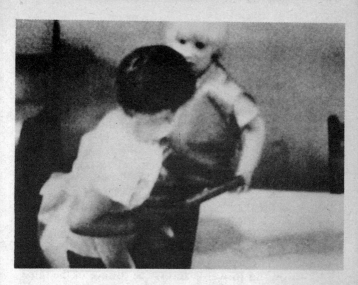

Picture Seven

John looks anxiously at Robert, who seems about to launch an attack on him. He touches the edge of the table with his left hand. Barry is still keeping a careful watch on the situation and holding his roller at the ready.

Picture Eight

John now breaks eye-contact by looking down. In silent speech this is a submissive gesture which acknowledges that Robert has won. The other boy stands in a defensive posture, not attacking but guarding his territory. As John looks down, he begins to sweep his left hand very violently backwards and forwards across the surface of the table.

Picture Nine

John's hand-sweeping gesture continues for several seconds. In this way he releases the aggression which had built up during the brief encounter. Barry, sensing that the aggression is subsiding, places his roller down on the table. Robert, although still wary, starts to sit down.

Picture Ten

The boys look at one another again. Robert, who has now almost regained the seat, smiles appeasingly. John is far from happy with the way things have turned out, but most of his anger has been absorbed by his brisk hand movement. Barry is no longer interested in the encounter, and starts to use his roller on the pastry once again.

If the adult had not been present and intervened on

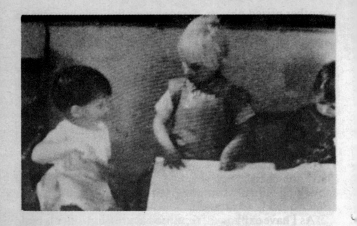

Robert's side, it is likely that the pushing and shoving would have continued, until either there was a clear winner or a compromise was reached. Submission by a *Dominant Aggressive* child is rare, unless the exchange is distorted by the interference of a third party. If either John or Robert had been dominated children, the outcome might have been quite different. Neither a frightened nor an isolated child would have contested the seat in the first place. Even if such a child had already been sitting there, either of the dominant boys could have taken it from him with a minimum of fuss, again provided that a grown-up did not take the submissive child's side. A *Dominated Aggressive* infant might have contested the seat at first, but would probably have retreated in the face of determined attack.

Infants come to blows for much the same reasons that inspire aggressive responses in adults, as a result of disputes over property or territory. The third type of violence, which arises from redirected anger, is usually much shorter in duration.

The most common cause of arguments are toys, games

or other prized objects. Simon, aged five, has brought his own box of cars to the group. He refuses to let Alison, aged four, play with them. After watching him for several minutes, she grabs one of the cars and takes it to the other side of the room. Simon runs over and confronts her angrily. He shrieks, frowns, and bends forward with his arms tensed. "Naughty Alison!" he shouts. He beats at the air. She drops the car abruptly and walks away.

Anthony, aged three, wants to sit next to his friend Rachel during lunch. He has already sat there on several occasions, and clearly thinks this gives him a prior claim. Peter, another three-year-old, decides that he wants to have the chair. They struggle, pushing one another and shrieking. Finally Anthony falls over and starts to cry. Peter quickly sits down.

As I have explained, ritualised aggression-signals build on one another, increasing the menace of the message as each new threat is added. An exchange escalates from bodily tension and cold stares to symbolic blows in a hierachy of hostility. Is the same aggressive progression found in the ways actual blows are struck? Is the type of attack made, and the part of the body to which it is directed, merely a matter of chance? Or does an element of calculation and communication enter into it? My impression is that however random such blows may appear, they are not struck in a haphazard manner. Although the attacking youngster may be very angry and intent on hurting the other child, the big guns are never brought into play immediately. There is a gradual rise from the tentative to the ferocious, and it is only rarely that the worst violence of which a child is capable ever appears.

The meaning of the blow can be varied in one of three ways. The most obvious is by the force with which it is delivered. A *Dominated Aggressive* child, driven to strike a *Dominant Aggressive* infant, may slap at them in a weak and rather ineffective manner, with no real intensity to the attack. Often these appear to be symbolic blows which were meant to lash the air and landed by mistake. On the other hand, *Dominant Aggressive* children frequently grab one another with considerable determination, and pull or push with all their strength.

The other variables are the ways in which blows are struck and the part of the body to which they are directed.

In ascending order of aggression the target areas are:

1) Legs or arms.
2) Back.   Increasing
3) Chest.   Aggression
4) Back of head or neck.
5) Face.

Types of blow are even harder to categorise in this way, but an approximate order of intensity is:

1) Pushes or shoves.
2) Slaps.
3) Kicks.   Increasing
4) Pinching or hair pulling.   Aggression
5) Biting.
6) Punching with the clenched
   fist.

When trying to interpret an aggressive exchange where physical violence has been used, it is important to remember the details of the fight itself. The amount of crying at the end of the encounter is not a reliable measure of how ferocious it was. An already frightened or anxious child might burst into tears after being lightly pushed in the back. On the other hand, a *Dominant Aggressive* child may not cry even though he has been punched fairly violently in the face. In both cases, tears are more likely to result if there is a sympathetic grown-up in ear-shot. As every parent knows, small children are only too ready to sob in order to attract attention, evoke affection, and possibly bring down adult wrath on the aggressor.

Notice the type of blows struck, for example pushes, kicks, slaps, punches; how they were delivered, whether violently or timidly; and where they were directed, at the opponent's back, chest, face and so on. This will give you a general guide to the degree of aggression being expressed. You should also observe how the fight escalates, and who steps up the violence of the attacks. At the end of the encounter, see how both victor and vanquished behave. Analysing fights amongst the under-fives in this way provides useful insights into the structure of the group and the personalities of individual members.

Usually the struggles are short and sharp, finishing without any physical injury having been sustained. In this respect small children, like the majority of wild animals, behave in a far more rational way than human adults. The youngsters pull their punches for the same reason that an animal rarely goes straight for its opponent's jugular vein during a fight. They understand that the real purpose of combat is to win as quickly and easily as possible. Every aggressive encounter, whether in the nursery or the jungle, represents an investment of energy and risk to those involved. The risks are not only those of a weakening injury, which could place even the victor at the mercy of other enemies, but the loss of status which will result from a defeat. The latter is clearly the more important consideration in nursery fights. A small child who is high in the pecking order often places his whole reputation at stake in every aggressive encounter. Fighting can only payoff if a victory seems likely with a minimum investment of time, energy and risk. Adults often castigate the playground bully by demanding of him: "Why don't you pick on somebody your own size!" In fact, by concentrating their violence on smaller, younger or weaker children, the *Dominant Aggressives* are behaving in a very rational manner. To some extent, the weaker the opponent the easier and more certain is a victory. But a law of diminishing returns operates here, which helps to protect the weakest members of the group, the *Frightened* and *Isolated* children, from constant attack. A victory is socially valueless if it has been gained *too* easily. There is little point in an aggressive child coming to blows with an opponent who offers only instant surrender and appeasement. Such an encounter will do nothing to help him—and it usually is a boy—in terms of status

Fights Are About Status—Not Things

At a superficial level, most of the disputes, struggles and fights which take place amongst any group of boisterous under-fives, seem to be about things. The children argue over the ownership of a popular toy or game, or they push and squabble to be first on the slide or climbing frame. If any position in the room is especially popular, then a number of the more dominant children are bound to wrestle for the right to sit, stand or lie there.

In fact, it is not usually *possessing* the desired object which is most important, but being seen by the others to have possessed it. The toy or game will of course provide a reward in terms of amusement, interest or excitement. But by gaining something which the others want, the child is able to establish or maintain a superior social position. This is of more lasting value than temporary enjoyment of the object itself. Fights are about status—not things. Time after time in the nursery school or play group one can see children struggling bitterly over a disputed toy, or the right to monopolise a popular game. Yet, once victory has been achieved, the successful child will often lose interest and abandon what has been so energetically wrested from the others.

Gaining something which the other children wanted, either through threats or actual violence, enables the *Dominant Aggressive* to maintain his social standing, while serving as a warning to the others not to dispute his rights. Such struggles also enable aggressive but previously dominated children to establish themselves as dominant members of the group. The frequent but usually minor disputes which are so common in a group of under-fives should be regarded not merely as random expressions of violence, but as a way of structuring the social order. They are a necessary and effective means by which power is distributed and maintained.

This is one of the main reasons why adult interventions can be so harmful. The child who has won a scuffle, secured a toy and so asserted himself, suffers a severe loss of face if a grown-up then comes between him and the fruits of victory. A slap or a sharp word may appear a fair punishment for aggression. Restoring a toy or game to a vanquished and weeping child may seem like a kindly act. Physically removing a boisterious child from the head of a slide queue can look like the best method of giving the others a chance. There are occasions when such drastic interventions may be unavoidable. But they should always be approached with caution. My view is that, however well-intentioned, these actions are frequently unhelpful and even harmful in the long term. Aggressive children who have been thwarted by adults tend to respond with greater violence a short time later, probably in order to regain lost face. This clearly makes life even more difficult for them, and can lead to further adult intervention. Isolated or frightened children who have been helped to win enjoy only a brief advantage over their companions. They have not learned how to manage aggressive exchanges any better, nor has their self-confidence been boosted. In fact, quite the opposite may have happened. The dominated children can turn increasingly to grown-ups for assistance, instead of finding ways to win through by their own efforts. What they need are swimming lessons, not a series of handy life-rafts!

This is not to say, of course, that adult help and guidance is other than extremely valuable, when provided at the right time and in the right way. Dominated children need to be shown how to respond in a more assertive manner, so that they can develop into leaders. For their own happiness, as much as for that of the group, aggressive youngsters must be helped to resolve the stresses and tensions which often lie at the basis of their violent behaviour. But always approach every situation with patience and understanding. Changes should be brought about in such a way that the child is guided, rather than manipulated, into a more socially successful approach to life.

Aggression and Anxiety

Even the most dominant and self-confident child becomes anxious at times. But some infants are in an almost constant state of anxiety when mixing with a group. These are the youngster who remain solitary and watchful, never able to bring themselves to join in with the games and activities going on around them. Isolated children are so obviously unhappy, and sometimes so transparently anxious, that even the least perceptive grown-ups realise that all is not right with them. Anxiety signals sent out by other infants are often less blatant, and consequently harder to detect.

As we have seen, even during aggressive exchanges the children involved are usually mixing anxiety signals with their threats. Torn between the urge to stand and fight, and the desire to run away from the frightening situation, they experience a considerable level of stress. The variations in hormone levels detected by Professor Montagner are a measure of that stress.

Small children also become anxious when watching aggression between other infants, or observing adult threats towards a child in the group. Finally they may become extremely anxious if they are the victims of an attack, actual or threatened, by another child or an adult.

The kind of secret language signals produced by these fears fall into two categories. There are some which have a clear communicative intention. The infant makes them in order to broadcast his or her anxiety to others. Then there are those signals which are a vivid reflection of inner emotions, but not made with the deliberate purpose of letting others know about them. Two examples will help to make clear this important distinction.

Smiling, as we saw in Chapter Four, is often used as an appeasement signal. *Dominant Leader* children with smile when others smile at them, or when they are making an appeasement or solicitation gesture towards an equally dominant child. Dominated children smile more frequently, and always do so when starting an exchange with infants who are higher in the pecking order than themselves. These smiles are combined with other body signals, all indicating non-hostility. The secret language message being sent is: "Don't hurt me. I am not going to be any threat to you."

When a child is anxious about whether or not to take part in a game, he may stand for a few moments watching what is going on, while at the same time massaging or sucking different parts of his body. Small boys and girls may push a comforting thumb into their mouths, rub their heads or tug at their clothes. Small boys will often play with their genitals, or pull at the edge of their trousers. Girls seldom seem to manipulate themselves genitally, preferring to clutch at the hem of their dress or twist their fingers together. Even when it involves genital contact, this kind of self-manipulation is not sexual but fearful in origin! Very anxious children sometimes suck their thumbs for such lengthy periods that small cracks appear in the skin. The presence of such fissures is a good indication of high level anxiety. Persistent head rubbing, scratching or massaging of different parts of the body, especially the hands and face, are also indications that the child is excessively anxious. Sometimes extensive self-manipulation leads to minor skin disorders, raw patches and rashes, which although trivial in themselves may be the external evidence for deep internal fears. All these signals reflect tensions about the situation or lifestyle which the infant is currently experiencing. They are primarily made as a source of comfort. Holding, stroking, feeling and manipulating parts of their own body, are all methods by which the infant can reduce or at least contain his or her anxiety. Nervous adults use similar types of body language, combing their hair, touching their faces, fiddling with shirt cuffs, rubbing their hands together, picking their noses, or carrying out any number of small fidgety movements. The next time you travel by air, watch out for those who deep down are terrified of the flight, yet determined not to show it. Their features may be calm, they may even appear relaxed. But every opportunity to self-manipulate in minor, socially acceptable ways will be taken.

In children, crying may or may not accompany these anxious movements. As I have already mentioned, tears on their own are not an accurate guide to anxiety, because small children may sob for a variety of reasons totally unconnected with fear. They may cry to elicit adult attention, to bring down grown-up wrath on an aggressive child, to express pain after a tumble, or simply to show solidarity with another bawling youngster. Contrary to popular belief, girls are less likely to cry than boys. But both sexes are more inclined to burst into tears as a result of social confrontations than solitary injuries. A child who trips and falls will probably not cry unless there is an adult close by. An infant who is pushed over by another is more likely to start sobbing, whether or not there is a grown-up in earshot.

Anxious crying sounds very different from angry or vengeful sobbing, and is accompanied by much greater self-touching.

The behaviour of children being introduced to a play group or nursery school for the first time is usually watchful and anxious. Fears will be less if the infant has an older brother or sister already in the group, or if they are already familiar with the other children. But otherwise a great deal of anxiety can be generated on these first encounters with such an unknown environment. There is a good deal of manipulation, combined with lengthy periods during which the new children remain motionless and watchful. They may suck their fingers or thumbs, or

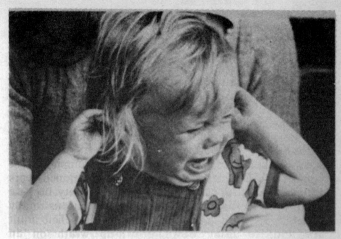

Touching, stroking and massaging different parts of the body is a sure sign of anxiety in the child. The arm movements of a twelve-month-old and a three-year-old are very similar. Kiran manipulates his ears as his mother leaves . . . Tony rubs his forehead miserably when left at the start of his first day in the play group.

some comforting object like a handkerchief or favourite doll. They may chew their lips and tongue and make frequent shrugging movements with their shoulders. If another child attempts eye-contact with them, they swiftly look away, usually glancing quickly and submissively downwards. Some very anxious newcomers spend most of their time looking down, so as to avoid the gaze of others. They walk or stand around with their chins tucked into their necks. They explore their new surroundings uncertainly, moving slowly and keeping their arms close to the body. They sometimes shuffle, but very seldom run. Their main ambition is to avoid any confrontations, whether hostile or friendly, and find a quiet corner where they can be left in peace. For the first few sessions, they will probably cry and cling to their mothers, and seek the attention of an affectionate supervisor once they have been left. Girls usually adapt more quickly than boys and as with crying make less fuss over being left. Within two or three sessions, however, most of the children will have settled down and will no longer appear so anxious. Only those who are very young or especially timid, in other words those who are destined to fill the role of the most dominated and isolated group members, still avoid any contact with others.

The response of boys to newcomers is largely to ignore them. They tend to study them briefly, with a somewhat disinterested air, before returning to their games and their companions. Girls are more friendly, and smile frequently at fearful strangers. They often go over and lead the new child into the group, taking their hand and touching them reassuringly. But even boys are prepared to treat newcomers rather more gently than established members of the group, at least during the first few sessions. This is probably because the infants are sending out such powerful anxiety and submission signals that it is clear they offer no competition for toys or territory.

Aggression and anxiety can be seen as two sides of the same coin. There is seldom one without a good measure of the other. Before condemning the infant bully, one should look carefully for any anxieties which may be causing his frequent outbursts of violence. Before concluding that a dominated child is lacking in "strength of character", we must relate their submissive behaviour to the situations in which they occur. Most parents try to be understanding. But sympathy and a desire to judge the child fairly will not, by themselves, help the situation very much. The first task is to find out exactly why excessive anxiety or aggression are present. This means examining the infant's lifestyle, not in general, but in specific terms. Keep a written note of the situations in which the child seems especially fearful or pugnacious. Use your knowledge of the secret language to spot the signals which indicate these conditions at even a low level. Once you have found out when and where difficulties are most frequently encountered, it becomes possible to take practical steps to make changes. One might find, for example, that a child is dominant at home with younger brothers and sisters, but isolated at play group where there are mostly older children. An infant may be aggressive in a large group, but more appeasing in a smaller one.

Aggression cannot be curbed by scoldings. Submissive behaviour is seldom responsive to such exhortations as "stand up for yourself." Both approaches are likely to make matters worse by increasing the levels of stress. Some of the ways in which you can help the child most effectively, by use of the secret language, will be described in Chapters Eight and Ten.

Hand washing accompanied by tears and a sad expression send a message of anxiety and distress. Infants frequently signal inner fears by self-manipulation of this kind. Tony was unhappy during his first day at the play group.

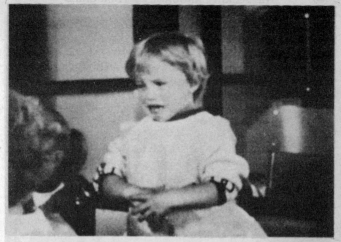

The powerful solicitation signal described in the last chapter is used by a sensitive adult to cheer him up. The smile and head tilt produced a rapid change in his behaviour and he started to smile himself for the first time.

7 The Meaning Of Gestures and Gaze

Small children talk to us with their eyes, their arms and their hands. They ask questions, express doubts, show weariness, and discover what's going on in the world around them, by means of a language of gestures and gaze. All too often, however, adults either miss these silent speech signals or dismiss them as being of little importance. Frequently we do not even realise that the child has attempted to say something to us.

Jane, aged eighteen months, is playing in her back garden when she suddenly stands still, points towards some bushes and looks intently at her mother. Ronald, aged fifteen months, is exploring the countryside with his father. He stops abruptly, sucks his thumb and looks around. When the adults were asked if these movements meant anything to them, they replied in bewildered tones: "No, nothing at all. Should they have done?" and "Of course not! He was just thinking about things."

This kind of response is not really surprising. We are used to seeing some types of expression, such as smiles or frowns or certain gestures, as being obvious attempts at communication. But random activities, like those described above, usually seem too disorganised and spontaneous to be silent speech signals. Yet in many cases that is exactly what they are. Messages can be sent in the most unexpected ways, and it is quite easy at times to mistake body talk for childish games. The first lesson to learn, when it comes to studying exchanges between the very young and adults, is that no movements should be automatically dismissed as meaningless.

What Toddlers Try To Tell Us

The kind of mutually unsatisfactory exchange which can take place between a grown-up and an infant is illustrated by what happened when twenty-three-year-old Sally took seventeen-month-old James on an outing to the park. James is Sally's first child, so she is possibly less alert to infant body talk than a more experienced mother.

She pushes James to the park in his buggy. Once there, the little boy is allowed to wander where he likes under Sally's watchful gaze. She sits down on the grass, and he toddles eagerly away to explore some tree stumps, he squats down and starts to pick up stones. He puts one in his mouth, which provokes an anxious cry of: "Naughty James... don't do that", from his mother.

After a few moments he flings away the stone and starts to suck at his fingers. Then he takes his hand away from his mouth and scrapes at the ground. This amuses him for several minutes, but finally he loses interest and gazes back at his mother. Sally waves. James then stands up and pops his right thumb into his mouth. Immediately after this, he starts back towards her. When he is still about ten feet away he stops, straightens up, and glances briefly at the busy main road beyond the gates. Then he stares hard at his mother and points towards the traffic.

"No, James," she calls urgently. "Not that way. Go over there..." She points towards a safe, grassy bank which slopes gently towards the lawns. James gazes at her, but makes no move to obey. Sally waggles her hand in an attempt to make her meaning obvious, then indicates the lawn even more firmly with a thrusting finger: "Go over there..."

The little boy stands motionless, then he drops his arm

and sucks his thumb again. After a moment he stoops and picks up a flower, which somebody has torn from a nearby cluster of daffodils and thrown away. He toddles eagerly towards his mother, who smiles delightedly at the offering: "Isn't that lovely Jimmy," she says eagerly. "Is that for me?" When he is a couple of feet from her, however, the small boy suddenly discards the flower and wanders away again. His mother looks disappointed, reaches down and picks up the bloom.

James plays on the grass for ten minutes, then he walks back to his mother, stops and waves.

"No, don't disappear again Jimmy," Sally tells him with a laugh. "We are going home now." James then comes over to her and is rewarded with a welcoming smile. He raises his arms, and Sally responds almost immediately by stooping and lifting him up.

During this short excursion, James made many of the most frequently observed infant gestures. Some of the movements were deliberate attempts to communicate with his mother, others occurred as a result of his eagerness to explore unfamiliar surroundings.

What were these silent speech signals intended to tell his mother, and what do they tell us about his development?

Pointing

Small children frequently make gestures which look very similar to adult pointing movements, and are often seen as such by their parents. We point to emphasise or clarify questions and statements such as: "What's that?" or "You go down the street to that corner." When an infant raises hand and arm in a purposeful way, a grown-up may regard it as a sign that the child wants to go in a certain direction or is drawing attention to something. But toddlers, who make frequent use of pointing gestures, seldom use them in the same way as we do.

Points of Balance

When James started to toddle away from his mother, he raised his right arm and held it more or less parallel to the ground as he walked. His fingers were lightly clenched, with the forefinger pointing towards tree stumps. If an adult had made that signal there would have been little doubt that the message was: "I am going over there." But James was not, at that moment, trying to say anything at all in body talk. The raised arm was there simply to help him stay on his feet across uneven ground. Infants who have only just learned how to walk, and James had been toddling for less than a month, often use an upraised arm like a tight-rope artist's balancing pole. It helps them maintain what is usually a rather precarious gait. It may also reduce any anxieties they have about tumbling over on their faces, so long as the outstretched hand is there to break the fall. Even after children have mastered walking they will sometimes return to the earlier balancing movement when chasing one another or hurrying to meet an adult. This kind of movement is usually quite easy to identify. The arm raise mostly occurs when the ground is especially uneven, and the hand waggles slightly, just as a tight-rope walker's pole sways to maintain balance. During this time the child may be looking almost anywhere. The direction of gaze does not appear to be linked to the arm movement.

Points of Conflict

An almost identical gesture, made when the child is standing still, often precedes a change of direction or the start of a new game. A small child who has been toddling or playing happily will suddenly stop, become upright and motionless, then make the arm raise movement while looking uncertain about what to do next. The puzzling feature of this signal is that it does not seem to be triggered by anything in the surroundings. Although the infant will point in a particular direction, he does not necessarily intend to move that way. This gesture, which is normally accompanied by shifting gaze, seems to be a reflection of internal conflicts rather than external events. It is as if the child is translating doubts about what to do next into a vague body movement. This movement is only seen in the very young. It has normally vanished from the repertoire of silent speech by the age of two.

Points For Self-Preservation

Infants under one year old hardly ever point to something they have seen, or imagine they have seen, in their surroundings. But by the age of fifteen months almost every child uses the pointing movement in this way. Here again, however, the point is not identical in meaning to the adult gesture. Nor is the message sent in quite the same way.

If we raise a hand to indicate something of interest, the movement is often brief, and eye-contact shifts between the person we are with and the direction of point. For example, words, gesture and gaze might be combined like this. A woman sees a familiar face at the other end of the street. She turns to her friend:

"Isn't that Doreen Brown?" As she asks the question her hand comes up, elbow slightly bent, forefinger aimed in the direction of the person in question, and then back at her friend. Her eye-brows are raised to emphasise the question. If her friend cannot spot the right person, she may extend her arm in an attempt to pin-point the target more accurately. Another glance to make sure the outstretched finger is positioned correctly, then a return of eye-contact to her friend: "No, the woman in the blue hat by the parked car!"

The infant's sequence of arm raise and gaze is quite different. He lifts his arm, points with a finger, and glances briefly in that direction. Then he looks away and attempts to make eye-contact with his mother. Once mutual gaze has been established, the child will usually continue to stare at his mother while pointing. Infants invariably look towards their mothers when producing this very specialised signal. If both parents are side-by-side, it will be the wife and not the husband who receives eye-contact.

This consistent desire to relate to mother something seen, or imagined, is one of the unique features which distinguishes this silent speech signal from all others. Pointing which results from internal conflicts and precedes a change of direction can be sent to either parent, or even to strangers. The infant will also wave at strangers and relate to them with many other secret language signals. But this never happens with "point and gaze". If the child is close to the mother when the message is sent, he may pat her arm or thigh with his other hand to attract attention. At a distance, steady gaze is used in an attempt to catch the mother's eye. So reliable is this signal in linking infants with their mothers that it can be used as an infallible guide to which child belongs to which adult, when large numbers of mothers and children are gathered together.

Another distinctive feature of point and gaze is that the mother never attempts to mimic it, as she does almost every other piece of body talk. By repeating her child's gestures and expressions, a mother teaches the infant to make a signal correctly. Imitative teaching is the main method by which children master a whole range of silent speech movements. But not only do adults never copy this gesture, they frequently misunderstand it. In an earlier example of a mistaken body talk message, I described how sixteen-month-old Karen was scolded when she pointed towards a paddling pool. Similarly, in the other example James made his mother Sally equally anxious when he pointed to the main road. Both mothers assumed the "point-and-gaze" message meant that the infants intended to go in that direction. But the gesture does not normally take on this more adult meaning until around the age of three. Then the gaze is directed not at the mother, but in the intended line of travel. By this time, "point-and-gaze" has almost vanished from the silent speech repertoire.

When making this signal, the child usually stands motionless, with a tense, alert posture. Although no sound is made, it is certain they are trying to say something important. Just what this might be, it is frequently impossible to decide. The infant has obviously been attracted, and either alarmed or puzzled, by something and wants to communicate this fact to his mother.

But what exactly it is that may have caught his attention is often far from clear. One can search the surroundings in vain for something unusual, exciting or unexpected which could have intrigued or frightened the child. Even mothers are usually unable to say what, if anything, might have caused the purposeful movement and intense gaze. Many just shrug it off as a babyish gesture which has no significance. But this is incorrect. The signal does have an important meaning to the child. It is a gesture linked to self-preservation.

It may be that adults fail to see anything of special interest for the excellent reason that there is nothing to see! While the children are still learning to make sense of the world, the dividing line between fantasy and reality often blurs. Their sudden interest may have been aroused by something which only exists in their imagination.

Another possible explanation could be found in differences in visual perception. Seeing objects in terms of perspective is a skill which takes quite a long time to develop. Small children often fail to realise that objects which appear quite small may really be big things at a distance. They tend to see these objects as being nearby and tiny, rather than a long way off and large. So when a child points eagerly, he could be attempting to direct the adult's attention to something which is in fact several hundred yards away. Because of its remoteness, the grown-up thinks that it can be of no significance. But to the toddler it seems within touching distance. Finally, the adult may fail to see anything of interest because everything in the surroundings appears to be so ordinary and familiar. We must remember that our vast experience of the everyday world is not shared by the very young. Things which are commonplace to us—blown leaves, an unusually angled tree, cracks in a wall, a dog sniffing along the grass—may all look extraordinary and appear of importance to the infant.

The early years are a time of maximum learning, when tasks of great complexity have to be mastered quickly and efficiently. Everything is strange, mysterious and potentially dangerous. The only ways in which the child can find out about the world is through exploration and personal experience. Much of that knowledge is acquired by investigating things: sucking, tasting, touching and gazing at them. If any doubt arises in the child's mind, it is resolved by an appeal to the person who has been most involved in loving and caring for him. Usually this means his mother, the source of all knowledge, protection, and security. For almost invariably it is the mother whom the child feels can be trusted above all others; the constant Pole Star in an environment which is unknown and often seems both bewildering and irrational.

So what probably happens is this. The infant sees, hears or imagines something which cannot be identified. There is no information stored away in his memory which quite matches it. Perhaps there has been a sudden movement, an unknown sound, a peculiar-looking object. It may only be a confusion between fantasy and reality. *What* it is does not matter. The crucial questions the child need answered are: "Will it harm me? Should I fear it?" The mother is the only person who can be relied on to tell the truth.

To a child of the Stone Age, getting the right information in the shortest amount of time could really have meant the difference between living and dying. This is when the inborn "gaze and point" signal originated and acquired its particular form. Every component of the message is geared to ensure the best chance of survival.

The child remains motionless. This makes it harder for a potential enemy to spot him. He becomes tense, an indication that the fight or flight mechanism has been tuned up ready for action. Not a sound is made. The slightest noise could attract potentially lethal attention. The infant remains alert and watchful. After a quick glance to fix the position, he gazes at his mother. Her reaction will tell him all he needs to know about the mysterious sight or sound. Does she look scared or come to his aid? Does she remain relaxed? Usually, of course, the reply he gets is one of indifference, based on complete ignorance of what is going on in his mind. But this too is a perfectly satisfactory response. She is not worried, so he need not be anxious. The child relaxes and starts another game. "Point and gaze" usually marks the end of one activity and the beginning of something new.

The sequence of movements is always the same. Playing stops, a "point and gaze" signal is sent, then a fresh bout of play begins. Some children use "point and gaze" signals every few minutes. Others send out the message much less frequently. As the child grows older, and more and more information about the world is stored away in the memory, there is less occasion to query things. But all children, from the moment they start crawling actively until the time they are almost thirty months old, find out about the world by means of this primitive and powerful signal.

In the sunny park and friendly playground, we are watching an eerie reflection of mankind's evolutionary past—when an infant's precarious existence might depend on the speedy identification of every crack in the undergrowth and each brief movement in the forest shadows.

Points To Go

As "point and gaze" declines, the gesture is used increasingly to indicate that the child wants to move in a certain direction. The arm is raised as before, but like the adult movement, it is normally kept up for merely a brief moment. The child looks only quickly at the adult and then in the direction of point. This signal is often made just before the first step is taken, and seems to be a throw-back to the earlier "point and balance" gesture.

Adults often point when they want a child to go in a particular direction. Frequently this message is misinterpreted. Children of less than fourteen months have great difficulty in grasping the idea that a pointing movement can be associated with a distant object. To them they are two completely unconnected entities. Even when the child is standing close to the grown-up and given a large number of other clues, such as encouraging words, finger waggling and gaze in the same direction, he may not be able to understand what is happening. Ten months later, children have usually learned to link point and a distant object when standing close to the adult. But confusions may still arise if the gesture is made from a distance. When James seemed about to head for the main road, his mother called sternly and pointed to a safer part of the park. The boy, who was asking a question about something, was clearly puzzled by this response. Instead of doing what she expected, he stood and gazed intently at her, trying to make out what message she was sending and how it reacted to his urgent question. His bewilderment revealed itself in a thumb sucking expression of anxiety (see below).

Waving

Adults wave to say "hello" or "goodbye". But small children have to learn how to use the signal in this way. It is not something that comes naturally. Until the lessons have been mastered, the gesture will be used in an entirely different way.

When we make vigorous hand and arm movements of greeting or farewell, our purpose is to draw attention to ourselves and to the other pieces of body language appropriate to the occasion. To be effective, the wave must be accompanied by the correct expression and posture. By about the age of three, most children have learned how to produce an acceptable combination of such silent speech signals, and are more or less aware of when they should make them. But it has taken many months training to achieve this seemingly spontaneous gesture. In Western cultures, the wave and the handshake are amongst the first social signals acquired. In any society which sets a store by good manners, lessons in the body language of politeness start early.

"Say bye bye to Granny," commands a mother, and waggles the wrist of her six-month-old baby. "Bye, bye poppet," coos granny, and repeats the waving movement in an exaggerated manner. By doing so, she provides the child with a biological mirror to help learn how a wave should look. After scores of repetitions, endless prompting, and some years of practice, the child makes the movement automatically in the right situations.

Before the wave has become firmly associated with a social occasion, a brisk waggling of the hands and arms is used to express feelings of excitement or frustration. Exactly which emotion is involved is usually clear from the accompanying facial expressions and sounds.

The pleasure which a toddler feels at the thought of going back to mother, produces some of the most intense waggling and flapping. A child who has been exploring boldly will suddenly decide that he wants to see mum again. As though overwhelmed by the excitement of returning to her, he starts to wave his arms vigorously up and down, flapping with hand, wrist and forearm while a delighted expression lightens his face. Then he toddles uncertainly towards her, still flapping enthusiastically. In body language the child seems to be chorusing the classic Al Jolson line: "I'm a coming, I'm a coming, I hope I didn't make you wait...."

Hand waggling and waving are a clear indication that the child will be returning quickly to mother. I have observed the signal more than three hundred times in five countries. The average delay between waving and starting back was ten seconds.

A child often interprets an adult's wave not as an instruction to return, but an invitation to play a game of imitation. In many cases the infant looks up, hesitates, and takes a few steps towards the grown-up. Then one arm is raised in a gesture which mimics the wave. If nothing further happens, the child wanders off in another direction or goes back to his game. Even clear adult beckoning signals can baffle the toddler. Some parents scold a child for being naughty when he takes no notice of their urgent, silent speech commands to return. But this is much more often due to a simple lack of understanding, rather than an obstinate refusal to obey.

Waving and flapping as a means of showing excitement at the return to a parent diminish as the child becomes better at walking and running. Then it is the speed of a return which expresses his or her delight, rather than hand signals.

Vigorous arm waving can also accompany a temper tantrum. The movements are similar to those made during the offensive—defensive beating gestures which I described in Chapter Six. They too indicate conflict in the child's mind, but unlike the slower and more deliberate arms raise signals, they are usually very quick and sharp. An angry infant will flap briskly up and down with one or both arms, fists clenched, as though beating a violent tattoo on a toy drum. The noise which normally accompanies this furious activity is equally unattractive!

Arms Raise

Sally may have had difficulty in understanding many of the body signals which James made. But there was no confusion in her mind over the last one. It would have been remarkable if there had been, because the arm raise is one of the most frequently used and successful messages which an infant can direct towards his mother. It says: "I want to be picked up." To produce it the child stands directly in front of the mother and looks up, if possible making eye-contact. The arms are stretched imploringly upwards. In most cases, the mother almost automatically stoops down and lifts the child into her arms. The signal is so powerful that a woman can be deeply preoccupied and still respond to it. I have seen many instances where two mothers have been talking earnestly when a child approaches and makes the arms raise gesture. With barely a downward glance, and scarcely a falter in her conversation, the woman stoops and gathers up the infant. In most cases the response occurs within two or three seconds of the signal having been sent. If it does not, the child may strike the mother's thighs to attract her attention, or thrust himself against her. A persistent refusal often causes the child to cling tightly to her legs and start to sob in protest.

It is not clear how children learn this piece of body talk, which appears to be very widely used. I have seen it produced and responded to in Western, African and Indian cultures.

A possible explanation is that it originates when the infant is starting to walk. When beginning to master this difficult skill, the toddler is only able to stand upright for a few seconds and take one or two precarious paces forward before collapsing in a heap on the floor. At this stage, both arms are sometimes held up to assist an uncertain balance, just as the "point and balance" single arm raise is used by a walking but still uncertain child. Just before a fall, or as the infant pushes himself up again after a tumble, he may again raise both arms producing a movement very similar to the: "Please carry me" signal. If there happens to be adults around at that moment, the child is frequently helped up, soothed and made a fuss of. This attention and encouragement is intended to reward the walking attempt. But it could also help to establish the arms raise gesture by reinforcing that piece of behaviour. Behavioural psychologists have long known that any action which is immediately rewarded is very likely to be repeated. In this way the arms raise becomes an established part of body talk, which the infant links in his mind with being picked up, carried and made a fuss of. This idea is supported by the fact that children often make the signal when they are not at all tired. Here their request to be carried clearly stems from a need to be held and comforted by the adult.

But there is some evidence which seems hard to fit in with this theory. For one thing, babies make an almost identical gesture long before they start to walk. This suggests that the gesture is not learned but innate. Another difficulty is that children will make a "Please carry me" signal when at a considerable distance from their parents. Since it only works at close range—the message is usually ineffective if it is made more than three feet away from the mother—the infant must realise there is no hope of it being acted on.

Another possible answer is that the arms raise is actually a form of pointing or reaching. The baby looks up at the adult's face and lifts his arms in a grasping movement. Research has suggested that pointing itself starts life as a reach and grab action, in which an infant tries to hold or touch something out of range. In time, the baby learns that by making that particular movement it is very likely to be picked up and made a fuss of. The mystery is why parents should see the two arms raise as a request to be lifted and held in the first place. But they almost always do, thus making the message an extremely effective one for the child.

Thumb and Finger Sucking

As I explained in the last chapter, these gestures are body talk reflections of anxiety or conflict. They are identical in both cases, but made in different situations and sent out in a slightly different way. Anxiety signals, produced by an infant who does not know what is going *to happen* next, can be made either when standing still or moving slowly and cautiously about. Conflict signals, produced by a child who does not know what *to do* next, are almost always made while motionless. Often they are combined with an intense gaze in the mother's direction, and frequently mean that the toddler will return to her within a few seconds.

Although thumb and finger sucking are amongst the most commonly observed expressions of both fear and indecision, they are not the only ones. The uncertain child, like the fearful one, may rub his hands together, massage his face, stroke his hair, pull at an ear, chew at his lips, or pluck fretfully at a piece of clothing. Boys will feel for their genitals in both types of situation.

These comforting pieces of body language are not confined to the under-fives. As we saw in Chapter Six, adults in conflict carry out a great variety of behaviour which has its roots in childhood body talk.

Conflict gestures are produced whenever the child is confronted by a difficult choice, or is unable to decide what is expected of him. They also occur when something happens to prevent an infant from doing what he wants. Often these signals provide the only visible clue to the opposing desires in his mind. There are four main kinds of situation which can give rise to such a response.

Conflicts of Emotions

These arise when the child is subjected to equally strong but conflicting emotions, such as anxiety and pleasure, delight and fear, or happiness and misery. A child watching a cartoon film in which the hero mouse is being chased around the room by a frying pan wielding cat, often experiences equal amount of laughter and terror. A Punch and Judy show where the alligator is creeping up on an unsuspecting Mr. Punch also arouses deeply conflicting emotions, and leads to all sorts of self-manipulation by the watching children. Likewise, tensions arise when the child is confronted by alternative courses of action, both of which seem compelling. For example, three-year-old Tom is following his mother across the playground when his attention is caught by a game. He stops and joins in. His mother, not realising that Tom has been left behind, walks briskly on. When the boy glances up a few moments later, he sees her moving further and further away. The enjoyable activity and his vanishing mother present Tom with an agony of choice. He is caught up by two equally powerful emotions—pleasure at the game, and a fear that he will be left behind. He stands up and begins to suck his right thumb. His left hand goes down to the edge of his trousers and he tugs anxiously. For a moment nothing else happens. Then he makes up his mind, and either resumes the game or runs hastily after her.

Conflicts of Desire

The need to choose between equally desirable alternatives produces a similar conflict situation to the one described above. A two-year-old girl offered either an ice cream or a chocolate bar may agonise over her choice. As she glances first at the ice and then at the chocolate; she sucks her thumb, translating indecision into body language.

Conflicts of Command

If two people in a position of equal authority give you simultaneous but contradictory orders, you cannot hope to win. Obey one and you will inevitably disobey the other. These are known as double-bind situations, and they can produce considerable anxiety in children who like life to be clear-cut and consistent. Young children need a reliable framework on which to build. When this is denied them, they are uncertain about any correct course of action.

Double-binds often occur when the child becomes the victim of antagonism between the parents. For example, a mother tells her daughter that she can get down from the table once she has stopped eating. The father, attempting to exert authority over his wife via the child, says that she must remain seated until they have all finished. The mother immediately insists that the girl obey her. The father warns of the consequences if *he* is disobeyed, and it becomes impossible for the little girl to do right. Older children often become expert at exploiting this kind of conflict between their parents. "I want to go to Mary's party, but Mum says I can't," the manipulating teenager tells her father, knowing that he is likely to receive permission to do anything which his mother opposes. But the under-fives are usually unable to understand, let alone capitalise on, a bad relationship between their parents.

Adults placed in frequent double-bind situations over a long period of time, for example by working for an overcritical employer who manages to find fault in everything they do, may respond to the anxieties created in a number of ways—by becoming physically ill, excessively irritable, depressed or indifferent. The same kind of symptoms can be seen in small children who have been subjected to frequent double-bind commands. The incidents themselves may appear trivial to their parents— disputes over whether the child should be allowed to stay up late, watch a particular TV show, eat sweets between meals, and so on. But however minor the points at issue seem to the adults concerned, the conflicts arising from not knowing which course of action is the correct one can make the infant depressed and disturbed.

Conflicts of Frustration

Children who are unable to do what they want, often produce conflict signals. The frustration may be caused by an adult saying "no", or as a result of their own lack of alertness or skill. For example, a child who insists on trying to finish a painting when very tired, or an infant attempting to work a toy intended for the abilities of a much older child, may suck his thumb or fingers in the early stages of irritation with himself. As the frustration increases, beating gestures, crying, frowning, pouting, and an attempt to destroy the offending objects, can occur alongside the earlier conflict messages.

When a situation is proving too much for the child to cope with, an element of withdrawal may come into the body talk. A tired child, or an infant torn between equally important alternatives, may cradle his head in his hands, half-close his eyes and suck a thumb. If a cloth doll, handkerchief, blanket, or some other soft comforting object is to hand, the child will cling to it.

These signals provide a useful barometer of the child's responses, warning of forthcoming storms. But they should only be regarded as being of real significance when frequent or prolonged. If they do occur with this kind of intensity, try to discover exactly how and why the conflicts are arising. Then work to reduce the problem or help the infant make a choice. But always remember to look at the world through the child's eye. Because a

Rapid beating movements indicate frustration and conflict. Eighteen months-old Kiran wants to play with a toy train but the older boy takes it from him: (Picture One)

Kiran looks towards the train and then reaches to grasp his left hand in his right (Pictures Two and Three)

These drawings were made from still photographs taken from video-recordings.

He then raises both hands abruptly and turns away. As he does so his left hand goes behind his head in a clear conflict signal. His right hand clenches into a fist (Picture Four and Five)

He then waggles his hands vigorously copying the right hand raise left arm across the body by raising his left arm and bringing his right across the body. The whole sequence lasts less than three seconds and is typical of the very brief, abrupt movements made by small children in conflict situations. (Picture Six and Seven)

situation seems trivial to you, does not necessarily mean that a small boy or girl will see it in that way. Reflect back over recent events, and see if any of the four major areas of conflicts are present.

Gifts and Giving

Small children often pick things up and bring them to adults. But it is a mistake to regard such offerings as a form of communication, in the way that a gift between their elders says something special about their relationship. Sally was delighted when James picked up the discarded daffodil. She responded as if the little boy was bringing her a present. "Is that for me?" she enthused. When her son abruptly threw the flower away, Sally looked upset and disappointed. By regarding James' initial action as the proffering of a gift, she could only see his refusal to hand it to her as a personal rejection. This kind of response might be justified between grown-ups, but it is entirely the wrong way to look at the actions of an under-five.

I hope that I am not being guilty of the kind of adult elitism which I have already condemned, when I say that at sixteen months it is most unlikely James had any concept of beauty. To him, objects were simply interesting or dull, mysterious or unimportant. Everything had to be examined, investigated and filed away in his memory for future reference. The main question which needed to be answered about anything unusual or unexpected was—will it hurt me? To the little boy the flower was merely an unknown object. He picked it up for the same reason that he had earlier gathered stones and put them into his mouth. Carrying it towards his mother was just another way of finding out what the thing was. He wanted to test her reaction to it. Should he be wary of objects which looked, felt and smelled like that in the future? Would it cause him harm? Sally's encouraging smile and warm tone gave him the answers which he sought. Mum said it was OK. He made a mental note that things of that shape and colour might be picked up safely, and then discarded the flower. The idea of giving something to another person in order to make them happy or win their favour was outside James' range of social concepts. It is not until the age of two, or later, that most children discover how to use gifts as a way of gaining co-operation and appeasing aggression. Until then all offerings should be regarded as information-seeking tactics, rather than presents.

Picking things up, feeling, tasting and stroking them, trying to chew them or pull them apart, are all frequent activities amongst toddlers. In one series of observations, approximately 50 per cent of small children carried the object back towards their mother, but less than 20 per cent actually handed it to her for inspection. Most either dropped the thing when they were close to her, or carried it away again without attempting to hand it over. When they throw something away, toddlers usually do so casually, with an air of bored indifference, as if the object no longer held the slightest interest. Children over the age of two, however, tend to fling unwanted objects away from them with a vigour which suggests they are pleased to be rid of them.

There is a big difference between the child bringing something towards his mother, and the offering of a toy or game to the child by an adult. The first, as we have seen, stems from a need for information; the second from a desire to stimulate, amuse and give pleasure. Frequent gift-offerings and shared games have an important role in the development of the child. They can not only improve the rate of mental and physical growth, but also help them learn many of the important rules of communication.

Gaze and Glance

We look at other people and things in order to find out about them. The more interesting, unusual or unexpected facts there are to be discovered, the harder and the longer we are likely to look. At least part of the attraction, which draws crowds of curious onlookers to road and rail accidents, is that the scene offers a great deal of unusual information. Much of it may be unpleasant and disturbing, but our urge to find out about the world is often so powerful that it overcomes these considerations. However, the dramatic effect which a prolonged stare has on others shows that gaze is regarded as indicating more than mere curiosity. It is seen as a threat. So great a threat, in fact, that few people will tolerate being stared at for lengthy periods, unless they have had professional training as actors or public speakers.

The power of the intense stare to intimidate is universally recognised; which is why witch-doctors so often paint their faces to emphasise the eyes. Although the ability of the "evil eye" to produce terror and sickness is mainly confined to more primitive cultures, we are all to some extent vulnerable to the disturbing influence of an unblinking stare.

Strong gaze is such a powerful way of sending out a threat that it works even when combined with otherwise non-hostle body language. This was dramatically demonstrated during an experiment in which volunteers were asked to stare hard at motorists who had stopped at red traffic lights. As soon as the lights changed to green, drivers who had been subjected to intense stares roared away as though in mortal danger. Even when volunteers combined their stares with a warm smile, the drivers they gazed at still made better times away from the lights than other motorists!

Autistic children have such an aversion to gaze that it is one of the factors used to define this type of mental disturbance. Although they will sit on an adult's lap or play with grown-ups, they constantly avoid making eye-contact, either by looking away or by hiding behind their hands and peering out through gaps between their fingers. Clearly these children find the threatening nature of gaze far more intense and arousing than non-autistic children.

Gaze is regarded as threatening because it is one of the ritual aggression signals used as a prelude to any hostile encounter. Watch two contesting dogs or cats shaping up for a fight, and you will see that they fix one another with unblinking stares. The purpose of this gaze is mainly to gather every possible piece of information about an opponent's behaviour, and to spot at the earliest moment any dangerous manoeuvres. But, like many other pieces of ritual behaviour, this has become detached from its original function, although not from the response it generates.

Children are discouraged from staring as they grow older, because of this association in the adult mind with aggression. We may explain away our dislike of the stare by saying that it is "rude" or "impudent", but the underlying motive is the avoidance of a threat.

Yet while prolonged gaze is disliked, a complete avoidance of gaze is seen as equally disturbing. The amount of gaze we receive from another person plays an important part in the way we assess their personality. To test the influence of varying amounts of gaze, two researchers made a film of actors speaking. As the actors spoke, they stared out at the audience for different periods of time. Some gave direct eye-contact with the camera for 80 per cent of the time, others for as little as 15 per cent. A cross-section of the public then viewed the films, and described the impression which the actors had made on them. Those actors who gave minimal eye-contact were, without exception, judged to be cold, evasive and unattractive. They were described as "indifferent", "immature" and "pessimistic". Those who gave 80 per cent eye-contact were assessed as friendly, mature, sincere and self-confident. The influence of gaze is not as powerful as this in real life, but in general people who give a lot of eye-contact tend to be looked on as confident and dominant, while those who avoid eye-contact convey the impression of being unreliable and lacking in confidence. Most men enjoy longer periods of eye-contact with woman than with members of their own sex, a finding which will surprise no one. Rather more unexpected, perhaps, is the discovery that women prefer longer periods of eye-contact from both sexes, and find the absence of mutual gaze much more disturbing than men.

Very little experimental work has been carried out to explore the use of eye-contact in the under-fives. But it seems likely that the conclusions drawn from studies of adult gaze can be applied to children older than five years. Probably the greatest difference is that young children normally make far greater use of eye-contact than adults. They look directly at one another more frequently and for longer periods at a time. This probably stems from a need to obtain as much information as possible from the surroundings, combined with their uninhibited attitude towards all forms of contact. Not only do they look more intently at one another than adults, but they also touch, stroke, hold, feel, caress, kiss and embrace each other far more than the average adult member of Western cultures. Mutual gaze is, in addition, an important part of silent speech.

Gaze is a key part of many secret language messages, and close observation is essential if important visual clues are not to be missed.

Variations in the use of gaze provide an interesting clue to a young child's place in the pecking order. It also indicates how they achieved that position. *Dominant Leaders,* of both sexes, use equal amounts of gaze to establish their social status. But having achieved the rank of the leaders, they avoid using it, again to a more or less equal extent. This is because the leaders spend far more time appeasing and soliciting co-operation from others than threatening them. Non-hostile body language exchanges involve initial eye-contact, but no prolonged stares. *Dominant Aggressive* children use gaze during confrontations, but tend to avoid eye-contact at other times. *Dominated Frightened* and *Isolated* infants are usually fearful of prolonged eye-contact, however friendly the body language which accompanies it. When other children start to look intently at them, they often move to another part of the room.

Prolonged gaze may be used when the pecking order in a group of under-fives is being decided. Lengthy eye-contact need not be accompanied by any other kind of hostile body language in order to convey a threat. Children frequently indulge in trials of strength, trying to out-gaze each other so as to assert their dominance. Like contesting adult males locking their arms in an Indian wrestling match, the competing infants fix one another with intense stares to see who will give way first.

The loser is the one who breaks eye-contact. But the degree of submission varies according to the direction of the break. The clearest indication of surrender is a downward glance. This is the body language equivalent of the white flag, and gives victory entirely to the other child. The infant who regularly submits in this way drops quickly in the pecking order. Downcast eyes, a sign of deference in the adult world as well as the child's, always convey a humble or penitent attitude. In the sequence of pictures accompanying Chapter Six, where Robert and John clashed over the right to a seat at the table, John ended the exchange by hastily looking down. This was a rare confession of defeat by a normally dominant infant. It showed that he had been seriously alarmed by the determined stance of a boy armed with a dangerous looking weapon. On this occasion he preferred dishonour to a blow across the face with a wooden roller!

But one can break gaze equally effectively by flicking the eyes to either the left or right. This is an acceptance of temporary defeat, rather than an unequivocal surrender. The message is: "You win the battle—but not the war. I

will be back!" Because the signal is lacking in appeasement or submission, it may not be sufficient to bring an
angry confrontation to an end.

The decision to break eye-contact by glancing to the
right rather than the left, or vice versa, is one which is
made with remarkable consistency, although women are
less reliable in this respect than men. It is not certain at
what age the pattern is established, but there is some
evidence that our unconscious decision to be right-sided
or left-sided eye-contact breakers is reflection of our
personalities. Left-side breakers tend to be sociable,
thoughtful individuals, more interested in philosophical
speculation than practical activities. They are frequently
musical or artistic, and they are also easier to hypnotise
than right-side breakers. On the other hand, right-side
breakers are often very self-confident, capable people
with a greater interest in science and mathematics than
music and the arts. They are frequently very logical, and
have an objective, unemotional attitude towards life.

Such a link has not been proved; but if there is an
association between direction of eye-break and personality, it is probably due to one side of the brain being more
dominant than the other.

We all possess a "double-brain", two hemispheres of
identical appearance which fill the vault of the skull. They
are separated by a deep cleft at the top, but joined at the
base of this fissure by means of a thick band of nerve
fibres. As long ago as 1864, it was discovered that
language skills are located in the left hemisphere. But it
was not until the 1960's that the brain's division of mental
labour was analysed in detail. In brief, the left side of the
brain is concerned with analytical tasks, the right with
more creative and intuitive thinking. Those who have a
more dominant right hemisphere, usually possess a talent
for artistic subjects and a greater interest in painting,
music or creative writing. Because the optic nerves cross
over, the right hemisphere receives images from the left
eye. The left hemisphere, which is sent pictures from the
right eye, is concerned with mathematic and logical skills.
People with dominant left hemispheres are usually more

scientific and less emotional in their approach to life. It may be that we tend to break eye-contact in the direction of the most dominant eye—which really means the more dominant side of the brain. Practical, left hemisphere individuals look away to the right, because this is the eye associated with the left side of the brain. Imaginative, right hemisphere dominated people look away to the left—that is, in the direction of the eye linked to the right side of the brain.

So far as I am aware, no detailed investigations have been made into the consistency or otherwise with which small children break eye-contact. Nor has any research been carried out into possible connections between direction of break and personality in the very young. Anyone with patience, and an interest in making original and potentially valuable observations, might well start by gathering accurate data on this subject.

While prolonged gaze is seen as menacing, brief eye-contact is an essential element of silent speech. As James played happily at a distance from his mother, they occasionally exchanged short glances. These joined them for a second or so, creating an invisible thread which linked their otherwise unconnected activities.

Gesture and gaze are silent speech signals in their own right. Each can be used in the absence of the other. When they are combined, the effect is either to strengthen the force of the message or to change the meaning of the gesture. For example, pointing with gaze directed at the mother asks a question, and pointing with the eyes turned away usually indicates an intention. When watching gestures it is important to look carefully at the way the eyes are used. Notice the direction and length of gaze. Try to spot whether the break-off is made to left or right, or downwards.

Always remember that body language consists of a flow of signals, just as this line of print is made up of a stream of letters and words. You can only fully understand either by placing each separate element of the message in its correct relationship to the rest.

8   Your Part In The Secret Language

So far in this book, I have concentrated on the ways in which the under-fives use silent speech when talking amongst themselves, and describe how the solitary child communicates using gestures and gaze. This emphasis on the role of the child may have left an impression that adults have no active part to play in the secret language, implying that they are never more than spectators passively observing the wordless exchanges.

Nothing could be further from the truth. Whether they realise it or not, everybody concerned with looking after the under-fives is involved in the development of infant body language. By our own use of non-verbal communication, we provide young children with body language blue-prints from which they can construct many of their own silent speech signals. By encouraging the use of these signals, we can ensure that the child uses body talk regularly and fluently. Such an ability is fundamental to the growing infant's social success.

In Chapter Four, I noted that children who smile a lot have parents who also smile a lot. Those who remain fearful and uncommunicative for long periods after being introduced into a play group or nursery school, are usually those whose parents are tense, impassive or unresponsive to body language. Aggressive children are often found to have parents who produce a large number of abrupt, threatening or hostile signals.

The responsibility for helping young children to become non-verbally articulate is shared, to some extent, by relatives, close family friends, nursery school teachers and play group supervisors. But of course the main burden falls on the parents, and in most cases especially the mother. We have already looked briefly at the importance of mother and baby being able to form a close bond as soon after birth as possible. Delays in bringing the two into physical contact, however unavoidable, can prejudice their future relationship, and the infant's subsequent development. This is something I will be looking at in more detail later in this chapter. But one should never forget that however vital the first hours of life, the months and years that follow are no less important. The period from birth to the age of five has long been recognised as crucial to the child's social and mental growth. Some experts even believe that personality, temperament and intellectual ability are all irreversibly determined in this first-decade.

What does seem certain is that children who are fluent in the secret language have a head-start in life. They integrate more quickly into groups, and rapidly become *Dominant Leaders*. They are more confident, friendly, and better thought of—both by other children and adults. *Dominant Aggressives* frighten their companions and are regarded as bullies by grown-ups. *Dominant Aggressives* suffer the same fate, without gaining the extra degree of self-confidence which comes from remaining high in the group pecking order. As a result, they can become unpredictably aggressive, struggling to bolster up their lack of confidence by outbursts of rage. *Frightened* children find it harder to make friends because they have so little experience in attempting to do so. *Isolated* infants do not even try.

So *Dominant Leaders,* with their fluent body talk, are in a class of their own. The idea of appeasing others, and winning their co-operation to achieve a desired end, usually proves so successful in the nursery that the same softly, softly approach is followed throughout adolescence and adulthood. When combined with the kind of self-assurance which social success and popularity generate, it can be enormously effective.

The *Dominant Aggressive* child also scores many victories but through intimidation. This makes him think that threats and aggression are the best weapons in life. Every time another, more submissive, infant gives in to him, the idea gets a boost. So this form of behaviour is followed in primary and secondary school. It may well continue into adulthood, often with dire personal consequences.

For the aggressive child, as for the *Dominant Leader,* example is as important as practical experience. The infant does not learn merely by being placatory or threatening, but by watching others, especially adults, in action. A recent survey into school bullying carried out by Dr. L. F. Lowenstein, a British psychologist, showed that 75 per cent of the violent children came from homes where the parents had marital problems. Almost a third of them had been bullied by their parents, or strictly brought up.

There are of course a multitude of inter-relating factors which determine how each individual responds to others. But I am quite certain that a child, if he is deprived in early infancy of sufficient chance to learn enough good silent speech signals, will find it much harder to become personally and socially successful later in life.

The Face of Failure

A chilling, and hopefully apocryphal, story is told about a certain Prussian monarch who considered himself to have a scientific turn of mind. He was especially eager to discover which of all the world's languages was the "natural" tongue of mankind. Children only spoke as they did, he believed, because they were taught to do so. If the child was never spoken to, he would never become "contaminated" in this way. Then, if he began to talk

German, or Greek, or Latin, one would know for certain which was the most fundamental human language. To test this theory, he obtained a dozen babies and gave them into the charge of experienced nurses. These women were told to lavish every possible attention on the infants. They were to be well nourished and painstakingly cared for. But, on pain of death, no nurse was allowed to cuddle, caress or—above all—talk to any of the children. The experiment, it is said, was a failure. The king never discovered which language the babies might have spoken, because none of them survived for more than a few months. They perished, not through physical neglect but from social starvation.

From its first days of life, every child needs a close involvement with other humans. The baby arrives in this world biologically prepared for social communication, just as it is equipped with a digestive system capable of dealing with food and a breathing apparatus in tune with the atmosphere of the environment.

So far as you, personally, are concerned, I am confident that this will be a statement of the obvious. The fact that you feel sufficiently interested and involved to read this book, suggests that you are aware of the real needs of the developing infant.

But sadly, not all parents either realise or are prepared to recognise the full extent of their responsibilities. It is not a matter of education, wealth or social position. The kind of neglect I am concerned with here can be found just as easily in a palatial mansion as a decaying slum. In fact there is slightly more chance of it occurring amongst the affluent and professionally preoccupied, than in a less wealthy family.

Sarah is the only child of articulate and intelligent parents who both have successful careers. Her father is a sales director for a major drug house, and travels abroad frequently. Her mother works as a full-time colour consultant for an interior decorating firm. She too has to travel in her job, and spends many weekends away from home. As a baby, Sarah was looked after by a succession of nurses, au pairs and baby-sitters. By the age of two, she had grown into an attractive child, but she seldom smiled, and invariably hid from strangers. On the few occasions she got the chance to play with other children, Sarah stole away into a corner of the room and watched them fearfully. There was no question of any physical ill-treatment; but the paid caretakers were usually too busy, or insufficiently interested, to devote much time to the little girl.

When her mother looked after her, it was with an air of bored detachment. As a baby the girl had been bottle-fed, and held in such a way that there was the minimum possible body contact. As she grew up, Sarah's chief companions were the dolls and toys which her wealthy parents lavished on her. When a psychologist was called in to advise on the child's frequent temper tantrums, he suggested that she was isolated and desperately lonely. Whereupon the mother 'solved' the problem by having a colour television set installed in the four-year-old's bedroom.

"Now she can have hours of company every day," said the mother. And she was perfectly serious. It never even crossed her mind that a small child could need human companionship. "She'll have plenty of friends when she is old enough to go to schoool," the father said. "Toddlers don't make real friends anyhow."

This may seem like an extreme case. Unfortunately it is all too common. Doctors, psychologists and social workers are painfully familiar with that increasingly common phenomenon of the twentieth century, the infant who has everything money can buy. But almost nothing else.

More than twenty-five years agao, Dr. John Bowlby, a psychologist working in the Child Guidance Department at the Tavistock Clinic in London and a pioneer in the study of infant social needs, said bluntly: "When deprived of maternal care, the child's development is almost always retarded—physically, intellectually and socially . . ."

What concerned John Bowlby was not so much the

more obvious aspects of deprivation and cruelty, involving physical neglect or baby battering, but an indifference to the child's needs for love, attention and the sympathetic interest of a caring adult.

The effects on children whose mothers are emotionally incapable of adequate communication has been carefully documented by British child psychologist Joyce Robertson. With her husband, she runs the Robertson Centre in London, an internationally recognised educational trust which they set up to promote an understanding of the emotional needs of infants and young children. Two cases, drawn from her records, graphically illustrate the kind of psychological damage which can be done:

PETER

When first seen at a few weeks old, Peter was a picture-book baby, contented and round, delicately coloured and presenting no problems. His mother handled him competently, but appeared harassed and depressed. She was conscientious, devoted to her son, and pleased with his development. But she was an unhappy woman, seriously inhibited in her ability to express feeling or to witness it in others.

Peter first smiled at about six weeks, but did not progress to the free smiling which is typical of babies between two and three months . . . His mother did not try to elicit smiles from him, and she became uneasy when I tried to do so. When he wriggled in response to my talking to him, she said, "He is embarrassed," and thereby gave the first clue to her inhibition. We were to become very familiar with this inability to elicit, or to answer to, an emotional response.

She did not talk to her baby or play with him. By the time Peter was seven months old his lack of facial expression, lack of bodily movement, and lack of expression of feeling were conspicuous.

When he cried she would hold his shoulder as one might do a strange school child found crying in the street. Inadequate comforting led in his case to the gradual development of an exceptional ability to control his tears when in pain. He would tremble, flush, screw up his eyes, and swallow his tears. By the time he was a year old this meagre response had gone; even injections did not make him cry.

He was slow in attaining the usual developmental steps.

It became clear that subdued unresponsiveness was what his mother wanted. The attention and stimulation that came his way during illness, or on family holidays, brought about more demanding behaviour. This behaviour was more normal, but it invariably caused his mother to complain.

Peter always looked healthy, but there was no animation or pleasure in his body movements or in his facial expression. His watching sometimes had a self-protective quality, like that of a petrified animal—eyes staring, body tense and stiff—waiting and watching for danger.

At three years his nursery school teacher recorded:

"He takes little notice of the other children and his teachers. He makes no spontaneous move to amuse himself, but stands rather near his mother looking about in a dazed, inhibited way, not really watching anything, not looking for anything to play with. Peter makes a queer impression with his rapid alternations of joyous excitement and inhibition. He does not seem to know how to communicate with his mother, to express his wishes verbally, or to be aware of what to expect from her."

BEATRICE

Her mother was conscientious but lacking in intuition, warmth, and identification with her baby.

At three months, mother and baby made a curious impression of dullness. They would look at each other silently, with expressionless faces, and there was little evidence of contact between them. Beatrice had less bodily movement, less expression, and was less responsive than is normal for babies of her age.

At six months she was serious, and her gazes had a staring, intense, and apprehensive quality. She looked with interest at toys, and was aware of the person offering them, but she showed no pleasure and rarely any movement toward them. A glimmer of a smile appeared very occasionally. . . .

This mother did not fulfil the role of comforter. When her child cried, this brought no response. When Beatrice wanted attention—wanted to be lifted from the floor, for instance—the mother would look away to avoid responding. It was painful to witness a baby trying to get protection and response from a mother who defended herself by being blind to these demands.

The reason for this mother's looking away was not difficult to understand. Her own mother had for many years suffered from disseminated sclerosis, and Mrs. A. had been much affected by her erratic movements. She remembered as a school-child being ashamed and afraid that her mother would behave badly in front of her friends. So when years later she was faced with the jerky, uncoordinated movements characteristic of babies, all her old feelings were revived—hence, the need to look away.

But when toward the end of the first year the baby's movements became more coordinated, the mother was able to respond more adequately. Beatrice showed some improvement too, though she was still tense and lacking in animation. A tight-lipped little smile was the only sign of pleasure.

As a result of her wide experience of the emotional needs and social development of the infant, Joyce Robertson concludes: "A baby mothered in this way, without warmth or empathy, will develop broadly along the same lines as other babies. He will focus his eyes, smile, babble, find his limbs; but he will do it largely alone. There will be no fusion between the baby's achievements and the mother's pleasure and support; and for lack of mother as intermediary there will be less reaching out to the environment... As early as eight to ten weeks the consequences are low quality and quantity of body movement, slow responses, serious facial expression, with eyes incongruously alert and watchful. The mother will say, "But he is so contented," meaning that he is undemanding; or 'He is happiest when alone in his cot,' unaware that her baby may be withdrawing. With the passage of time these deficiencies become more gross. The uncomforted baby who swallows his tears at seven months may not cry at twelve months."

What makes some mothers so cold and unresponsive to the needs of their children? We still cannot give a complete answer to that crucial question. But there are some clear indications that the trouble often starts very early, perhaps within an hour or so of birth. A recent report, prepared for the British Department of Health, suggested that the warning signs of a bad relationship between mother and child might even be present immediately after delivery. Evidence gathered from midwives, nurses and doctors has shown that mothers who are unable to make eye-contact with their newborn babies, are more likely to treat them with indifference, neglect and even physical cruelty at a later stage. Amongst the factors seen as dissociating mothers from their children are early induction of labour and the excessive use of pain killers during delivery. There is also a risk in the enforced separation of mother and baby, because of illness or prematurity, immediately after birth. Statistics indicate that premature infants, who have to be kept in incubators for some days after delivery, make up a disproportionately high number of battered babies, and also account for a large proportion of those who fail to survive although there seems to be nothing physically wrong with them. There is some evidence to suggest that even the shorter period of separation which follows a caesarian birth makes it more likely that the child will be at risk.

But why should the period immediately after the child has been born have such a powerful and long-lasting effect on the mother's behaviour? Here again, it must be said that the complex biological and psychological mechanisms involved are far from understood. In a report on the effects of separation, Dr. John Kennell of the Department of Pediatrics at Case Western Reserve University in Cleveland, comments: "Maternal behaviour is determined by a multitude of factors, including the woman's past experience with her own mother, the patterns of her culture, whether or not the baby was planned, and the qualities of her relationship with the baby's father. In some cases, the intellectual abilities of a mother may enable her to bridge potential difficulties such as an early separation from her infant."

What can be said with certainty is that bonding between mother and child must take place as soon after birth as possible, if a good relationship is to be achieved. There is a period of some hours following delivery in which this bonding occurs most easily, strongly and surely. This has been termed the "sensitive period". It is, arguably, the most critical time of our lives.

The Vital Hours

Not long ago, an unfortunate mistake occurred in the busy maternity ward of an Israeli hospital. Due to a labelling error in the delivery room, a number of mothers were sent home with somebody else's baby. A fortnight later, when the mix-up was discovered, embarrassed hospital administrators began to sort out the confusion. At that point, what had been merely an unfortunate mistake took an unexpected turn. The officials found that most of the women were extremely reluctant to give up another mother's baby in exchange for their own. Rather than part with an infant they had looked after for only a couple of weeks, they were prepared to bring up a stranger's child as their own. The fathers, on the other hand, were only too eager for the situation to be rectified.

Those who have studied the ways in which mother-child bonds are formed will not find the reaction of those Israeli women particularly surprising. The attachment created during the sensitive period is so powerful that it can override all other considerations.

Zoologists have known for some years that if a female animal is deprived of its young immediately after birth, it may be unable to recognise the offspring as its own a few hours later. One of the shortest "sensitive periods" is found in the goat. Unless the nanny and her kid are kept together for the first five minutes after delivery, no maternal attachment is formed. Without this bonding, the goat will be very unlikely to care for the youngster, and may violently reject it. The anthropologist Konrad Lorenz, who made a special study of the effects of the sensitive period in different species, called the bond which is formed between the new-born and adult animals "imprinting". He found that some species could be "imprinted" on an astonishing variety of animals and objects, provided these were presented to them in place of their real mother during the sensitive period. An illustration of the powerful nature of imprinting, which proved especially popular with press photographers, was when Dr Lorenz convinced some ducklings that he was their real mother. They obediently followed him in single file, and even swam after him when he went for a dip. Such imprinting is a permanent process, but it can only be achieved within a specific amount of time after birth. In ducklings, the critical period seems to be about fifteen hours. Even animals like cats and dogs, domesticated for many thousands of years, still have to be imprinted on humans shortly after birth if they are to become tame and affectionate. Once the sensitive period has passed, it becomes much harder to domesticate them.

Three American doctors, John Kennell, Mary Anne Trause and Marshall Klaus, all of the Case Western Reserve University, made a special study of mothers and babies in the United States, with the intention of exploring the nature and extent of the sensitive period in the human animal. The twenty-eight women involved were divided into two groups. Half of them received the normal treatment provided for mothers in the maternity departments of North American hospitals. They were allowed a glimpse of the baby at birth, brief contact for the purposes of identification between six to eight hours after birth, and visits for feeding every four hours, each visit lasting between twenty and thirty minutes. The remaining mothers were allowed to hold and caress their nude babies for one hour in the first two hours after birth, and for an extra five hours each day during the following three days.

The behaviour of all the mothers towards the babies was then closely observed during routine visits to the hospital in the months that followed. From the first, clear differences could be seen in the responses of the two groups. Mothers who had been given sixteen hours extra contact with their babies tended to relate to them much more strongly. They stood closer to them, and gave more eye-contact. They stroked and massaged the baby more often. Clearly, touching and holding the child had become a natural and spontaneous reaction.

After twelve months the differences remained. Those who had been allowed extended contact during the first three days showed far greater empathy towards the infant. They held them more reassuringly, involved themselves actively with the medical examination, and were reluctant to leave their babies in the charge of others. The overwhelming impression was of women who were deeply responsive to the needs of their children. When the final observations were made, two years later, the close relationships persisted. These mothers used more words when talking to the toddlers, and gave them fewer commands. They also seemed to be extremely sensitive to the body language of their children. These findings have been supported by other long-term studies, some of which have strongly suggested a link between early contact and the subsequent intellectual abilities of the child.

In a study carried out at Guatemala's Roosevelt Hospital, nine mothers were given their naked infants immediately after leaving the delivery room. A second group of women was separated from their babies in accordance with normal hospital routine. After the short period of initial close-contact, all the babies were sent to the newborn nursery for twelve hours, before being returned to their mothers for the first breast-feeding. A doctor, who did not know which pairs of mothers and babies had spent additional time together in skin-to-skin contact, was asked to observe all the mothers and note such indications of close bonding as kissing, fondling, clasping, holding, massaging and intense gaze. The observer had no difficulty in identifying those mothers who had been given additional early contact with their babies, so significant was the increase in these responses.

So there does appear to be a crucial link between what happens immediately after birth, and the relationship which mother and child later enjoy. Experiments have proved that babies are extremely sensitive to their mother's body odour, and are able to distinguish it from the odours of other women, with considerable consistency. Research has also shown that the infant is able to distinguish the mother's voice from that of strangers. These highly selective preferences form part of the powerful bond which is, ideally, forged within moments of delivery. They are elements in the natural process of biological attachment. A process with which, in the view of some doctors, medicine had already interfered too extensively. In a discussion at a CIBA conference on parents and infants, Dr John Kennell told his colleagues he believed that such interventions were often excessive, and potentially harmful to successful attachment: "Drastic things are done to mothers and healthy babies in hospitals," he said. "We put solutions in the baby's eyes that blur his vision and cause swelling of the lids, which sometimes closes the eyes. We wash and wipe the baby's skin and the mother's nipples, which probably changes the odours. Our procedures interfere with many parts of the mother's specific behaviour with her baby at this particular time. These interferences as well as the separation may drastically disturb the attachment process... The mother is given drugs that dull her perceptions and cause amnesia during a period when heightened responsiveness may be needed for attachment to occur."

Such practices are gradually disappearing from many hospitals, as doctors come to accept that the less interference with natural childbirth the better it will be for both mother and baby. Women too are better informed and more vocal in demanding their right to remain in control of their bodies during delivery.

The work of Dr Lorenz has demonstrated the importance of the sensitive period and the value of a bond being formed during this brief time after birth. With some animals, as we have seen, there must be an attachment at this time if the mother is going to accept and rear her young. But while contact between an alert mother and her naked baby immediately after childbirth greatly assists in the formation of such a bond, the sensitive period is not the only consideration where human beings are concerned. Our ability to reason and control our emotional states means that even when the sensitive period is missed it will still be possible for successful attachment to occur. Mothers who have been separated from the babies for days or sometimes even weeks after birth, are subsequently found to have formed a deep and lasting attachment to them. Parents who adopt children are capable of loving them just as much as if they are their own babies. On the other hand, women who are given every chance to form a biological attachment with their baby immediately after birth may still reject and even hate their infants. In other words a mother's love is quite powerful enough to surmount a biological disadvantage, but a biological advantage is not usually sufficient to overcome a psychological refusal to accept the baby.

Research has indicated that rejection and hostility are more likely to occur if the baby was not planned, or born illegitimately. Money worries, an already large family, poor housing conditions, and a bad relationship between the parents, are problems which the baby's arrival can make worse. But it would be a mistake to regard rejection and social deprivation as being invariably linked. The case of poor-little-rich girl Sarah, described earlier, shows that parental indifference does not depend on class, education or income.

A more consistent relationship can be found in a mother's rejection of her baby and that woman's treatment at the hands of her own mother. In many families a dark thread of rejection, hostility and neglect runs from generation to generation. Women who have been emotionally starved as children possess a remarkable ability to seek out and attract men with a similarly unhappy background. With neither partner ever having learned how to respond to the psychological needs of others, the chances of their children developing into warm and responsive adults are greatly reduced. When they grow up and marry, it is very likely that those children will become equally unsuccessful parents.

There is a widely accepted view that the blood-tie is so important to the happiness and well-being of a child that it must override all other considerations. Time after time the courts and welfare services will return a fostered child to natural parents in the belief that they are best suited to bringing the child up. It is a notion which has caused much unhappiness amongst the foster parents, and sometimes led to tragedy for the children. But even where the child has not been obviously ill-treated by a mother who initially rejected him, there may be less visible damage. This is the conclusion to be drawn from a study carried out by Dr Barbara Tizard of the Thomas Coran Research Unit of London University. She examined 65 children who had been taken into the care of the authorities at about the age of two, and subsequently either adopted or returned to their natural parents. Dr Tizard found that those who had been sent home were *more* likely to experience psychological difficulties during adolescence than those who had been adopted.

Small Changes—Major Consequences

In the three case histories looked at so far, there was a major break-down in communication. Contact was negligible, warmth non-existent, and social starvation almost complete.

But a lack of responsiveness need not be as obvious and dramatic as this to influence the baby's development. Small changes on the part of the mother can bring about major consequences for the baby.

As the infant becomes more socially effective, the early biological attachment must mature into an intimate personal relationship. In this, both mother and child play an active role, sharing and co-operating in social exchanges of the kind described in Chapter Three. It is during these play dialogues and periods of cuddling and comforting that a woman's responsiveness to the needs of the baby is of paramount importance. Unless the two can maintain a precise and sympathetic synchrony, the baby may become distressed and uncertain. Even at a few weeks, the infant is keenly aware of even the smallest changes in expression, posture and voice tone. The tension in the muscles of an anxious woman is communicated to the baby as he is held. Disinterest or a withdrawal of attention from the baby's signals, during face-to-face exchanges, will be instantly recognised by the watchful and perceptive infant. Of course this is bound to happen at times in even the most relaxed and successful relationship. But if the negative responses are frequent, and persist over long periods, then the baby can suffer emotionally, although the symptons of distress may be far less obvious than in cases of major rejection.

To find out what happens when a mother fails to respond sensitively to her baby, researchers have deliberately distorted exchanges between them. Instead of the woman being allowed to react naturally and normally to the infant's body language, she is asked to switch off her own silent speech signals and to remain blank-faced and motionless. She can gaze steadily at the baby, but his gurgles, kicks, wriggles and smiles must be studiously ignored. When these instructions are followed, and most mothers find them extremely difficult to obey, the effects on the baby are traumatic.

In Chapter Three I described a vigorous, mutually satisfying exchange between nine-week-old Josey and her mother. On another occasion the woman was asked to turn herself into a statue, and not to react at all as the baby girl tried to start a play dialogue. This is what happened.

Josey glanced up delightedly as her mother came into the room and sat down so that they were brought face to face. After a moment Josey smiled, inviting a game. Normally her mother would have immediately replied with a smile of her own, and excited words. This time she simply stared silently back at the little girl, her face a mask. Josey looked quickly away, and remained motionless for a moment. Then she glanced back again, as if unable to believe the cold, impassive response. She smiled for a second time, and when her second request for a game was as brutally rejected as the first, she looked away for a longer period. The baby was puzzled and hurt that her affectionate greeting should have been so badly received. Looking back for the third time, she scanned her mother's emotionless features. There was no smile this time, only an alert watchfulness. She started to kick her legs rapidly. On previous occasions, these movements had been smooth and integrated with gestures and head shifts. Now they appeared abrupt and uncoordinated. She thrust a hand into her mouth, and looked away for a much longer period than before. She yawned and beat with her clenched fists. Her body was tense. When she again returned her gaze to her mother's face, Josey managed a small, almost beseeching smile. But once more her eyes met only blank indifference. Her fingers clutched jerkily at the woollen material of her jacket. She glanced away for the last time, and curled up in her chair looking utterly dejected. As her mother got up to leave, Josey cast a final, almost furtive, glance in her direction. There was no smile. Just a rapid, bewildered look which did not seem to expect any response.

Sometimes the mother cannot help responding with apparent indifference to her baby's signals. Dr Brazelton studied the effects on a baby girl whose mother had been blind from birth, and so never learned to use facial expressions. When the mother spoke to the infant, her features were often blank and mask-like.

"At four weeks of age the infant was visually very alert," says Dr Brazelton. "Yet she would glance only briefly at her mother's eyes, and then avert her eyes and face from the mother as the mother leaned over to talk to her."

The child's father was also blind. But he had lost his sight at the age of eight, by which time his mastery of body language was complete. When he talked to the baby, his facial expressions were identical to those of a sighted person. As a result, the baby's response was entirely different. "She watched her father's face and sightless eyes carefully for long periods as he talked to her," reports Dr Brazelton. "With us she greedily watched our eyes and faces and followed every move."

This was an especially tragic situation, because the baby's mother was a devoted and extremely sensitive woman. She was aware that the baby refused to look at her when she was talking but gazed at the father, and asked the researchers why this was. They explained, and then queried how she could possibly know which way the child was looking in either exchange. "I can tell from the direction of her breathing," said the mother.

John Tatam and Lynne Murray, researchers at the

University of Edinburgh, have shown that even very slight, subtle changes in the mother's response can cause babies as young as eight weeks to become confused and distressed.

In their experiments, they used special lighting techniques and an angled glass window to switch a mother's attention from her baby to another adult without altering her position. An exchange began with the mother looking at the infant and responding warmly to his movements. Then, by altering the direction of the lighting, the image of the second adult was reflected onto the window between mother and baby. Now, although the mother could still see her child, she could also see the face of the third person—and it was to this that she responded. Immediately, her body language altered to match the rhythm of the new exchange. It was then in tune with the adult dialogue, but completely out of synchronisation with the infant's silent speech signals. The baby continued to see his mother exactly as before. To him, the second adult was invisible, and the shift in response inexplicable. Nothing seemed to have changed, but suddenly his mother was no longer in sympathy with his movements. She did not merely ignore them, as in the other experiments, but responded to them in an entirely inappropriate way. To the baby, this was even more disturbing than a totally disinterested reaction. In a very short space of time, he became so dejected and bewildered that he withdrew from the exchange and refused even to attempt eye-contact with his mother.

This kind of laboratory-created situation may seem remote from what happens in everyday life. Yet, very often, a baby's attempts to communicate with his mother must be met with equally negative responses. Overwork and anxieties of all kinds can make it hard for a busy woman to devote sufficient time to what she may regard as unimportant games. So long as the child is well nourished and neatly dressed, the parents may feel that they have done everything necessary to ensure their child's happiness. However, research has clearly shown that frequent and mutually rewarding exchanges, between a baby and responsive adults, are not merely desirable but essential to his successful social development. An upbringing which satisfies all the infant's material needs, but is devoid of the special kind of stimulation provided by human contact, can retard, probably permanently, that child's psychological growth. There is also strong evidence to suggest that where the environment is more than usually rich in all kinds of stimulation, a baby's mental and physical development is more rapid. In recent years, child care specialists have been exploring the considerable benefits to be derived from a procedure known as "early learning."

Early Learning and Silent Speech

Masaru Ibuka, a leading Japanese industrialist and author, has made a special study of the needs and abilities of the very young. In his book *Kindergarten Is Too Late,* he argues that children should begin active learning about the world within a few weeks of birth. If the lessons only start around the age of three, when the youngsters go to nursery school, their mental and physical potentials may never be achieved.

The value of early learning has been demonstrated by Dr Jaroslav Koch, a clinical psychologist working at Prague's Institute for the Care of Mother and Child. During twenty-five years work with the very young, Dr Koch has developed a wide range of exercises for stimulating the infant's physical and psychological progress. The emphasis of such early learning is always on helping each youngster to achieve everything which he is capable of achieving, not to make him attain artificially forced skills and performances. Dr Koch's training programme starts with simple exercises in the early weeks of life, and continues throughout the first year. What all the suggested activities have in common is that they seek to stimulate and interest the infant, through movement and the use of exciting or attractive objects. In his book *Total Baby Development*, which lists 333 different exercises, Dr Koch reports that babies who have been subjected to this kind of early learning schedule gain a wide range of benefits: "The exercised children doubled their birth weight in the fifth month; the control group in the sixth—and the accelerated weight gain of the exercised group was in muscle, not fat." These children had a better appetite, slept more soundly, and cried far less than the control group of similar babies.

There was also an increase in the rate of intellectual development. "And why not?" asks Dr Koch. "The entire process of physical stimulation makes good anatomical sense: as he becomes motivated to move physically, the exercised infant's brain is supplied with more than the normal amount of blood; the increased blood supply, in turn, makes the child more receptive to stimulation."

By ensuring that your baby has plenty of warm human contact, and frequent games with a variety of interesting and stimulating toys, you will be providing valuable early learning which can only have a beneficial effect on his total development. As Joyce Robertson comments: "The baby whose responses are answered, who is helped from the very beginning to get pleasure from his early strivings and to master them, progresses smoothly from one achievement to the next. He is not content to babble to himself or to play for very long with his own fingers and feet. The baby who has been given attention, whose responses have been answered, continues to demand these responses. Not all mothers are able to have such an intimate life with their infants. Those who have done so produced babies who are alert, active, communicative, and expressive, on tip-toe for new experiences."

At this point, a word of warning may be advisable. The stimulation should not be overdone. The best advice to follow here, as in so many other areas of life, is the ancient Greek maxim: "Nothing in excess." Too much stimulation can actually retard a child's progress, as was demonstrated by an experiment carried out in the 'Sixties, by Burton White of Harvard and Richard Held of the Massachusetts Institute of Technology. They used three groups of infants in hospital wards. The first, which acted as a control, was given routine hospital care. This involved spending much of their time lying flat on their backs in cots. They had nothing to look at except plain walls and a white ceiling, nothing to play with except their hands. The second group was played with for twenty minutes a day, from the sixth to the thirty-sixth day of life. The third group was exposed to what the experimenters termed "massive sensory enrichment." They could look around the wards, their plain cot liners were changed for brightly coloured ones, and their cots were strung with beads, balls, mirrors and rattles.

The results were intriguing. As expected, the control group babies discovered their hands before any of the others, simply because they had nothing else to distract them. The second group found their hands about a week later than the controls, but they were far more visually alert. The least expected response came from the highly stimulated group of infants. Far from being made alert and interested in their surroundings, they became confused and miserable. They cried more than the other babies, and were less visually perceptive than even the control group. It was a case of sensory over-kill. When the investigators reduced the amount of stimulation, by replacing the colourful cot liners with plain ones and removing some of the dangling toys, there was a rapid increase in their mental and physical growth. The favoured babies were soon far more mature than any of the others. In mastering some important motor skills, for example, they had a sixty day lead over infants in the first two groups.

So the lesson would seem to be that on days when the baby is likely to be especially stimulated, by visits from relatives or friends, trips away from home or some other interesting activity, the early learning sessions can be reduced. Otherwise they should be as frequent and regular as possible. Six or seven periods of around ten minutes each day, seven days a week, are by no means excessive. During this time the baby should be talked to, held, caressed, played with, and allowed to explore as wide a range of toys, games and safe objects as possible. Preferably these should be brightly coloured, shiny, produce a pleasant noise, feel interesting, or have some other specific quality which makes the rewarding to handle and investigate. And these early learning sessions ought not to depend on the mother alone, the father's role is equally important. Close relatives should also be brought in to help whenever possible.

In this way the baby is able to learn, from the earliest possible moment, how to relate to a familiar group of adults, and so gain confidence and experience in a secure, caring and affectionate atmosphere. During these games, try to allow the child to take as active a part as possible. Respond *to* him, rather than expecting him to react all the time like a passive spectator. Let him accept challenges which are within his capabilities. Do not try to spoon-feed all the activities so that there is no challenge to his capabilities. For instance, toys should not always be pressed firmly into his hands. Put them within reach and let the baby find them for himself.

Dr Koch recommends that the infant be naked during these sessions whenver the room is warm enough to allow this to be done safely. A baby unhindered by clothes will be able to use his limbs far more easily and freely.

So far as mastering silent speech is concerned, one of the main advantages of early training is that you help to establish a sound foundation on which this, and any other skill demanding visual alertness, efficient co-ordination and precise muscular control, can be built. In this way the baby becomes used to using his limbs actively, which greatly improves the fluency and confident of later non-verbal communication. The consequent increase in intellectual abilities, reported by Dr Koch and other researchers, are of course equally helpful. No less important is the fact that the infants learn *how to learn*.

They develop a curiosity about life and an interest in the world around them which greatly assists in mastering all kinds of learned behaviour. Dr Koch reports, for example, that children who have been exercised according to his programme for twelve months are far superior in the verbal skills than unexercised children. After one year, his exercised group had learned twenty words and used them regularly, while the control group of infants knew only five. The gains in non-verbal skills are equally significant. Finally the infants enjoy the experience of frequent human contact from the earliest weeks of life. In this way they develop a psychological appetite which leads them to seek out social exchanges. This motivates them towards early interactions with other children, and so enables them to acquire a wide vocabulary of silent speech signals early on.

How Adults Misuse Silent Speech

Adults misuse the secret language when they use silent speech signals unintentionally or incorrectly. This can lead to confusion and concern amongst the very young. Most of the time we intend to send out the non-verbal messages directed at children. We smile to welcome or reassure, frown to convey annoyance, nod or shake our heads in agreement or refusal, and so on. All these are simple, everyday signals which are usually unambiguous and easily understood.

But difficulties can arise for one of three reasons:
1) Because the adult is incompetent in body language. Bad body talkers can be unsettling for adults and children alike, because they use inadequate or ineffective signals.
2) If an adult is trying to deceive a child, his body language may be out of tune with what is being said verbally. The conflict between words and actions, when this happens, is especially noticeable to young children.
3) An adult is unintentionally using body language which,

while it might seem unremarkable to other adults, has a disturbing effect on the young child for whom the signals can have a powerfully different meaning.

Bad Body Talkers

We have already looked at a case in which a baby was unable to respond to the ineffective body language of his blind mother. But you do not have to be visually handicapped to be incompetent at non-verbal communication. Sometimes people who can manage to use body language quite well when they are relaxed become so tense and anxious in certain situations that they are no longer able to respond physically. This often happens to the under-confident mother, who becomes so frightened when handling her new baby that she freezes up. I will discuss ways of overcoming these difficulties in Chapter Ten.

More often, however, bad body talkers got that way because they were inadequately trained as children. Perhaps they were brought up by stern parents who regarded expressions of emotion as a sign of weakness. Maybe their mothers and fathers never mastered successful body talk themselves, and so were unable to teach these essential social skills to their children. Whatever the reason, being in the company of an incompetent body talker can be an uncomfortable experience for other adults. Their range of facial expressions may be so limited that you never really know how they are responding to your attempts at communication. They may either avoid your gaze entirely, or fix you with an unblinking stare. As we have already seen, both these incorrect uses of eye-contact are unsettling. Also the movements of bad body talkers are frequently abrupt and unpredictable. They may use gestures which are out of context with the words they speak. Their grasp of proximity is poor so, that they either stand claustrophobically close, or too far away, for easy conversation.

The effect of such behaviour on young children is often more than merely unsettling. It can be traumatic, since the under-fives depend to a far greater extent than grown-ups on non-verbal clues and signals. Some people only have to walk into a room where a group of toddlers are playing, to produce an immediate atmosphere of tension. Children who had been happy and uninhibited only a few moments earlier, become suddenly alert and uncertain. Interestingly, I have noticed that adults who have an unsettling effect on children are often equally disturbing to domestic animals, especially horses and dogs. Like the children, these animals have to make important decisions about a human being's personality and intentions on the basis of silent speech signals.

Lying With Our Bodies

A few years ago, I had the distressing experience of driving a small boy to a residential home for disturbed children. In view of the child's unhappy background, it was hardly surprising that he was maladjusted. His father had been a drunken bully who beat his mother. In the end she had run away from home to a refuge for battered wives. As she was unable to cope with the boy, it was decided that he would be happiest living away from her for a short time.

When we arrived at the home, the boy was greeted by his house matron, a plump smiling woman, who hugged him affectionately and assured him she was very pleased to see him. Nobody could have made the little boy more welcome. But as I carried his case to the bedroom, he whispered miserably: "She's horrid. I hate her." At the time I felt that this reaction stemmed from a general hostility to his new surroundings, and to being separated from his mother. Perhaps that *did* play a part in the boy's response. But a few months later, the woman was abruptly dismissed from her job for cruelty to the children in her care. Beneath an outward show of gentleness and warmth, she had been chillingly sadistic. That little boy had seen right through the convincing veneer, and had made an accurate assessment of her real personality.

Because young children are so familiar with silent speech signals, they can often pick up clues about an adult's real attitudes and feelings which another grown-up might never notice. We are so concerned with assessing the truth of the spoken word, that we often fail to spot the give-away signals of silent speech. However soothing the tone and friendly the words, a small child almost always detects insincerity or deceit, anger or indifference, because the body language is all wrong. The adult is too tense or too relaxed. The facial expression is too fixed. The look in the eyes fails to match the movement of the lips and limbs: "I am so pleased to see you," is the verbal statement. But the body is telling a completely different story. Parents who fight with one another but "never in front of the children", sometimes express astonishment when told that their constant rows are making their offspring tense and unhappy. "But we are always so nice to one another when the kids are about," they protest. Probably they do say polite, even pleasant, things to each other when the children are in earshot. But they cannot hide the signals of hostility sent out by their bodies.

When We Use The Wrong Signals

Sometimes the silent speech signals an adult sends out frighten children without them ever realising the fact. When trying to offer reassurance and love, adults may combine soft words with threatening body language. Since the adults are completely unaware of what they are doing the child's frightened response seems unreasonable and inexplicable.

After sessions of filming children at different nurseries

and playgroups on video-tape, I would always try to make a recording of the greeting behaviour of their mothers when the time came to go home. A study of their welcome by the adults revealed a good deal about relationships within the family, and also provided clues as to why a child behaved as he did within the group.

Let us look at one recording to see how different methods of greeting can effect the overall behaviour of the child.

Allison, the twenty-seven-year-old mother of Lucy, greets her daughter with joy and affection. As the dark haired three-year-old runs eagerly forward, her mother kneels down and holds out her arms. She spends a few moments cuddling the child, smiling and giving her eye-contact. As she does this, their faces are very close. After the greeting Alison stands up slowly, takes the child's hand, and they walk side-by-side towards the cloakroom to collect the girl's coat. They both look animated and happy. Lucy is a *Dominant Leader*.

Alex, aged four, is a *Dominant Aggressive*. His twenty-three-year-old mother, Brenda, greets him in a completely different way. As the boy runs towards her, Brenda places her hands on her hips and leans forward at the waist. She smiles briefly, then straightens up and turns to talk to another woman. She reaches out absently and takes Alex's hand in a casual way. Without another glance in his direction, she turns abruptly and leads him towards the cloakroom.

Lucy's welcome was warm, animated and unhurried. For the few moments of their meeting, Alison devoted all her attention to her little girl. They both smiled and looked at one another a great deal. As Lucy ran up, Alison knelt down so as to bring their faces level. This is the only way of ensuring a relaxed and mutually rewarding exchange. If an adult remains standing, towering over the infant, the posture conveys an air of superiority, if not of downright threat, no matter how friendly the smile. If we had to communicate with people who were so tall that we could only either look at their waist or stare up into their nostrils, we too would get a feeling of being overwhelmed!

Brenda not only sent out a rather intimidating signal by remaing standing, but as Alex hurried towards her she made the situation worse by unintentionally using an infant aggression posture. As we saw in Chapter Six, the act of bending forward at the waist is one of the components of a threat message. Alex probably realised that his mother was friendly, but even so the unfortunate use of aggressive body language must have robbed her greeting of any warmth. The boy then received only a cursory glance, before his mother's attention turned elsewhere. Her physical contact with him was equally minimal. She led him quickly into the cloakroom and hastily tugged on his coat.

During any kind of exchange with a small child, we must remember that body language which is intended to be friendly, and would probably be seen that way by another grown-up, can disturb and intimidate an infant.

Movements should be made smoothly rather than abruptly, especially when greeting a child for the first time. The adult should kneel or sit, to bring their faces level. Above all, avoid the leaning forward posture. Smiling, eye-contact and an animated face are equally important. Do not be afraid to show your feelings. Touching, holding, stroking and cuddling convey more to the child about your love than words can ever do.

If you intend to send out playfully aggressive signals, by making a mock-threatening face or a loud sound, then make certain that you precede it with a great many friendship signals, so that the infant is absolutely certain you are doing it as part of a game. Some adults, especially males who are unused to small children, tend to be excessively boisterous. What may seem like no more than good-natured fun to them, can be extremely alarming to a small child. Remember that all adult behaviour is magnified by our greater height and strength.

Minimal body contact gestures, such as light touches, holding the child's fingers instead of his hand, briefly patting his head and so on, say nothing to the infant about your liking them. They are, at best, neutral messages. If sent by an adult from whom the child expects comfort and reassurance, they can be distressing. Patting a child's head, for example, is sometimes regarded by adults as an effective way of expressing affection, but children will seldom see it like that. Mothers instinctively realise this, and research has shown that they very seldom use the gesture. Fathers and close relatives pat the child's head rather more frequently, but it is mainly used by distant relatives and casual family friends.

To be psychologically close to a child, you must at times get physically close. If a child wants to demonstrate fondness or friendship for another, he or she will move beside them and hold them. To make a child feel comforted, reassured and loved, the same kind of intense physical contact is needed. "I often tell her I love her," the young mother of a three-year-old reassured me. "Isn't that enough!" The answer is simply—no, it is not!

Getting It Right From The Start

As we have seen from this chapter, the secret language of infancy is not just about children. Anybody involved in the care and upbringing of the young has an important role to play in helping the child to develop, use and respond to silent speech.

The consequence of neglect in this area of the infant's life are certainly less immediately obvious than equally severe cases of physical deprivation. But while the scars may be invisible, the damage is likely to be deeper, longer lasting and far harder to rectify.

I have already described some of the uses to which responsive adults can put their knowledge of the secret language. In Chapter Ten I will be looking at other ways in which such an understanding is invaluable.

The first step is always to analyse the current situation,

through an accurate interpretation of body language, in order to pin-point and correctly assess any difficulties the child may be encountering. The only effective way of doing this is by direct observation. Use the procedures already detailed to help you carry out the observations and make the analysis. But in addition to actually watching the child, there is a useful indirect method which can sometimes be used to provide helpful additional information. Its value lies in the fact that you gain a better perspective on current family interactions, through an examination of what has happened in the past. To carry out this kind of analysis we don't go into the playground or nursery school, but to the living room sideboard or attic chest, in search of those fascinating storehouses of family memories, the snapshot albums. How old photographs can be turned into a source of information and insight will be explained in the next chapter.

9 Hidden Truths In Family Snaps

You can use a knowledge of the secret language to discover hidden truths in family snapshots. These very personal photographs are always more than straightforward records of happy events and special occasions. Snaps are mirrors with memories. They are time capsules in which fragments of silent speech have been permanently frozen. By carefully studying the body language of those portrayed, one can gain important insights into the personalities of individuals and the dynamics of families. This type of analysis is especially valuable where young children are concerned. A series of pictures, taken over a period of years, can provide as much information about the present as about the past. The snap album can become, to the perceptive observer, what a rich archaeological site is to the historian. By painstakingly digging back through the years, we can plot the evolution of current attitudes and relationships, the development of personalities and the growth of antagonisms. By enabling us to make a realistic appreciation of the way things were then, these permanent records of times past can help us to a better understanding of the way things are now. Let me give you a couple of examples of what I mean.

Not long ago I was approached by a young mother who was desperate to get her six-year-old daughter into show business. She had convinced herself that the little girl had all it took to become a child star—looks, personality,

charm and talent. For nearly a year she had trailed the girl
from agent to agent and audition to audition, spending a
small fortune on professional photography, drama
coaching, elocution lessons, deportment classes and
travelling expenses. The results were utterly depressing. A
few auditions but no offers of work. The only time the
child had appeared in front of the cameras was when her
mother had paid the photographers. Now she wanted my
advice about what was going wrong.

The mother saw her child as an outstandingly pretty
girl, with a lively and vivacious personality. In reality the
child was attractive, but not especially photogenic, with a
quiet, rather introverted manner. Being famous was her
mother's idea, and the child had done her best to please.
Failure after failure had made them both miserable. "She
looks so beautiful in her photographs", sighed the
woman, and handed me a collection of carefully posed,
professionally lit prints. They did look good. But I was
more interested in any spontaneous unposed snaps which
might have been taken of the girl with her family. A few
days later, the mother returned with a large album. It
contained scores of pictures of the girl and her brothers,
the last one having been taken some twelve months
earlier. This was at about the time her mother decided to
embark her daughter on a showbusiness career. It was
easy to see why the mother had turned to professional
cameramen for help. They could disguise the facts, and
convert reality into a fantasy which matched her dreams.
The casually taken snaps told the real story. On page after
page were the home truths which the mother had rejected
in favour of soft focus lenses and flattering lighting. We
spent about twenty minutes looking through the pictures
in silence. Then she said suddenly: "No. She hasn't got
what it takes". She made the admission with something
close to relief. The dream was finished, but so was the
constant need to blind herself to the reality of the
situation.

Photographs can be as brutally frank about relationships. After a lecture, I was approached by a man in his

mid-thirties whose life was being made wretched by
feelings of guilt about his relationship with his step-
mother. He explained that his real mother had died when
he was three years old, and twelve months after her death
his father had married again. "She treated me just like her
own children. I could not have wanted a kinder or more
loving mother," he said. "But I have never been able to
return that love. The truth is I dislike her . . . hate her even.
But why? I sometimes think I must be a terrible person to
have these kinds of feelings about such a good woman."

As we talked, it became clear that he and his
step-mother had actually seen very little of one another.
His parents had sent him to boarding schools, and many
holidays had been spent with an uncle who ran a farm.
"But that was only because I was weak as a child and the
country air was good for me," he explained. From what
he said, it seemed unlikely that his relationship with his
step-mother had ever been close. To test this theory, I
asked if he had any snapshots of them together. At a later
meeting, he showed me more than thirty photos—which
confirmed my initial feelings. He had lied to himself for
more than fifteen years. Those snapshots demolished the
fantasy in less than fifteen minutes.

There were eighteen photographs of his step-mother
with her own children, twins who were born a year after
the marriage. There were eight shots of himself with his
father, and just four pictures taken with his step-mother.
In none of these was there a shred of evidence for the
warm and loving attitude which he claimed to recall so
vividly. In fact, the snaps told a completely different
story. The tall, rather severe looking woman was literally
keeping the boy at arms' length. There was only a
minimum of body contact, and she was not looking at him
in any of them. Even in two candid shots, one taken at a
picnic and another on the beach, the woman remained
tense and stern. The snaps of her with the twins were
exactly the opposite. She held them tightly and protectively, while looking relaxed and happy.

The black and white images destroyed the colourful

dream of a loving and caring woman. In four fading snaps one could read the true story of his isolated and unhappy childhood. It was a reality which the boy had denied. He had refused to accept that his step-mother was indifferent to him and only loved her own children.

The fantasy mother he had created had probably helped him to endure the loneliness of boarding school and holidays with an uncle. But as an adult it made him guilt-ridden. He was quite unable to reconcile his hatred for the woman with the warm and loving figure of his dreams. As a result he felt anxious and at fault. He was convinced that he had failed her, when on the contrary she had failed him.

In America, some psychoanalysts are starting to examine snapshots in order to help them dig back into their patients' family histories, using the lens of the camera as a reliable window onto an imperfectly remembered past.

Looking at snaps need not be such a serious business. Nor will it necessarily produce the kind of dramatic revelations described above. But one does usually turn up at least one or two previously unseen messages. These have remained hidden for the same reason that silent speech stayed a secret for so long—because we do not normally look at either photos or infants in the right way. As I explained in Chapter One, once you know that the secret language exists you begin to see it in action, and infant exchanges take on new meanings. It is the same with family snaps.

What is your usual response to other people's photographs? Probably an inward groan of boredom as soon as the family album is taken out, or the slide projector plugged in! You glance through the snaps as quickly as possible, commenting politely on how attractive the subjects look, or the pleasant colour of the print. Even when those involved are members of the family and your interest is genuine, your attention is most likely to be focused on superficial details. "Hasn't Peter grown quickly...doesn't Jane look like her mother

...did it rain all the time?" In other words you concentrate on the more obvious points, and fail to see the rest of the image.

To analyse a photograph takes time and patience. You have to study the images with the same careful attention to detail that you need when watching infant silent speech.

Snapshots Hot and Cold

No matter how quickly and casually they were taken, snapshots say more than is usually realised about their subjects. In fact, a hastily posed group can be much more revealing than a picture where the photographer has carefully directed everybody into an "artistic" pose.

Photographs tell us quite a lot about the people who took them, as well as those involved. Family snaps are usually taken by the husband, who becomes a frequent absentee from the pictures. Sometimes a self-timer is used, which enables the camera operator to press the shutter release and then hurry over to join the others. After ten or fifteen seconds, a clockwork mechanism fires the shutter automatically. When this has happened, there is often a certain amount of hilarity in the group as the photographer squeezes in at the very last moment.

If the photo was taken by a husband or wife, their relationship and attitude towards those in the group can often be discovered by examining expressions and postures. Do they look relaxed and happy, or tense and uncertain? Is the group posed with military precision, everybody being told where to stand, when to smile and how to look? Is the pose haphazard but spontaneous? Are the smiles genuine, or the frozen cheese grins which I described in Chapter Four? Remember to look out for the give away wrinkles beneath the eyes. Do the children look bored, watchful or indifferent? Their attitude provides a clue as to what went on before the picture was taken—whether it was quickly posed and snapped, or fussily and tediously organised.

Start by gaining an overall impression of the photo. First feelings are usually an accurate indication of what I call the image's psychological temperature. Some snaps come over instantly as hot, others are just as obviously cold. Many more seem tepid. What evokes this response?

It is seldom any one thing in particular. Usually the psychological temperature is made up of a whole range of silent speech signals, some obvious, others much harder to pin down. It is composed of expressions, postures and the relationship between members of the group. Background and foreground details also have a part to play. Sometimes these evoke such a powerful response that it drowns out every other message. During a lecture in New York, I showed some slides of children playing in the slums of Lisbon. Their faces were dirty and their clothes ragged. In the foreground was rubbish and in the background a decaying slum tenement. The immediate response was: "Oh God! Look at those wretched, miserable kids." It was an understandable reaction, but the photographs did not justify that conclusion. Far from looking unhappy, the children were obviously enjoying themselves enormously. They were smiling with delight as they played with a wrecked car.

I am not saying their conditions were desirable, only that the pictures did not support the comment that they looked miserable. By projecting our own attitudes and prejudices onto a photograph, we may become blind to the truth of picture. Pay attention to the surroundings. Let them give you clues which will help analyse the snap. But do not allow yourself to be overwhelmed.

The illustrations on pages 233 and 235 provide examples of *hot* and *cold* photographs. The first was taken by a Victorian studio photographer, the second I took myself a few years ago. The psychological temperature of the nineteenth-century group strikes most people who view it as close to zero, while the modern family is seen as radiating warmth.

Victorian family group. A stern faced mother and serious children produces a cold picture.

It is very likely you share this view—but what is it about the photographs which produces such a response? The most ovious difference between the two pictures lies in the expressions. The Victorian mother and her children look grim and unfriendly. The modern mother and her family are relaxed and smiling. They send out a welcome. We feel instinctively that it would be an enjoyable experience to meet them, while an encounter with the nineteenth-century family was probably stiff and formal. Whether or not we can relate to the subjects of a photograph, plays a big part in our assessment of the psychological temperature.

Now let us consider the direction of gaze. In the nineteenth-century photograph the two children are looking straight into the camera, and so meeting our eyes. But the mother avoids the lens. Something to the left of the photographer appears to have caught her stern attention. As we have seen, eye-contact is a vital component of body language. Those who continually refuse to meet our gaze appear cold, evasive and unfriendly. Jill, pictured with her four children, looks directly towards the camera, and so her gaze meets ours. It is probably the first thing you saw when looking at the photograph. Only after the details of her expression had been absorbed, did your eyes move to the children's faces.

Even when the grouping is haphazard and the snap spontaneous, a certain amount of posing may occur as the photographer tries to include everybody in the view-finder. This distorts natural proximities. We all tend to stand much closer to others when having our photographs taken, than we would do normally. But the posture and distance can still provide a certain amount of reliable information about the relationships within the group.

Before the frock-coated Victorian photographer exposed his plate, he probably told the children to: "Get in close," to make certain the group would fit into his oblong picture area. I asked Jill's children to do the same before taking my picture. But so long as they were all included in

A happy mother with her children, Jill defied the doctors to have her babies. Their obvious affection for one another makes this a hot picture.

the shot, neither I nor the nineteenth-century camera
operator cared how this was achieved. This is what often
happens when a family snap is taken. The grouping may
be partly dictated by the photographer's need to see
everybody in the viewfinder. But within these outer limits
the subjects have complete freedom to pose where and
how they like. They can choose who they want to stand
beside, and decide whether to fold their arms defensively
across their chest, tuck them neatly behind their back, or
rest a companionable arm on the person next to them.
They can lean in for greater physical contact, or outwards
to reduce contact to the minimum. Because of this
element of individual choice, even posed groups can tell
us a great deal about the personalities and relationships
involved.

In the Victorian photograph, the children are leaning
in towards their mother. When this is a spontaneous
gesture it implies warmth and affection. But here the pose
looks stiff and artificial. The brother and sister lean
uncomfortably against their mother, as if she was a post
or wall. The boy on the right rests his arm across his
mother's dress. But his fingers are clenched. He is simply
posing, not trying to make any kind of intimate or loving
contact with her. Even so, his relationship seems to have
been closer than the girl on the left. The boy is actually
resting his weight against his mother. The girl only
appears to be leaning against her. Her balance remains
firmly on her two feet. The woman is not attempting to
associate with the children in any way. It is almost as if she
remains unaware of their existence. Her hands are tightly
folded, and rest across her waist in a defensive posture.
The children are dressed alike and are sexually ambiva-
lent. Unless one knows, it is hard to tell whether they are
boys or girls. While it is not unusual to find small children
similarly dressed in nineteenth-century photographs, the
lack of any individuality here is striking. It is as if their
personalities were being firmly suppressed.

Jill's children are grouped closely around her. Their
arms reach out for one another so that they are joined in a

chain of mutual affection. Linda and Sean have their hands touching and resting on Jill's shoulder. The boy puts a protective left hand on his sister Vanessa's shoulder, while the little girl reaches out to hold the baby. The impression one gets is of a happy and united family.

What are the stories behind these pictures, and how do the facts compare with the deductions one can make from analysing the images?

The Victorian photograph was taken in the 1890's. It was given to me by the man who was the small boy in the picture. Now in his eighties, he recalled his childhood as bleak and lacking in affection. His mother was an intensely private woman, who seldom showed her emotions. His father, a modestly successful businessman, was a strict disciplinarian. Both he and his sister were frequently thrashed for the most minor misdemeanours. His mother was rather closer to him than to his twin sister, but he does not remember her with any great affection. The girl grew up very much like her mother: withdrawn, shy, and undemonstrative.

Jill's story is a long battle with pain, rejection and physical disability. It is a triumph of one woman's determination to live a normal life against almost hopeless odds—and to have the family which medical opinion considered impossible. At the age of five she caught polio, and became paralysed from the waist down. Doctors warned her that she could never have children, and as a teenager she tried to put all ideas of marriage from her thoughts. But eventually she did get married, and confounded the doctors by becoming the mother of four healthy active children. Her experiences might have left her feeling bitter, instead they gave her strength. These two photographs show how similarly posed groups can send out entirely different messages.

Now let us look at two pictures which have quite a lot in common, even though they were taken more than sixty years apart.

The adults are smiling and looking directly at the camera in both photographs. Because of this, the pictures radiate a certain amount of warmth. Yet there is little of the spontaneous feeling of welcome that one finds in the photo of Jill and her family. A careful analysis of each snapshot reveals that this difference is due to small but crucial variations in smile and gaze.

The Edwardian lady named Mary was photographed around 1910. She is giving us an upper smile and direct gaze. This combination of body signals should produce a happy expression. Yet although she comes over as a friendly woman, one also gets the feeling that she was slightly tense and uneasy when posing for her picture. The upper lip is horizontal and there is very little upturn to the corners of the mouth, which reduced the intensity of the smile. But there is something else as well. A careful examination reveals that her upper teeth are lightly resting on the lower lip, at the right side of her mouth. As I explained in Chapter Four, this is a silent speech signal conveying doubt and uncertainty. I would hazard a guess that it was the fact of being photographed at all which made her uneasy. Perhaps she was reluctant to have her picture taken and had to be coaxed into posing with her children.

Joanna, the young woman in the modern snap, narrows her gaze to shade her eyes from direct sunlight. This has diminished the intensity of her simple smile, which appears very diffident. One senses that she is holding herself back, and like Mary does not feel entirely at ease before the camera.

Mary, despite her slight uncertainty, looks out boldly from the photograph. She appears to be a strong and dominant personality, who would make a loyal wife and a capable affectionate mother. Joanna seems kind and sociable, but much more restrained. The snap shot says that here is an easy-going young woman who would not push herself forward.

Now let us examine the relationship between the children and the grown-ups in each picture. Mary is holding her new baby firmly, but there is no sign that the little girl, Loraine, has been thrust into the cold by his

This Edwardian lady with her two children looks slightly anxious. What gives us this impression and what else does the snap say about her?

arrival. Mary leans towards her daughter, and draws the stiff and rather tense infant into the group. Loraine is sitting very still and looks quite serious. But her legs hang down in a way that suggests she is only waiting for the picture to be taken in order to jump off the bench and start playing. Her hands come together in a rather defensive position across her body. The fingers are not clutching at one another, but nervously tweeking at the dress. Perhaps this anxiety signal was produced by uncertainty over having her picture taken. The baby is sitting up and looking intently at the camera. Mary has taken hold of his arms and is grasping them firmly. This is probably to prevent him from moving during the exposure and so coming out blurred on the print.

The fact that Mary had to hold his arms so tightly suggests that he was a vigorous baby who disliked having to sit still for long.

Lee, the three-year-old boy pictured with Joanna, looks questioningly up at his mother. She holds him gently and protectively, inclining her head towards in his direction. The girl, six-year-old Kim, stares into the camera and keeps her arms behind her back. Because there seems to be less contact between Joanna and Kim, somebody unfamiliar with the family might assume that mother and daughter were on less affectionate terms than mother and son. Such a conclusion pin-points one of the dangers of trying to analyse snapshots in isolation. In fact, the girl is Joanna's niece, not her daughter. Although they are close, they obviously do not have the same kind of intimate relationship as a mother and her only son.

When studying other people's snapshots, make sure you have all the relationships sorted out before you proffer any opinion about what the body language is saying. If you fail to take this precaution, an embarrassingly inaccurate analysis can result.

Loraine, who gave me the photograph, thinks she was about five when the picture was taken. She remembers her mother as a strong capable woman, who ran her house expertly and was devoted to her husband. Her little

Joanna, snapped in a back garden. What does the different attitude of the two children suggest?

brother turned out to be as active and independent as his first picture suggests. She told me that her mother hated having her photograph taken, and only agreed because of the new baby. Her father was a competent and enthusiastic amateur photographer, but it always took all of his charm to coax Mary in front of the camera.

Joanna is described by her mother as a serious and rather shy young woman, who prefers to keep herself rather in the background. She is very close to Lee, her only child, and has a good relationship with her cousin Kim, a direct and dominant little girl who knows what she wants from life and intends to get it.

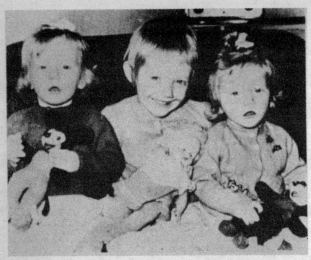

Carol, aged three sits between her eighteen-month-old twin sisters Jacqueline and Lisa. She radiates warmth and attachment to her sisters.

Time Travel

While an analysis of the silent speech signals captured on a single snapshot will tell us quite a lot, a comparison between photographs of the same children taken over a period of years can be even more revealing.

By travelling through time in this way we can watch changing personalites and relationships within the family.

The pictures on pages 242–244 are all taken from the same album, and show three little girls over a time span of eight years. In the first, Carol, in the centre, is aged three; and her twin sisters, Jacqueline and Lisa, are eighteen-months-old. The older girl's warm and affectionate nature shines from the snapshot. She gazes directly at the camera and gives a joyful upper smile. Her arms reach

Three years later Carol still stands protectively between the twins. Notice the different way she holds them and their expressions. These small points tell us a great deal about family dynamics and personalities.

protectively around her sisters, who unknowingly mimic one another's expressions.

The second picture was taken on a family outing three years later. The pose is similar. Once again Carol stands in the centre of the group and holds her twin sisters affectionately. She draws them to her, and dominates the picture by direct gaze. She is giving a warm upper smile, and the folds of skin under each eye confirm that there is nothing artifical about the grin. Jacqueline, on the left of the picture, is also smiling; but hers is a slightly mischievous expression, and she gazes out to the right as though there is something very interesting just beyond camera range. Lisa is looking towards the camera, but her expression is serious.

Notice the small but significant differences in the way

Five years after the last picture the family pose for a group snap. Carol still stands between the twins. But her personality has changed and so has that of the twins. This snap also says a lot about the other members of the family.

Carol is holding her sisters. Her right hand, the fingers outstretched, clasps Jacqueline's right shoulder. The grasp is quite firm, almost as if she was physically restraining the little girl from running away. This feeling is strengthened by Jacqueline's posture. Her left foot is raised from the ground, her right hand clenched into a fist. One can imagine that, as soon as the snap was taken, she dashed excitedly off towards whatever has attracted her attention. Carol's left hand rests on Lisa's shoulder. But here her fingers are folded into a fist which presses hard against the girl's cheek. She is not restraining Lisa, but very firmly drawing her into the group.

Five years after that photograph, a family group picture was taken. It tells us a great deal about the personalities of the whole family, and I want to examine it in some detail. But first let us look at Carol and the twins, who are standing behind the sofa. By the age of eleven the openly friendly child who dominated both the earlier snaps has become much more reticent. She stands right at the back of the family group, still close to her twin sisters but no longer touching them. She seems to have withdrawn into herself since the previous photograph was taken. Her gaze is still direct and friendly, her upper smile is warm and genuine. But there is none of the spontaneous eagerness and delight, which was so apparent in the other photos. Jacqueline, on her right, also seems to have drawn in on herself. Her arms are folded defensively across the back of the sofa.

From these three snaps, spanning eight years of the children's lives, we can discover quite a lot about their changing personalities. Carol is clearly an affectionate child, who is fond of her sisters. She always stands close to them, and in the two earlier shots wraps protective arms around them. Interestingly it is always Jacqueline who is photographed on her right, while Lisa stands to her left. This suggests that Carol found Jacqueline rather more of a handful to look after than Lisa, so she kept her close to her stronger and more dominant right arm. In the first two pictures, Jacqueline seems a more active and eager child than Lisa. But by the age of nine, she has become quieter and more passive.

Their mother, Wendy, who is included in the family group, told me that the behavioural profiles which I had been able to draw up from the snaps were very close to the truth. Carol, now a married woman of twenty with a baby of her own, had always been a friendly loving child who acted as a second mother to her twins. Until the age of about eight, she had been an extrovert. Then she became increasingly shy and began to dislike having her photograph taken. The twins, although they looked alike, were quite different in temperament.

Jacqueline was described by her mother as a warm and compassionate child, while Lisa had a much less emotional and more pragmatic approach to life: "She knows what she wants and is determined to get it."

At first it was Jacqueline who used to take the lead and dream up games for the two of them—games which often ended in minor disasters, as they were both high spirited and mischievous children. On one occasion, Wendy recalls, they decided to "landscape" a neighbour's garden. In a few minutes they had managed to pull up every flower in sight. Little wonder that Carol felt the need to restrain the eager Jacqueline when they posed for their picture. Later on, it was Lisa who became the more dominant of the two and dreamed up their games. This switch in the leadership role can clearly be seen between the second and third photographs.

Now let us see what the group snap tells us about the other members of the family. Wendy gazes happily at the camera. She looks directly into the lens and makes a warm, upper smile. Her eye-brows are slightly raised in a quizzical expression, as if she was demanding whether the photographer was going to take much longer! Her husband, Eric, avoids the camera lens and looks slightly downwards. This rather submissive signal suggests a shy and retiring man who dislikes confrontations. But at the same time his posture is a strong and direct one, and there is an air of determination about the set of his jaw. He is clearly the exact opposite of Wendy, who bubbles warmly out of the photograph.

Once again, the camera has revealed more about the people in the picture than they realised. Wendy confirmed that she and her husband do have completely different personalities. She loves being photographed, he would prefer to be left out of a shot. She never avoids a confrontation or a row if one is necessary. Eric is a quiet self-effacing man, who prefers to walk away from unpleasant encounters. But he still remains very much the master of the house. "I leave all the decision-making to him," says Wendy.

The three youngest children sit close to their parents. Four-year-old Kerry snuggling up against her mother, seems to be a child who enjoys a great deal of physical contact. She leans happily against Wendy, who is resting one arm on the child's shoulder and another on her knee. Kerry touches herself too, placing her left hand on her bare leg. Even today, as a teenager, the girl adores being cuddled by her mother.

Eight-year-old Toni holds the family's pet cat, and seems to be less interested in having her picture taken than in what her baby brother is up to. Apart from her father, she is the only member of the family not looking into the lens. But, while Eric has deliberately avoided doing so, Toni simply seems to have glanced down when the shutter was fired. Other snaps in the album show the little girl as a serious child, who seems older and more mature than her sisters. Wendy agreed that these snaps accurately reflected her daughter's personality. She is a highly intelligent and articulate child, who held lengthy conversations with her mother before the age of two. But in this, and other photographs one gets the impression that she was less involved with her family at that time than the other girls. Carol and the twins form a self-contained group. Kerry obviously relates strongly to her mother. Toni is left to play with the cat.

The youngest member of this large family, ten-months-old Bradley, wriggles in his father's arms. He seems eager to make his escape and go back to a more interesting game. One gets the impression of a strong, restless child who is not going to take kindly to being bossed around.

How To Analyse Family Snaps

If you are looking at snaps of your own family, then try to adopt the same objective attitude which I described in Chapter Two for looking at silent speech. You will find this easier to do if you study the pictures methodically, concentrating on every small detail.

If the pictures are of strangers, find out all you can about the relationships of those involved before you start. This will give you a guide about what to look out for. But avoid asking for opinions about the personality of the subjects. Other people's views may influence your analysis. It is nearly always possible to read what you want to see into photographs!

Start by taking the image's psychological temperature. Do not try to work out what combinations of expression, gesture and proximities are giving you a particular impression at this point. Just assess the photograph as hot, warm or cold.

Now ask yourself why the picture was taken. Is it a casual snap of some family event, or a carefully posed photograph intended to bring out the subject's best features? Has the camera been used to capture a personal occasion, or was the main idea to impress other people? The father of two small boys once showed me some "casual" snaps he had taken of his children. They were playing with brand new pedal cars in a room which was so neat and tidy that it looked more like the toy department of a luxury store. Everything was carefully arranged to show a large number of toys and games at their best. There was no mess, and very little evidence that the children were enjoying themselves. "I made sure the place was put in order before I took the picture," admitted the man. "Usually it is in a terrible state."

It seemed clear that the pictures had been taken more as a means of advertising his wealth than as a private record of his sons at play. Details like this can tell you as much about the photographer as his or her subjects.

The next step is to look at faces. Notice the direction of gaze. If the lens have been avoided, does this appear deliberate or as a result of something catching the person's attention while the picture was taken? Glances to left or right of the camera are most often caused by the sitter being more interested in what is happening elsewhere. Downcast eyes are usually a deliberate attempt to avoid gaze. They can indicate a submissive and anxious attitude. But be sure to read this signal within the framework of posture and expression, or you could make a bad mistake about the subject's personality.

Study the expressions. Smiles will be formed by more than just the lips, if they are genuine. Look at posture and proximity. Are the people involved standing close together, or managing to distance themselves from one another? Do they seem relaxed or anxious, alert or bored? Once you have decided, try to discover whether this is a reflection of their personalities or the way in which the picture was taken. If people are holding or touching one another, look at their arms and the exact position of the hands. Are they tense, with clenched fists; or relaxed, with the fingers lightly curled around the other person's shoulder, waist or arm?

Remember to watch out for the kind of anxiety signals described in Chapter Six. Thumb sucking, finger chewing, self-manipulation, and a nervous tugging at parts of the clothing, are all indications that the subject felt unhappy about something.

Avoid jumping to conclusions or allowing your own attitudes to influence the analysis. Base your conclusions on what the snaps tell you, not what you believe they ought to say.

When using snapshots to study body language, always proceed with caution. Remember that it is the *flow* of movements which conveys the message with gaze, gesture, stance, posture and proximity all interacting. A snapshot provides you with a split-second extract from a continuous stream of signals. In some ways it is rather like trying to learn about a river by examining a bucket of water drawn from it at random! But an accurate analysis can be done, so long as you approach the task in the right way. Never take anything for granted. Only when a particular signal has been repeated in a number of pictures over a period of time, can one feel certain that it represents something typical about that person or their relationship with somebody else.

Finally, be cautious about expressing judgements too bluntly. Even if you are perfectly correct in your conclusions, you could still hurt or distress somebody quite unnecessarily. Just like labelling a child as aggressive or timid, you may produce a self-fulfilling prophesy.

But do not become discouraged if you find it hard to discover anything of fresh interest in a snapshot when you first start photo-analysis. Because the picture seems quite

Study these three photographs carefully and use your knowledge of the secret language to discover the hidden truths about the little girls, their personalities and relationships. Which is the most aggressive child do you think? What silent speech signals are they sending to one another? Who is the more dominant?

ordinary at a casual glance, does not mean it lacks the hidden truths contained in silent speech signals. Keep studying the picture and your efforts will be rewarded. Bear in mind that, in one important respect, snaps are like ice-bergs. To see everything, you have to look deep beneath the surface.

10 Helping You To Help Your Child

The secret language of infancy says things about childhood which no child can ever tell you. It reveals hidden anxieties and provides insights about aggressive exchanges beyond a youngster's ability to convey with words. It uncovers fears, pin-points the causes of frustrations, gives early warning of rising stress, and discloses difficulties in social adjustment. It helps adults to understand the needs of their children more perfectly, and deal with problems of early development more effectively. And it offers parents a means of expressing feelings of love, sympathy and reassurance more power-fully than the most beautiful words in the world.

I have already described some of the practical uses to which your new knowledge of the secret language can be put. In this final chapter I want to examine, in more detail, the ways in which an understanding of silent speech signals can help you to help your child in three key areas of human response—*Aggression, Anxiety and Affiliation.*

The Three "A's" of Life

The secret language has a great deal to say about relationships between the under-fives. It can also tell us quite a lot about the emotional states of children who are still too young to express their feelings in words. By themselves, such insights do not of course provide answers to problems of adjustment and social development. But they do allow us to start asking more penetrating questions about a child's lifestyle. In this way we can begin to respond to conflicts, frustrations, anxieties and refusals, in the most effective way. Instead of having to rely on guesswork, or fall back on standard remedies, we are able to monitor continuously changes in behaviour, and so accurately assess the consequences of our interventions.

Helping The Aggressive Child

I am starting by looking at the problems of the aggressive child, because this is the kind of behaviour most likely to provoke extreme adult responses. Very few of us can remain completely calm and detached when watching conflict between the under-fives. We are either moved to break up the exchange, usually by siding with the child who seems to be getting the worst of things, or if we are unable to take any active part, to form a very strong opinion about the personalities of the children involved. As I explained earlier in the book, the tendency is to label one of the contestants a "bully" and the other an "unfortunate victim".

Our reaction to aggressive exchanges between children is, to a large extent, a reflection of our own response to aggression. Some people are only too willing and able to defend themselves—either verbally or physically—when they feel threatened. Often they will attack first at the slightest indication of disagreement or contradiction. Adults who are used to handling aggression in this way can watch a quite violent exchange between young children without feeling at all anxious. Their attitude is usually: "Let them sort things out. They've got to learn to stand up for themselves." While they may not actually side with the aggressor, they frequently express some contempt for the victim, whom they tend to see as cringing and spineless. It is an attitude usually—but not exclusively—found in men, especially fathers.

At the other end of the continuum, there are adults who intervene at the first sign of conflict, even if it never looks like escalating beyond a minor squabble. These are usually people who find it very difficult to come to terms with any kind of aggression. They may become so disturbed in the presence of hostile behaviour that they can be termed *aggression phobics*. The overwhelming anxiety and distress which they experience makes it impossible for them to remain relaxed and tolerant during any kind of conflict.

There are ways in which both these extremes of response can be modified to make them more flexible and socially effective. Aggressive individuals can be taught how to behave in an *assertive*, rather than a violent manner—so that they stand up for their own rights without attacking the rights of others. Aggression phobics can be trained to control their anxiety responses, so that mental confusion and physical symptoms of fear no longer prevent them from confronting and coping with hostility. These are just two of the areas of human response in which the procedures of the behavioural psychology have proved particularly successful.

How you respond to aggression in the very young will, therefore, vary according to your attitude towards aggression in general. If you tend to react in an extreme manner when threatened by hostility yourself, you may find it hard to view such conflicts from an objective standpoint. It is not possible here to describe methods by which, for example, excessive anxiety about aggression can be reduced, although I have written about it elsewhere.* You may, however, find it easier to adopt the degree of detachment necessary to make careful and accurate observations, if you understand more about the

* *The Anxiety Antidote*—Dr Robert Sharpe and David Lewis, Souvenir Press.

nature of specific conflicts and the general reasons for much infant aggression.

Specific aggressive encounters can best be analysed using your knowledge of the secret language. So far as the nature of aggression in young children is concerned, it is important to bear in mind that behaviour which we group under the heading of "aggression" or "violence" may have very different motivations.

One of the drives which produces a considerable amount of violent or destructive behaviour in the under-fives is simply curiosity. The two-year-old who tears a book to pieces, breaks a toy, or pulls the inside out of a doll, may well merely be satisfying his or her need to find out about the world. Most young children have a lively interest in everything going on around them. This is a very desirable character trait in many ways, because they can only discover how to make sense of life by constantly experimenting and experiencing the consequences of their actions. On the other hand, the effect of these activities can be extremely upsetting, especially where expensive adult property is involved. In these instances of *apparent* aggression, the ideal course is to try and sustain the curiosity which has motivated the act, while carefully channelling it into more constructive behaviour. As in so many other areas of childhood learning, adult example is of considerable importance. In a home where the grown-ups treat possessions as though they had no value, one usually finds that the children take a similar attitude. If the young child's environment is bland, monotonous and lacking in opportunities for creative exploration, he may be driven to more destructive experiments. Here again, adults and older children set the pace and provide the model. In this case, exploratory damage may be combined with a release of frustrations caused by insufficient stimulation. The same kind of boredom often exists in a home where the mother is fanatically houseproud. If she constantly grumbles and complains when a toy is out of place, or the apple pie order of a room is even slightly disturbed, the young child's scope for satisfying natural curiosity will obviously be limited. If an activity which such adults consider to be an act of "motiveless vandalism" does occur, they may be quite unable to grasp how and why they were to blame. Frustration aggression can also arise when a young child's lack of skill prevents him from performing some difficult mental or physical task. The three-year-old who has struggled to put together a construction kit may suddenly fly into a rage and break the parts to pieces. In all these cases adults might describe the behaviours as "violent", "destructive" and "aggressive". While these may seem entirely appropriate words, such labeling does little to resolve the basic difficulties which have produced them. Furthermore, they can add to the impression that a particular child is "violently aggressive", even though the motives were not really aggressive at all.

In all these situations, silent speech signals can provide important clues about what is going on in the child's mind. This applies both to the solitary infant and to groups of children who direct their "destructive" actions against mostly inanimate objects. Look out especially for body talk indicating conflict, frustrations, and anxieties, and consider the meaning of these signals before deciding on your best response. If the basic drive is curiosity or frustration due to lack of stimulation, then you should be able to improve the situation by providing a more interesting and challenging environment. On the other hand, it may be that the child is trying to cope with problems beyond his capabilities. In this case the best course of action could be to introduce new and slightly less taxing activities. You should also look honestly at the example being set by yourself, and other adults, before putting the blame on the child, or seeking refuge in some comfortable label such as "disturbed", "maladjusted" or "naturally aggressive"! Remember that such labels, however scientific they may seem, are not answers to anything. Often indeed, they are a means of avoiding the real issues and taking a detour around reason.

Even if we accept that some behaviour which is called

"aggressive" may stem from non-violent motives, no one can deny that the under-fives do have frequent clashes. They squabble, fight, shout, shriek and dispute amongst themselves far more frequently than older children and adults.

A study carried out amongst American children infants in 1935, by Arthur Jersild and F. V. Markey, showed that conflicts occurred at the rate of one every five minutes. Twenty years later a second investigation, this time involving Australian children between the ages of two and four, recorded one conflict every six minutes. In both studies the encounters were quite brief, lasting less than thirty seconds on average. My own recent observations of children in a similar age group, made in Britain, Europe and America, suggests that this pattern and duration of conflict remains unchanged. Some people might argue that in order to protect the weaker children from excessive bullying, frequent adult interventions may be unavoidable. There are undoubtedly occasions when this can happen, although these are less frequent than one might think, because the most vulnerable children seldom become involved in aggressive clashes. They remain isolated and take care to avoid any kind of social exchange, whether or not it is likely to be aggressive. By removing themselves to the outer edges of the group, they minimise the risks. In addition, they frequently get some protection from the more dominant children.

Aggressive clashes are most likely to involve *Dominant Aggressives* in conflict with *Dominated Aggressives* and *Dominated Leaders*. They may also confront *Dominated Frightened* children, as will those in the other two groups of dominated youngsters. *Dominated Leaders* do fight with one another and with children in other groups, but by definition these clashes occur less frequently than acts of friendship and appeasement.

Experience of the behaviour of groups of young children helps one to adopt a more detached attitude. Even adults who become very anxious when they are involved in aggressive encounters, can quickly learn to tolerate clashes between the under-fives. This is partly because one soon realises that little actual violence is usually involved. More often than not, only a child's pride is hurt. When a clash does escalate to the point where real injuries are caused, an element of unlucky chance is frequently involved. A child *happens* to be holding a wooden skittle when striking a blow. A toy used to push another away has a jagged edge which causes a cut. A child falls heavily and bangs his head.

When this happens, the aggressor is usually as distressed, frightened and tearful as the victim. Neither of them ever meant things to get out of hand. Faced by blood, a nasty bruise, or a child who is clearly in pain, it is very easy for adults to lose control, explode with rage and vent their own anxieties about the incident on the child responsible. Such a response should be avoided, if humanly possible. A reprimand is clearly necessary, but any over-reaction is only likely to make matters worse, by further frightening and humiliating an already miserable child.

Try to analyse conflicts, by means of the secret language, so that you can understand the way the clash developed. Look at each encounter in terms of the behaviour of those involved. First consider the actions of the prime mover in the conflict—that is, the more aggressive child who snatched another's toy, tried to take away a game or shoved to the front of a queue. Then study the responses of the child, or children, in the line of fire. How did they react? Did they try to back away from a confrontation, or quickly escalate the clash to a point where physical contact was made?

Only when you understand what is happening should you take steps, where necessary, to try and change the overall behaviour in such a way that the children who need help to become more socially effective receive it. This means guiding the aggressive child towards appease-ment and affiliation skills, so that dominance previously achieved by means of physical force can be maintained through friendly leadership. Children who are unable to assert themselves, should be assisted in becoming more dominant and less anxious when faced by aggressive tactics.

To achieve these goals it will be necessary to look closely at the child's whole lifestyle before making any changes—such as reducing sources of stress, or increasing the child's feelings of security. Unfortunately, such an approach is far more difficult and time-consuming than the usual short-term "answer" to conflicts, which merely involves comforting one child and punishing the other. "Anytime Nicky gets into a fight, we have a session with the hairbrush at bathtime," the father of a lively four-year-old told me. "The strange thing is that he never seems to learn a lesson from it."

It would be remarkable if Nicky did stop fighting as a result of physical punishment. The main thing a beaten child learns is that violence is an acceptable form of behaviour.

I suggest that you proceed as follows when coping with an "aggressive" child. Start by making quite certain the term is justified. As we have seen, it is used very widely, like a sheet of brown paper, to wrap up a range of very differently motivated activities. The best way to discover whether it really is aggression is by through careful observation, and the keeping of written notes. These will help you to look back, after a week or ten days, and examine each of the situations which at the time struck you as aggressive. Disregard destructive behaviour which arose from a sense of curiosity or feelings of frustration, and concentrate on aggressive acts within the group. The other problems can be dealt with in ways which I have already suggested. Use Professor Montagner's system to compare incidents of aggression with exchanges where the child demonstrated leadership qualities. If it turns out that domination is being achieved through co-operation and friendship, as much as by aggression, strengthen this behaviour in the way described later in this chapter. If the child does initiate conflicts, and behaves in a generally bullying and overbearing way, then examine each of these clashes as they occur. Your notes should include as much accurately observed data as possible, because information about *where* and *when* conflicts most frequently occur can often provide important clues as to *why* they may be taking place.

In psychology, a great deal of research has been carried out into the influence of our surroundings on the way we behave, an effect which has been termed *stimulus control*. An everyday example of stimulus control in action can be seen in the behaviour of some motorists. Away from their cars they are reasonable, tolerant and patient individuals. But once behind the steering wheel, they rapidly adopt aggressive and impatient responses which show little consideration for their fellow drivers.

Stimulus control can make an important difference to the way a child behaves. For example, a youngster may become more aggressive in the company of slightly older children, because of a feeling that he must impress them. The child might also be more than usually aggressive when playing in his or her own home, where the familiar territory provides an extra sense of security. On the other hand, aggression may decline as a result of changing from one nursery school to another, or in the presence of adults the child sees no point in trying to impress.

Dominant Leaders sometimes become more aggressive after a move to a different playgroup and unfamiliar children. This may be because the previously successful appeasements and co-operation-winning behaviour no longer appears to work so well. It may also be that the child is fearful of offering appeasement until a high pecking order position has been achieved through physical dominance.

A story is told of a young teacher who taught in a number of tough schools. At the start of his career he was quite unable to control his disinterested students, and every lesson disintegrated into a shambles. Then he developed a different approach. The first time he ever went into a new classroom, he would select two or three of the biggest, toughest boys and flog them savagely for no real reason at all.

I recount this story not out of approval for his actions,

but because it illustrates a technique adopted by some youngsters when first introduced to a group. By initiating aggression, they seek to achieve the same kind of authority as the master. By provoking disputes and deliberately introducing conflicts into the group, they are hoping to establish their place at the top of the pecking order quickly and firmly. After this status has been recognised, they may well revert to more appeasing forms of behaviour.

There are two risks attached to this approach. The first is that the group may refuse to accept the child's right to rule by aggression, so the level of violence escalates. It is rather like the old Western gun-fighter who could never afford to relax. There was always some younger sharp shooter ready to challenge his position. The second danger is that if the initial ploy fails everything can be lost. If the boys had assaulted the master in return, or even refused to accept unjustified punishment, his position in the class—and probably in the school—would have quickly become untenable. The same thing can happen to the child who tries to bully the others into submission and meets defeat.

When you collect information about conflicts, make certain to note the day and the time. Professor Montagner's studies of changes in hormone levels has shown that there is often a pattern to aggressive behaviour based on these physiological variations. Your records may show, for instance, that a child is especially aggressive on Monday, Tuesday and Wednesday, but becomes more appeasing and friendly on the last two days of the week. If so, an examination of what happens during the weekend could prove helpful.

Armed with accurate facts, rather than conjecture and supposition, it is possible to plan any long-term changes in the child's lifestyle which you feel may reduce aggressive behaviour, eliminate excessive anxieties or reinforce leadership skills.

One of the first questions to answer is whether the child is receiving sufficient parental attention. Young children, however independent and self-reliant they may seem, need an enormous amount of interested and affectionate attention from a small group of intimate adults, especially their mothers and fathers. They can only be made to feel loved, wanted and secure through frequent and regular periods of close contact. It is never sufficient to toss the child a crust of comfort by means of a casual verbal assurance. "Of course I love you darling," murmured from the depths of a magazine or newspaper, is just not enough.

When we feel something very strongly ourselves, there is a tendency to believe that the object of our interest and love must realise our deep feelings by means of some kind of telepathy. The implication is: "I shouldn't have to tell him that I love him. I'm his mother. He should *know* I love him." This seldom works, at any age. And it is especially ineffective with the young child, for whom actions always speak louder than words.

So far as actual conflicts are concerned, these are usually best ignored and allowed to take their course. Watch carefully, but do not interfere unless it is absolutely necessary. Any such interference normally has three effects. It distorts the social structure of the group, it damages the status of the dominant child, and it only temporarily helps the victim of the clash. As I said earlier, in the long term you may be doing the more dominated child a disservice. Instead of learning how to interact assertively, the child comes to believe that an appeal to the grown-ups is a better, safer and more certain answer. So it may be. Until the day when there is no adult present, and the helpless youngster is left to sink or swim alone.

How To Help The Anxious Child

So far we have looked mainly at ways in which the aggressive youngster can best be helped. I have left until now any discussion about those children who are more often at the receiving end of conflicts, because what we have to consider are ways in which they can become more assertive and less anxious.

This is not to say that it is always the *most* anxious children who are the victims of aggression. Aggressive youngsters are sometimes very anxious and express their fears by initiating conflicts. Furthermore, *Isolated* children, who by definition seldom become involved in conflicts, are usually very anxious. They will best be helped in ways which are unlikely to be of much benefit to the three dominated groups of children, who are most often involved in clashes and usually come off worse. Here again an understanding of the secret language can prove invaluable in helping towards an accurate analysis of each situation.

As with aggressive children, it is important to base your response to their problems on reliable information. This means observing, making notes and discovering when and why such children behave in an especially anxious way. Stimulus control can influence anxious behaviour, just as it can increase or reduce aggressive activity.

Once you have this information, such children can be guided towards more effective kinds of behaviour. By this I do not mean that they should be manipulated, through threats or bribes, to adopt a different approach to life. Promises of rewards, warnings of punishments, and exhortations, are some of the main weapons in the armoury of many adults. They seldom have any lasting effect, and often produce fresh problems which are more serious and harder to resolve than those they were trying to eliminate.

Let us look, for example, at the effects of the commonly encountered "You make me so unhappy by being unhappy..." strategem. "Won't you join in with the others," pleads a mother. "Look what a lovely game they are having. If you don't play with them you are going to make Mummy very, very sad. You don't want to make Mummy unhappy do you!" This is basically a punishing approach, although many adults may not recognise it as such. The child is being punished by being told that he is responsible for hurting the most important person in the world. At the same time, the child's anxieties about joining-in may be so great that it is too frightening for him to do what is being demanded of him. A *double-bind* situation is created. Whatever the child does, it will cause distress. The outcome is heightened conflict, frustration and anxiety.

Another common line of attack is the unashamed bribe. "Go and play like a big boy, and Mummy will buy you a nice ice-cream." The obvious intention is to reward the behaviour of joining in a game. In principle, this is a fine idea, provided it is practised in moderation. But the way it is being used here makes it ineffective. Studies in the laboratory and clinic have firmly established that to increase the chances of a particular piece of behaviour occurring, a reward—or reinforcement as it is called in behavioural psychology—must be given *immediately after the desired action has taken place*. To delay giving a reinforcement by any length of time is to rob it of any potency. Nonetheless this reward technique does provide one line of approach if used correctly.

In my experience, it can be effective in persuading *Isolated* children to take the first steps towards joining group activities. The first essential safeguard is to make sure that a child's inappropriate and anti-social behaviours are not accidentally rewarded. This can easily happen without even perceptive adults being aware of the fact. We tend to see a reward as something positive which gives pleasure. But an effective reinforcer can just as easily be the avoidance of an unpleasant occurrence. This is what frequently happens when a child is first introduced into the group. Instead of taking part in games, the child creeps into a corner and refuses to become involved. By hiding away, the unpleasant feelings of anxiety are reduced to a minimum. The child's heart may still be slightly dry, but in time these symptoms of fear will decline. By avoiding the group, the child has rewarded himself in this negative way. A feeling of relief has been substituted for the feelings of fear. This is exactly the same kind of relief which phobics feel when avoiding the source of their fears. It makes it more certain that an avoidance response will take place the next time the frightening stimulus is present. With a phobic, this may be the presence of birds, dogs, spiders, bridges, open spaces and so on. With the anxious child, it can be other children, the room in which the nursery school or play group is held, the supervisors, games, and indeed anything connected with social activities. Instead of becoming easier to accept as time passes, the situation produces more and more anxiety.

Unless the child can be persuaded to take part in group activities he may learn, through avoidance, always to adopt a solitary role.

Fortunately playing is fun, and therefore a rewarding, or reinforcing, activity. Because the reinforcement is built into the behaviour you are trying to encourage, it is instantaneous and therefore extremely effective. The difficulty is to persuade the child to take the initial ice-breaking plunge. With most children this occurs naturally, after the first few sessions of crying for mother and looking miserable. But the child destined for an *Isolated* role never manages to take that plunge. If the mother, or some other equally comforting and affection- ate adult, is there to mop up tears and provide a safe haven, the necessary social integration is more likely to be delayed, perhaps permanently. Looking at what happens in terms of reinforcement, it is easy to understand why. The child hides away from others, cries and begs to be protected by an adult. An adult obliges. The result is effectively to reward, and therefore establish, the solitary and unsociable behaviour.

The need is to combine some comfort with an active participation in group activities. While the child's tears are being dried, he or she can be shown an involving game or some interesting toy which the others are familiar with. Playing with the toy, in the comforting grasp of an adult, makes the child forget earlier anxieties. Pleasure at playing rewards this new type of behaviour. At that point the child can be introduced to another youngster, so that they play together. This is the kindest, most effective and least traumatic method of gradually integrating the fearful infant into a group.

Dominated Leaders, Dominated Aggressive and *Dominated Frightened* children need a different approach. Here the problem is not that they refuse to participate in the group, but that their actions are often so ineffective. *Dominated Leaders* are usually the least cause for concern. Often it is only a matter of a few months, or less, before they discover the trick of dominating by a combination of friendly gestures and assertive responses. Encouragement can be provided, away from the actual conflicts themselves, for leadership qualities. This is best done by example. Adults should never use their superior size and strength to snatch, grab or demand things from young children. Respect their rights as human beings. If you want something which they have a just claim to, then make appeasement and solicitation gestures. And not simply with words—they may be quite ineffective with the under-fives—but by using the secret language signals yourself. Smile, use the head tilt, come down to their height. Slowly reach out a hand for what you want. But do all these things naturally and easily, not as if you are performing some strange ritual. Remember that it seems perfectly normal to the child to be solicited in this way. After a very short while, any initial self-consciousness you may have experienced will quickly disappear.

Dominated Aggressives must be gently assisted to overcome their two basic problems. The first is that they are following a course of behaviour which is not very socially satisfactory in the long term, and the second is that they are doing it badly! They lack the confidence and follow-through to make their initial aggressive approach pay off. As a result they often suffer a double defeat, for the same reasons that the schoolmaster mentioned earlier would have been in a much worse position had his pupils struck back.

Gather information about such children's behaviour.

Make notes of places, times, days, who was present and what happened. Do not rely on memory. Try to ease any stress-creating difficulties which they may be encountering. Are they receiving sufficient attention at home? Have any changes occurred in the family, or at nursery school and play group, which could be creating special difficulties? A *Dominant Leader* in one of my groups developed into a *Dominated Aggressive* child after his elder brother went away to boarding school. A *Dominant Aggressive* child became a *Dominated Aggressive* when his mother had to go into hospital for a minor operation. These are clearly important changes in family routine. But they do not have to be as obvious, in order to be significant. Sometimes the variations in routine which cause changes in behaviour are so slight that an adult may consider them unimportant. The loss of a favourite toy; a change in the husband's job, which meant that the start of the day had to be brought forward and meals rearranged; the redundancy of a father which kept him at home far more—these were all sufficient to produce marked changes in the behaviour of under-fives at one nursery school.

Nothing which might be of importance should be overlooked. But where changes are made for the benefit of the child, these should be discreetly and delicately introduced. What the mother or father must not say is: "You seem to be unhappy with so-and-so, so we've decided not to do it. Does that make you happier?" This is another potentially punishing situation, which may cause stress and anxiety in itself.

Dominated Frightened children are often extremely anxious. Unlike *Isolated* children, who may be treated quite kindly by dominant youngsters, these are more likely to be the victims of an attack than the recipients of a gift. They may be the innocent by-standers who get struck by an aggressive child seeking an outlet for his anger, or the target for a direct assault. Their toys are snatched, their building bricks sent crashing to the ground. They are bullied out of their place in a queue, shoved away from the slide or climbing frame, and generally treated with scant respect by the more aggressive youngsters. Most children in this group pass out of it as they grow older, stronger and therefore better able to take care of themselves. It is quite common, for instance, to find children between two and three in the *Dominated Frightened* category, but extremely rare to find a four or five-year-old.

These unhappy children are often supported by adults during conflicts, and comforted by them afterwards. "Poor little chap," sighs the playgroup supervisor, as she gathers up a sobbing youngster. "Everybody picks on you don't they, darling. It isn't fair!" Since these children are often verbally proficient, they usually get on better with grown-ups than their companions. This may have unfortunate long term consequences, as it is important that children learn how to relate effectively to youngsters of about the same age. As they grow up, it will be children, adolescents, and finally adults of their own age, who provide the most satisfactory friends, companions and potential mates. This is the inevitable result of similar interests and more or less equal physical, intellectual, social and sexual development. As we get older, the age difference becomes rather less important; but in early childhood, 'teens and young adulthood, the individual who finds it impossible to respond to his or her peer group will be placed at a social disadvantage.

This means that no matter how kindly disposed and well-intentioned they are, adults provide an unsatisfactory permanent haven for the frightened and dominated youngster. However hard it may seem at the time, the child should be encouraged to take part in the group activities, and not to constantly turn to grown-ups. The best advice which one can offer is to look at the child's situation as a whole, rather than concentrating on particular incidents. Instead of attempting to change the situation before, during or immediately after a conflict, try to take a wider view of the child's problems. For example, imagine an only child living in a remote country area where there are no other children. When that child is sent to a nursery school for the first time, the experience is going to be strange and probably frightening. Without practice in playing with other children, he does not know what is expected of him. After a time he becomes a dominated and frightened child, lacking the necessary social skills to establish himself in the group.

Instead of trying to improve matters in the school, where the needs of a whole range of children have to be considered and time is limited, changes should be made in the home environment. By introducing the child to companions of his own age, he can gradually be helped to master the repertoire of behaviour needed to function well in the larger and more boisterous world of the nursery school. "But surely he will know how to play with his friends," I can almost hear some mothers saying. "It's natural after all."

To state that man is a social animal is perfectly correct. We have an inborn need for the companionship of our own kind. But it is quite untrue to say that all the skill we need to perform as effective social animals is built into our biology, along with hair colour and skin pigmentation. There are inborn tendencies to behave in a certain way, but that is all. The actual mechanics of social exchanges must all be learned, and the earlier the better. We must learn how to make friends, learn how to persuade and placate, learn how to assert ourselves and handle the aggression of others. The under-fives can only master these intricate skills by practical experience. As they get better at doing all of these things, the rewards which result from successful social exchanges establish the behaviour which produced them. But until the first, tentative and often anxiety-producing steps are taken, no progress is possible. A child who never learns to make friends will find it increasingly hard to do so in later life, because as adults we become very good at finding intellectual justifications for any kind of lifestyle. The adult who is desperately lonely, but finds it impossible to establish rewarding relationships with others, may rationalise the situation to himself in any number of ways. He may, for instance, say that he is happier alone—by denying that other people are worthwhile, by refusing to accept that he is lonely, or by constantly reminding himself of the pain which a failed relationship can cause.

Behind all these, and the many other justifications given for a solitary existence, may lie the simple fact that before the age of five that person never found out how to make friends.

Affiliation

Making friends is important. The ability to make friends involves learning how to behave in an appropriate way. Fortunately these skills, although complex, are very rewarding. This means that, given the right start and sufficient opportunity, successful social behaviour is quickly established.

Dominant Leaders find that appeasing, co-operating activities produce good pay-offs. They have agreeable companions to play with. They are able to persuade others to hand over their toys and let them take part in games, without the need to resort to conflict. This makes them well-thought of by adults. They tend to be favoured, picked out for attention, and given responsibilities—such as handing around the morning milk—which further enhance their position in the group.

So long as this situation is maintained, there is no cause for adult help. But things can go wrong, and when they do the child may have great difficulty in regaining his or her old confidence. This sometimes results in a period of increased aggression, as more violent tactics are tried in favour of the discredited appeasement approach. Or it may mean that the child becomes excessively anxious and easily dominated by other members of the group.

A second problem that can arise, and here the difficulties may be long-term rather than immediate, is that the child becomes too self-confident and self-satisfied for his or her own good.

In the first case, the sudden rise in aggression should

not be regarded as anything exceptional—though it can come as a nasty surprise to grown-ups who are used to "little Susan" or "young Tommy" behaving in a consistently friendly way. Remember that even the most contented and well-adjusted youngster has fluctuating behaviour. It may be that some difficulties at home, a change within the group, or the onset of a minor physical illness, has temporarily upset his outlook on life. The important thing is to ensure that these changes do not last a moment longer than is necessary. The secret language can be a great help here, because it allows you to interpret exchanges accurately, and so monitor incidents of aggression and affiliation. If the level of aggression does seem to be rising steadily, then take steps to find out the possible causes. Very often some change in the child's lifestyle is responsible for the changes in behaviour. For example, in one of the groups I studied there was a boy who had been a *Dominant Leader* for many months. His mother became pregnant, and from her fifth month of pregnancy to three months after the birth of the baby, the boy became very aggressive. At the end of this period, probably because his mother began to devote more time to him and his homelife settle down again, he reverted to leadership behaviour.

Because adults tend to like children who offer others toys, play quietly and seldom cause a fuss, the *Dominant Leaders* benefit from a great deal of adult acclaim. The essential thing is not to make this praise too obvious. The kind of response some play-group supervisors make to a well behaved child, and I can well understand why, is to hold the child up as an example: "Look at Sally, isn't she a good little girl. Why can't you behave like that?"

Whatever the effects on the other children, a possible consequence for Sally is that she may come to assume she can do no wrong. If she is generally 'angelic', she will probably be given more latitude by adults, who will feel that the occasional lapse can be overlooked. Other children, quick to take offence over adult injustices, may start to dislike Sally. She will become isolated, and find it much harder to make friends. So, from the very best of motives, the adult response to her socially appropriate behaviour will have been to make her *less* socially effective.

Even if this does not happen, there is a danger that as a result of excessive praising a child will develop an unrealistic self-image. He may come to believe that he is superior to other children, and so deserving of special treatment. Any child who holds this opinion in nursery school at the age of four, is likely to be in for an unhappy surprise when he starts primary school a year later. From being amongst the oldest children in the group, the boy suddenly finds himself amongst the youngest. Instead of being a favourite of the grown-ups, the child is treated exactly like all the others.

This is a time when all children have to make several difficult and important adjustments. They must get used to the longer working hours, the more formal instruction, and the atmosphere of firmer discipline. If the need to drastically reconstruct a self-image is added to these major changes, it may prove too great a strain. Confidence vanishes, and a wary uncertainty takes its place. The child becomes frightened, unsettled, miserable and over-stressed. As a result school refusal, tantrums, and even psychosomatic illnesses may occur.

My own view is that small children should never be held up as shining examples to their companions, except in the most specific and limited way. No harm is likely to be done if an adult says: "Look at the way Tom holds his brush. Try it like that and you will find painting much easier." But there may be a harmful result if the adult then adds: "Isn't Tom a clever little boy to paint so well. Don't you all wish you were clever like Tom!"

The effect of such praise may be opposite to what was intended or desired. Instead of all the children being encouraged and helped, the resentments caused may create problems for the favoured youngster which he is quite unable to deal with.

Your Attitude Is Important

After lecturing on the secret language, and during private talks with the parents of young children, I occasionally meet two very different but equally unhelpful responses—namely hostility, and anxiety.

Let me deal with the angry reaction to begin with, if only because those who hold this view are usually the most vocal in their objections! They argue along these lines: "How dare you try to tell me how to look after my kids! All this psychological nonsense does nothing but harm. My mother raised perfectly normal happy youngsters, with nothing to help her but common sense and a carpet beater!"

While I can understand why some parents take this view, I have to say that I regard it as a depressingly negative attitude towards decades of real progress in our understanding of the child. To dismiss all the discoveries of child psychology as either a fad or a fallacy is to close the mind to knowledge of great potential and importance.

I am not suggesting that all the answers have been found. Most specialists would agree that, in some areas of child development, we are not yet even sure if we are asking the right questions! Nor am I saying that old fashioned ways must, by definition, be bad ways. Some of them certainly were, but others are as valid today as fifty years ago. Despite the dangers and challenges of modern society, I believe that the opportunity which most parents have for raising healthy, happy and well-adjusted children has never been greater. But achieving these goals demands an enquiring and receptive mind—one which is prepared to consider new ideas on their merits, rather than rely on a dogmatic rerun of personal childhood experience.

Anxiety about child-rearing is in a sense the opposite side of the coin. Far from refusing to consider fresh ideas, overanxious parents tend to seek out every new theory, and then worry that they have been doing everything wrong. "I've made so many mistakes," they admit unhappily. "My child is going to grow up aggressive (or dishonest, or amoral, or apathetic) and it will all be my fault."

Just as you will not give your child the best possible chance in life through an unthinking rejection of new methods, neither will you be capable of responding to the demands of childhood effectively if you are tense, under-confident and constantly worrying about "getting it right".

In his famous book *Baby and Child Care,* Dr Benjamin Spock gave mothers-to-be advice which cannot be improved on. "Trust yourself," he told them. "Don't be overawed by what the experts say. Don't be afraid to trust your common sense."

One aspect of this anxiety sometimes concerns the use of silent speech. When some parents discover there is a method for understanding children which they *could* have been using, they immediately feel that they *should* have been doing so. In fact, they will have been doing so without realising it.

You do not need to know that body language exists, in order to make use of it. Each day of our lives we unknowingly send and receive scores of silent speech messages, fluently and correctly. Take away the signals of non-verbal communication, and most of our spoken exchanges would be less interesting, informative and explicit. In Molière's famous play *Le Bourgeois Gentilhomme*, Monsieur Jourdain, the social-climbing hero, is astonished to learn that everybody speaks either in prose or verse. "Good heavens!" he exclaims. "For more than forty years I have been speaking prose without knowing it."

The same can be said about body talk. We all use it. We all see it being used. But we only start to take notice of the components of the unspoken messages once our attention has been drawn to them.

Simply knowing that children with little verbal ability can talk with their bodies, will not help a person to understand them better, or to help them more successfully. But it is the essential starting point for such a helpful understanding.

When parents ask me whether their lack of knowledge about silent speech can have harmed their child, I usually reply that this is most unlikely. While such questions may suggest a certain lack of confidence, they also indicate a deep concern and involvement with the child. Loving and being able to express that love openly is always the major consideration. It is indifference to children, rather than a lack of knowledge, which causes the most harm, and makes adults profoundly blind to the secret language of childhood.

Putting The Language To Work

Perhaps you feel that much of what I have proposed, while interesting, is impracticable. It may be all right in theory to suggest that children be carefully observed, and varieties of lifestyle interpreted and perhaps changed as a result of accurate notes and fresh insights. But how can this possibly be achieved, given the demands of a busy life? There is a house to run, perhaps an outside job to go to, meals to prepare, a partner and maybe other children to consider. The daily pressures are too great and the pace too fierce to take on any more chores.

While I am not saying that it is always easy; this extra trouble is usually possible, provided there is sufficient motivation. I have already discussed many of the benefits to the child. By watching, interpreting and making use of the secret language, you can understand the under-fives more perfectly and so guide them more effectively. By noticing signs of anxiety or increasing stress, at an early stage, it is far easier to correct the situation, just as it is easier to snuff out a match than to extinguish a bonfire.

There is increasing evidence that the first sixty months of a child's life are the most crucial in terms of physical, social and intellectual development. Neglect during this period can have profound and lasting consequences. An enrichment of the environment, on the other hand, can give the youngster a head start in life which is never entirely lost. The more stimulating, secure and loving the first five years, the more successful the child is likely to be in the years ahead.

Achieving these highly desirable goals is often more a matter of adjusting priorities and reallocating time, than finding more hours in an already hectic day.

For example, an outside job is important to most mothers, and not only because of the extra money. But by sacrificing her own interests for around 1200 days, a mother may be giving her child something which all the money in the world would be unable to buy. So a change in priorities could mean putting aside a career outside the family during this critical period. Another change in priorities might be to devote less time to caring for the house, and more time to the child. A comfortable, clean and well ordered home is very desirable. But if the price is being unable to give sufficient interest and attention to the child, then it will be far too high.

Reallocation of time simply means that you use periods already devoted to the children in a more effective way. Most parents look at their children, out of interest or concern, for several hours each week. In this case, observing the signals of silent speech need not take up extra time. It will simply involve watching and interpreting in a less casual and more constructive manner. Keeping notes takes only a few additional moments. Planning any changes you feel are necessary can be done at times when you would, in any case, be discussing the children with your partner. In his poem *In Memoriam*, Tennyson wrote:

"So runs my dream: but what am I?
An infant crying in the night:

An infant crying for the light:
And with no language but a cry."

We now know that Tennyson was wrong. Young children are able to speak without words, and their language is not limited to tears or confined to cries. It can talk to us clearly and honestly about the innermost secrets of growing up.

The widespread practical application of this new knowledge might enable us to transform not only childhood but society itself. By helping children to develop into self-confident, well adjusted and fulfilled adults, we could gradually create a society free from self-destructive anxieties and socially destructive aggression. So runs *my* dream. But, unlike Tennyson's helpless infant, I believe that we have the means to bring about such a dramatic change. It could be that the secret language of the child will help us to achieve one of the world's most splendid and silent revolutions.

Appendix
The Anatomy of Baby Talk

For quick reference to the most likely meaning of particular silent speech signals, refer to the listing below. Here you will find fifty of the most frequently observed facial expressions and body movements of the secret language. They are arranged under the main part of the body used to produce the signal, and these are in alphabetical order.

But remember, an accurate interpretation of any piece of body language is difficult in isolation. What matters is *the flow of movements* and the *context* in which the signal is made.

Arms and Hands

Beating: Rapid beating is used by children under twelve months as an indication of frustration or anger. Both arms are usually involved and flay the air rapidly. Beating as a conflict signal in toddlers indicates a mixture of aggression and fear.

When a single arm is drawn back, palm outwards, with the fingers touching the face or hair, the beat has a more defensive quality.

When the hand is held away from the head the beat indicates greater aggression. Note gaze, proximity, stance and expression. Modified beating gestures are used by adults in conflict situations, and appear as stroking or touching movements to the back of the head. (See Chapter Six).

Flexed: A component of a threat. Usually combined with clenched fists and a "leaning forward" posture. Notice direction of gaze and the shape of the mouth.

Pointing: The exact meaning varies considerably according to the direction of gaze. A brief glance in the direction of point, followed by intense eye-contact with the mother, asks a question about the surroundings. The movement is made silently, with a rigid posture and alert expression. It is almost always sent to the mother, and provides a reliable way of linking mother-infant pairs.

Pointing and gazing in the same direction indicate a desire or an intention to go that way.

Raise: Several kinds of raise occur. To determine the exact nature of the message, relate the arms raise to posture, expression and gaze. The newly walking child will raise one, sometimes both, arms to steady him. This signal reappears when confident walkers are hurrying towards somebody or chasing one another. Arm raise just before a child starts to walk forward, is probably a relic of the earlier balancing movement.

Arm raise when the child is motionless, signals uncertainty or conflict. The signal is not often used after the age of two. It often precedes a return to the mother.

Raised arms, accompanied by an intense gaze directed towards an adult, is a request to be picked up and carried. The child usually positions himself directly in front of the grown-up, at a distance of not more than two feet. If the signal is ignored, the child will tap the adult's thigh or thrust himself against the legs. It does not necessarily imply fatigue, but may reflect a desire for comforting and attention. The signal is sometimes made by children at a distance from adults. But it only works reliably at close range.

Reaching Out: The friendly child reaches out to solicit a gift or co-operation from another infant. Movement is often made slowly, with palm turned outwards and accompanied by a smile and eye-contact. The addition of head tilt makes the signal an even more powerful message of solicitation or appeasement (See Chapter Five).

Stiff: Arms held stiffly at the side indicate anxiety. This is seen in infants who have just been defeated in a confrontation, or by a fearful newcomer to a group. Seldom seen when the child is running. Usually associated with a shuffling walk or stiff-legged gait.

Waggling: Brisk waggling of the arms is a form of waving used by toddlers as they return to mother after an exploration.

Hands Clasped: Is sometimes seen as a submissive gesture made by a dominated child to assure the others that no hostility is intended. When the clasped hands are rubbed together in a washing movement, it is probably more of a comforting signal and indicates anxiety.

Hands-Concealing: Hand over eyes is used as a means for avoiding gaze, and signals embarrassment or anxiety when not being used in a playful manner. Autistic children, because of their aversion to gaze, will often peer between their fingers.

Hands-Grooming: Stroking of the hair or head in a grooming gesture indicates anxiety or conflict on many occasions.

Hands-Massaging: Rubbing of the face or body is a component of anxiety or conflict.

Hands-Manipulating: Pulling, touching, or fiddling with parts of the body or clothing, are used to provide comfort by anxious or uncertain infants.

Fingers: Chewing on or sucking at fingers after the age of about twelve months usually signals anxiety or conflict. The exact meaning of the message depends on the situation. Finger and thumb in mouth signals are often made just before the child returns to mother. (See Thumb section below).

Fingers: Splayed fingers over a toy or game show a clear intent to possess and retain. The same movement made with closed fingers is associated with a less assured claim. A dominated child about to claim a toy which still seems to be "owned" by a dominant infant may approach it in this way.

Thumb: Below the age of twelve months, thumb-sucking probably reflects an inborn need to suck. After that, it may be employed as a comforting gesture, during anxiety or conflict. When used by a solitary child in this way, it often precedes a quick return to the parent. Thumb sucking is also used by overtired children, and by those who have been put to bed when they want to stay up. Here it seems to indicate a conflict between the physical needs of the body for rest and the desire to remain awake. Thumb sucking gradually disappears around the age of four, but may persist to the age of six or seven in some children. Adults sometimes used a very modified thumb sucking movement in anxiety situations, chewing their knuckles or actually biting the top of the thumb.

Face

Eyes: Brief eye-contact is an essential element of all silent speech exchanges. It joins mother and child over a distance, greets, welcomes and sustains interest in a shared activity. Intense gaze is a threatening signal which is used during aggressive exchanges, or during gaze contests to determine the pecking order.

Eye-contact can be broken to left or right, or downwards. A left or right break finishes a staring match with neither side admitting defeat. Adults are fairly consistent in whether they break gaze to left or right, and this may depend on personality. A downward glance to end gaze, is a submissive signal. It is used frequently by frightened or anxious children who avoid gaze as much as possible.

Eye-Brows: Raised in a brief (approximately one fifth of a second) flash of recognition on meeting. Common in adults, but also seen in older infants (4-5). The movement can also be used to ask a question or query an activity.

Eye-brows are drawn together and upwards to signal doubt or surprise. Eye-brows are drawn down and together to signal anger or misery. The exact meaning is usually clear from the other body talk used at the same time.

Eyes-Pouch: A pouch or wrinkle of skin appears under each eye when an upper smile (see below) is a genuine reflection of pleasure or amusement. These swellings are caused by muscles which are not under our voluntary control, so they provide a reliable guide to the sincerity or otherwise of the grin.

Mouth

One of the most powerful signals produced by the mouth is the smile. It is associated with movements of other face muscles, gaze, posture and proximity. These are described in detail in Chapter Four.

Broad Smiles: Mouth opens, lips are drawn back uncovering both upper and lower teeth. Indicates great pleasure or amusement. The most intense smile which can be produced. Lips are tense however not relaxed as in play face.

Compressed Smiles: Lips are drawn up as in simple smile, but pressed tightly together. Signals a repressed and slightly embarrassed mirth.

Croissant Smile: Lips pulled up at edges, small aperture formed in centre. Seen in babies, and is a half-way stage between gastric and simple smiles.

Gastric Smiles: Produced by babies of only a few days old, during irregular sleep or when drowsy. Some believe these are caused by the infant breaking wind. But it is likely that they are a very early form of the smile. At least five minutes of non-smiling occurs between each.

Upper Smiles: Only the upper teeth are uncovered. By concealing the lower teeth the smile signals: "I am friendly". Watch for eye-pouches to indicate genuine smile.

Lower Smiles: Bottom row of teeth are uncovered more than upper teeth. An aggressive signal. May be accompanied by an intense stare and flexed arms.

Simple Smiles: Lips are drawn up, but mouth remains closed, and only a very small amount of the upper teeth is revealed.

Oblong Mouth: The lips are thrust forward, exposing the teeth in a threatening signal. Accompanied by intense gaze and other aggressive body movements.

Play-face: The name given to a relaxed and joyous expression seen during uninhibited play. The mouth is wide open with the teeth covered by the lips.

Biting: At first used during explorations of the environment by a solitary child. Most small children suck, bite and chew new things to find out as much as they can about them. Later used during aggressive confrontations, but declines rapidly because of adult disapproval.

Sucking: Fingers, thumbs, lower lip, a cloth doll, handkerchief or blanket. These are all comforting movements used by anxious infants, or those torn by inner conflicts.

Tongue: Tongue and lip movements are often seen in babies during play dialogues with mothers. They are pre-speech responses made as the infant begins the long, complicated task of controlling the organisation of verbal communication.

The tongue thrust into the front of the lower lip, or pushed into the cheek, indicates doubt. A child will make the signal when trying to decide what to do next.

Head

Grooming: Stroking or rubbing the head indicates anxiety or conflict.

Inclined: Produces a powerful friendship signal. It is usually combined with a warm smile and direct gaze, sometimes the body is also inclined at the waist. Infants respond to this signal from adults as well as other children. Even when the eyes are covered, it has been found to work effectively. It is the most intense way of saying "please" in silent speech.

Lowered: Head lowered, with the chin tucked into the neck, produces a threatening signal. May be combined with angry expression, intense gaze, flexed arms, clenched fists and a leaning forward posture to produce a very aggressive message. But the 'chin in' movement can also be seen in the unhappy child who wants to avoid gaze and appear submissing by keeping his eyes permanently down-cast. Which of these meanings it has, is usually made perfectly clear from the context and other body signals.

Tilted Back: Accompanies relaxed play-face, and is seen during very friendly and uninhibited games. Never seen in hostile or neutral exchanges.

Body

Genital manipulation: An anxiety or conflict signal made by boys. They will massage their naked organs or manipulate the crotch of their trousers. The movement is a comforting, rather than a sexual one, and is often made with a detached expression. Girls do not use this kind of manipulation, although they will pull and clutch at the hem of their dress.

Trunk: A rigid posture is one of the main components of aggression, but it is also present in anxiety signals. Which mood is involved can be seen from other body talk. To increase the threat, the infant can bend forward at the waist. This is a hostile signal which can intimidate infants when used inadvertently by adults.

Legs

Stiff Legs: Are seen in anxious children, or those who have just been defeated in a confrontation. This posture is often found in children who have just been introduced to a group, and is accompanied by a shuffling walk and down-cast eyes.

Stamps: Are a signal of anger or victory. A triumphant aggressive child may produce a loud stamp a few moments after the other infant moves away. Stamping and kicking are also redirected aggression movements.

Great Reading on the World's Most Popular Subjects From America's Most Trusted Magazine
READER'S DIGEST

I AM JOE'S BODY   04550-1/$2.50 _____
is based on the most popular series in DIGEST history, in which the various organs of the human body explain themselves

---

SECRETS OF
THE PAST   04551-X/$2.50 _____
explores ancient mysteries and tells about man's earliest adventures.

THE ART
OF LIVING   04549-8/$2.50 _____
contains practical and heartwarming advice, designed to help make life richer, more enjoyable, and more meaningful

---

TESTS
AND TEASERS   04552-8/$2.50 _____
is brimful of brain-wracking puzzles, quizzes, games, and tests. It promises hours of escapist fun and mental gymnastics

---